POLICE POWER

Police Abuses in New York City

PAUL CHEVIGNY

POLICE POWER

POLICE ABUSES
IN NEW YORK CITY

PANTHEON BOOKS
A Division of Random House, New York

FIRST PRINTING

Library of Congress Catalog Card Number: 68-26044

Manufactured in the United States of America
by the Book Press, Brattleboro, Vt.

Typography by Kenneth Miyamoto

*This book is dedicated to
the memory of my father,*

HECTOR CHEVIGNY

ACKNOWLEDGMENTS

A STUDY such as this depends so much on the help of others that it is practically impossible to give credit to all who deserve it. Among those too numerous to mention are the witnesses in all the cases discussed in this book; without them the issues would have been impossible to resolve.

My appreciation must first go to the Aaron E. Norman Fund and to the Civil Liberties Defense and Education Fund of the New York Civil Liberties Union, which made the work of the Police Practices Project possible.

Many lawyers contributed their time and advice, among them Henry Salitan, William Erlbaum, William Liebovitz, Sherwin Goldman, Margaret Taylor, Harold Rothwax, Stephen Nagler, Lewis Steele, Bert Perkel, Ruth Moscowitz, Arthur Gruder, Jacob Fishman, Lewis Mayers, Ernest Hammer, John Mage, Ernst Rosenberger, Paul O'Dwyer, David Drexler, and my colleagues at the Civil Liberties Union.

Law students and others contributed summers and hours of work to do indispensable research and investigation. They are Cliffton Johnson, Alan Lippel, Robert Croog, Lloyd McDonald, Stephen Sandler, Morton Grusky, Florence Gerber, David Bogen, Alan Church, Karl Haffenreffer, and Jefferson Chase.

Organizations which kindly informed me of relevant cases handled by their offices are the Legal Aid Society, the Scholarship, Education, and Defense Fund for Racial Equality, the NAACP Legal Defense and Educational Fund, and the NAACP.

Background material otherwise unavailable was supplied by Sol Rubin, Herman Schwartz, and Patricia Wald.

Eve Cary, my extraordinary assistant, contributed in more ways, large and small, than I can name, from interviewing Spanish-speaking clients to criticizing the manuscript.

My wife, Bell, urged me to write this book before even I wanted to and encouraged me to the last.

Finally, I would like to express a word of thanks to members and employees of the New York City Police Department, particularly at the Civilian Complaint Review Board, who dutifully investigated the cases described in the following chapters. I know that they will not agree with my conclusions, and I can only hope we will agree about the facts.

CONTENTS

INTRODUCTION

THIS IS NOT a book about sensational police scandals, either of corruption or of the third degree. It does not deal, and is not intended to deal, with the macabre excesses of the police as they are occasionally recorded in the newspapers, but rather with more routine denials of due process of law by false arrest, by unlawful search, and by "summary punishment"—police brutality. Most of the policemen in these cases are not detectives but patrolmen, involved in street-corner incidents. What I hope to tell is the genesis of these abuses and the reasons why so little is done to stop them.

On the other hand, this study is not a general survey of police work. It does not recount the many brilliant investigations by detectives, the acts of heroism by plainclothesmen in trying to decoy muggers, that were contemporary with the abuses recorded in this book. If it is not a "balanced" account, it was never intended to be one. This book is directed to finding out what is wrong, and the reasons for what is wrong, with law enforcement, chiefly in the streets. It concentrates upon police abuses in New York City during the two-year period of 1966 and 1967. The restriction to New York immediately raises a question about the general applicability in other communities of the patterns and conclusions described here. On the one hand, New York is the largest urban complex in the country, and it presents the most severe problems; on the other, the

New York City Police Department has long had a reputation
as one of the best departments in the country. I think it is
clear from other, more general studies than this, which will be
cited in succeeding chapters, that the problems explored here
are more pronounced in other cities. New York may not be
typical, but its police problems are typical of the police problems of the nation.

I first became concerned with police abuses in 1965 while
I was working in a neighborhood law office in Harlem. Although I had listened to a number of gruesome stories about
the police, I could not really begin to grasp what the problem
was until I had tried some criminal cases from the ghetto.

The saddest of these cases concerned a Harlem window
washer and his wife, a barmaid. On the wife's night off, they
were having drinks in a bar where she worked, and at the end
of the evening, she went out into the street to hail a cab. A
policeman, mistaking her flashy clothes for those of a prostitute,
ordered her to move on. A vituperative argument ensued, and
the wife was knocked down with a punch in the eye. When the
husband ran out of the bar with a friend to protest, he was also
knocked down. The wife was charged with assault and the
husband with disorderly conduct (breach of the peace).

A law student working in my office sat in that bar one night
for six hours, hoping to find witnesses, and finally succeeded in
giving subpoenas to three. But on the day of the barmaid's
trial, not one of them came to court—not on that day nor on
any of the three days to which the trial was subsequently
adjourned. At her husband's trial, the friend who had run out
into the street with him testified in his defense that there had
been no breach of the peace. The friend's credibility was poor,
not only because he was a friend but because he had a criminal record; the magistrate found the husband guilty and gave
him a suspended sentence.

After his trial, the husband said, "You know, I'm pretty good
with my hands. I bet I could have taken that cop. But when he
punched me, I just lay there and thought, 'Hell, I'll go downtown and tell it to the judge.' Well, I did tell it, but that cop
lied, and the judge didn't believe me. Next time anyone
punches my wife, man, I'm going to take him."

The window washer probably would not have done what he threatened; he was too respectable and civilized a man. But the important thing was that he had learned to believe there was no way to get justice except with his hands.

Similar criminal cases which I handled in 1965—of disorderly conduct, of assault, and often of resisting arrest—were just as discouraging; I lost four within the space of a few weeks. The result was that when I first heard about a plan for the New York Civil Liberties Union to study police abuses, I wanted nothing to do with it. I could imagine nothing more depressing than more of the same, over a period of two years. I had to see other lawyers win a few of these cases, and win a few myself, before I became convinced that such a project was useful; that it was sometimes possible to get the witnesses to come to court and to persuade the judges to acquit. I had to watch the defense of one such case by lawyers from Mobilization for Youth, the poverty project on the Lower East Side, in which social workers and neighborhood people appeared as witnesses, before I could grasp the enormous importance of community organization in helping to prepare those cases. The result this time was that when I was asked to work on the NYCLU project, by then called the Police Practices Project of the Civil Liberties Defense and Education Fund, I decided to try it.

The aim of the project was simple: to study police abuses, particularly police brutality, in New York City during the years 1966 and 1967, and try to find remedies. The method was even simpler: I went to work in a law office at the NYCLU, with an assistant, and began to collect complaints. We passed the word to literally hundreds of community groups, urging them to call us if they heard of complaints. I began to telephone lawyers, asking them to volunteer to represent the clients we agreed to take, or to tell us about cases involving their own clients.

The witness is the key figure in this book. The problem with complaints about police abuses in the past is that they have too often been based upon the unsupported allegations of the victim, himself usually charged with a crime. His reliability was thus easily impeached by the authorities, and his complaint could not be authenticated. To escape from this old dilemma, all complaints, however improbable, were recorded in our office, but cases were accepted for extended investigation or litigation only when there was an independent witness.

An "independent witness," for the purposes of this study, means a civilian who was not arrested. The policeman's fellow officers are not usually considered reliable witnesses because, as a presidential commission found nearly forty years ago, "It is an unwritten law in police departments that police officers must never testify against their brother officers." [1] This solidarity is nearly as strong now as it was when those words were first written. On the other hand, as we have seen, the defendant is not usually considered a reliable witness because he has too much interest in saving his own skin. As a practical matter, furthermore, when the defense in a criminal case attacks the character or veracity of the arresting officer solely on the word of the defendant, the likelihood of acquittal is very small. If we were to learn the facts about police abuses, and give any real help to the people abused, we were going to have to limit our litigation to cases with civilian witnesses who were not arrested. Even with the use of this rigid standard, we suffered a high percentage of convictions, either because witnesses we had interviewed at the beginning of the case disappeared, or because the judges refused to believe them.

When the project was planned, I do not think that anyone realized how much criminal defense work would be entailed. We received hardly any cases in which there was a naked police abuse without an arrest to cover the mistake. We were expected, in some way, to "study" the police, but we could not study anything at all unless we could get information, and unless we could begin to clear away the obstructions, chiefly criminal charges, in the way of corroborating the complaints. Obviously, no one was going to come to us and spend hours painstakingly giving us the facts of his case and the names of witnesses unless we proposed to do something for him. Furthermore, once a police officer had obtained a conviction on a charge which would explain a complaint—resisting arrest, for example—the complaint became worthless. Because of this, no cases are discussed here in which there was a conviction on criminal charges that seemed to explain the abuse, even when we disagreed with the court's decision. The purpose of this book is not to quarrel with the criminal courts, but to find out what we can learn about the New York City police under the existing system. The material of this study consists, then, of "authenticated" complaints: those in which no conviction covers the abuse, and in which a credible witness or other evidence (very rarely, a document) substantiates the complaint.

To obtain this material and attempt to get some redress for the complainant, we used a variety of methods and encountered the procedures of a variety of institutions, from courts to review boards. Here we will make just a brief survey of them, before we describe individual cases.

INVESTIGATION

This was simple legwork, done by me, by law students, by volunteers, and by Eve Cary, my assistant. It was not so difficult as it seemed at first, because in most cases the witnesses were either easily accessible or could not be identified at all. Quite often the complainant knew the names of his witnesses, and it was simply a matter of interviewing them. The alternative, which usually yielded no willing witnesses, was to drop in at the stores and houses facing the scene of the incident. In the end, it is an astonishing tribute to human patience that so many people were willing to take the time to go to court or to a hearing, or both, and tell what they had seen.

CRIMINAL COURTS

In New York City, during the period of this project, criminal penalties, apart from traffic matters, were imposed for felonies, misdemeanors, and offenses. Felonies generally included all serious crimes (with a maximum penalty of a year or more), such as burglary, grand larceny, assault with a weapon, and the like. Felonies were tried in the State Supreme Court, with a jury. Misdemeanors were less serious crimes (penalty less than a year) such as simple assault (e.g. a blow with the fist). These were tried in the City Criminal Court; there was no jury, but there was the option of a trial either by one judge

or by a three-judge bench. Offenses were still less serious infractions, including disorderly conduct and violations of city
ordinances and of subway and park regulations. These were
tried summarily, before one judge.

The typical pattern of charges covering an abuse in the
street included disorderly conduct, resisting arrest, and assaulting an officer. Resisting arrest is a misdemeanor, but assaulting
an officer in the line of duty may be a felony. Thus the bulk of
our cases involved misdemeanor and offense charges, although
sometimes we appeared in Supreme Court to answer a felonious assault charge.

After nearly all our material had been collected, the Penal
Law of the State of New York was overhauled completely as
of September 1, 1967. Under this revision, criminal offenses are
now divided into felonies (five classes), misdemeanors (three
classes), and violations. Although penalties for conviction in
most of the cases discussed in succeeding chapters might consequently be different, the legal doctrines and problems of
proof would be the same, with one major exception: at the time
the cases cited in this book occurred, it was lawful for a citizen
to resist an unlawful arrest. This extremely important right,
which placed the burden of proving the lawfulness of a defendant's arrest squarely on the police, was abolished by the
New York state legislature on March 6, 1968. The present law,
which makes it illegal to resist even an obviously unlawful
arrest, would make it considerably more difficult to win some
of these cases now than it was in 1967, as I shall show in detail
in Chapters 2 and 10.

DEPARTMENTAL REVIEW

This subject will be discussed in detail in the following chapters, because it is the chief means of redress for abuses. This
brings us immediately to a problem of definition that may seem
a little surprising: What is a policeman? Many city agencies
employ men in blue uniforms, but not all of them have the
powers of policemen. The Transit Authority, for example, employs men who are "peace officers" under state law; they have
the powers of policemen, except that they may not stop and

frisk. For purposes of our project, any peace officer who does police work (e.g. patrol) in New York City is defined as a policeman, and we investigated a number of complaints against transit patrolmen to compare them with complaints we received against the city police.

The question of definition arises here because every complaint against a peace officer or a policeman must be referred to the agency that employs him, and every agency has its own system of review. The Transit Authority disciplinary procedures, for example, are quite different from those of the Police Department. This confusing situation exists because all these officers are civil servants, and under the state civil service law none can be disciplined except after a hearing *within his own agency*. A city policeman must be tried by his department, and a transit policeman by the Transit Authority. This law was not affected in the slightest by the Civilian Review Board established by Mayor Lindsay in the summer of 1966 and abolished by the voters that November. The Board never had the power to do more than recommend a course of action to the Police Commissioner. Every investigation, every hearing, by any city agency about a civil servant ultimately boils down to preparation for a decision by the head of the agency. Thus every complaint made from my office about a city policeman had to be approved by the Police Commissioner before it could result in discipline.

AFFIRMATIVE ACTIONS

Many police abuses are themselves crimes; for example, police brutality usually constitutes a simple assault; if severe enough, it may be a felonious assault. Theoretically, prosecution by the District Attorney is a possible remedy, but as a practical matter, unless corruption or a killing is involved, the District Attorney does not often prosecute policemen. For the most part, discipline is left to the Police Department.

Civil actions for damages due to assault, false arrest, or malicious prosecution, or to enjoin future misconduct, can be brought in either federal or state court. As we shall see later, this procedure is much more effective than prosecution, but it

could be only briefly explored in our project, because civil
litigation consumes many more years than we had to give to
the entire study.

The results of this study have been influenced by all the
institutions through which the cases passed. For example, the
complainants and witnesses in a large percentage of the authenticated cases are middle-class people, without previous criminal
convictions. This is not because more people from the middle
classes than from the poor were abused, but rather because
middle-class people are more likely to register complaints, and
cases involving them are unfortunately easier to authenticate.
Because no case is considered authenticated if there was a
covering conviction in the criminal case, the results reflect the
decision-making process in the criminal courts. Judges find
articulate, well-dressed people without criminal records credible as witnesses, and are disposed to believe their testimony if
it is they who are defendants or defense witnesses. But once
a man has one criminal conviction, it becomes much easier to
get another; conversely, when his record is clean, the courts
are more inclined to let it remain that way.

For similar reasons, it is impossible for me to answer the
principal question on every reader's mind: How widespread
are police abuses? There are so many obstacles in the way of
authenticating any case that we cannot hope to give reliable
figures about the extent of the problem. It will be clear, however, that the patterns of abuse in the authenticated cases are
so repetitive (and so much like those that cannot be authenticated) that we have no choice but to believe we are faced
with pervasive problems of law enforcement.

In addition to the institutions with which we worked, the
methods of our project, as always, tended to define the subject
with which we finally deal here. In succeeding chapters, we
will consider assaults by the police, false arrest, deliberate
framing, and such violations of constitutional rights as unlawful search and seizure. We will consider only tangentially
abuses, such as coerced confessions, for which there are usually
no witnesses. Any abuse which is alleged to have occurred in
the precinct, in fact, is beyond the scope of the methods used

here, except in the most unusual cases. For the most part, we will be considering "street-corner" incidents, because they are the sort for which the facts are available. The precinct doors are closed to us.

It was not always thus. Forty years ago, police officers were not as well trained in the law as they are now, and in any case the courts were less restrictive of police misconduct. Precinct abuses like the "third degree" (coerced confessions) were relatively easy to study, because the police frequently did not bother to deny them. The Wickersham Commission, in its 1931 report on "The Third Degree," [2] said: "Brutality during arrests raises a more difficult problem of prevention than brutality thereafter, for the policeman always has the possible argument that the prisoner resisted arrest or tried to escape." The problem of establishing the existence of brutality during arrest is no doubt just as difficult as it was in 1931, but it is the major area of police abuse we will study here, because brutality in the precinct has become even more inaccessible to investigation. This is, if you like, the other half of Lawlessness in Law Enforcement.

My investigations have been further constricted in some cases by lack of cooperation from city and police officials. This problem springs from the natural secretiveness of public servants, particularly when faced with a representative of the Civil Liberties Union. Lack of cooperation was by no means general; the staff of the Department's Civilian Complaint Review Board, for example, was always helpful. But the Police Academy was not; we were permitted to attend only four classes, and therefore my comments on police training are sketchy. In two cases I was refused statistical information—once by the Police Department and once by the City Department of Law—although similar statistics for earlier years had been freely given to earlier investigators. Therefore, in some cases 1965 figures are used because 1966 figures were unobtainable.

This is a study of a social problem, and of the adequacy of the means now available to solve it. But the problem itself is a strange one, because many of the people concerned with it—

law enforcement officials and private citizens alike—do not admit that it exists. Thus, in each case, my aim has been first to show that the alleged abuse actually occurred, and second, to indicate what, if anything, was done about it. In other words, before redress of the problem can be discussed, I am in the position of having to establish that the problem itself exists.

The criminal charges which cover the police abuses cited in this book, however unfortunate for the defendants, afford us some special dividends here. Although these charges were often minor in the eyes of the courts, the trials give us an unparalleled opportunity to study the criminal process at work in petty cases. The process is interesting in itself, and an understanding of it is indispensable if one is to see why it is so difficult to remedy police misconduct. To give the reader a sense of the proceedings, I have made generous use of the minutes of the criminal trials in the first two cases which follow. But since such technical details do not easily bear repetition, even to lawyers, succeeding cases are described more briefly.

Our study of the way the criminal courts decide misdemeanor and offense cases, and the way the police testimony affects them, is an exercise in legal realism. If realism is the study of what the courts really decide, rather than of what they claim to decide, and the "fact-skeptical" branch of realism, as Jerome Frank called it, is concerned with the vagaries in the way judges and juries find the facts, then this book treats of one of the ultimate sources of fact-skepticism. It is concerned with the way the police prepare the facts to present to judges and juries; it deals with the vagaries of police testimony. The legal rules may be made by the courts, but the outcome of the cases is too often controlled by the police witnesses.

This is most emphatically not an attack on the police generally, or on the New York City Police Department in particular. I say this not only because a great deal of good and indispensable police work was carried out while these cases went on, but because in many if not most cases, the police were doing what society wanted them to do. It is my belief that society, and with it the police, can change enough to eliminate the sort of abuses that are recounted in succeeding chapters. This book is, in fact, a sort of backhanded tribute to the institutions of justice in New York City, including the Police Department. It is only because of their relative openness and fairness that we were able to authenticate as many cases as we did. One needs somewhat viable institutions even to investigate the facts in these cases. The standards of authentication applied in this study—a corroborating witness and the dismissal of the cover charges—could not be applied with any success at all in some American cities. The bias of the judges is so much greater and the defense of criminal cases so much more perfunctory in many cities than it is in New York, that I do not think a study such as this could hope for more than a handful of authenticated cases by the standards we used.

I must close with a note on the bewildering use of names in succeeding chapters. The names of police officers never appear. The actual names of complainants are used, except where a change is noted. These changes are made in cases where some fact might tend to embarrass one of the parties, and in cases where there were no court proceedings. The rules of the Review Board provide that no notation of a civilian complaint is to go into an officer's record if the complaint is found unsubstantiated, and the officer is entitled to the benefit of that rule. In cases, then, where the civilian complaint was found unsubstantiated and no criminal case was made by the officer against the complainant, the original names have generally been changed to accord with the spirit of the Board's rules.

May 1968

P. C.

POLICE POWER

Police Abuses in New York City

I

A PUERTO RICAN IN SEWARD PARK

IN THE SPRING of 1966, shortly after this study was begun, we had received only a few complaints of police abuse from the old Lower East Side. The handful that we had seemed bad enough—Puerto Ricans arrested for failing to move along fast enough and the like—but not extraordinary for a poor neighborhood. We were absorbed in an investigation and trial growing out of a riot in Brooklyn, to be discussed in Chapter 10, and at first we gave only desultory attention to complaints from the Lower East Side. We had no reason to expect serious conflict from that quarter.

At the beginning of June, my attention was finally distracted from the Brooklyn case by an agitated telephone call from the parents of a boy who had died in an East Side station house, apparently a suicide by hanging. They recounted a macabre but fragmentary tale of his death, with rumors of threats and assaults on other boys in the neighborhood. They said they had been referred to me by a Mr. Franklin, a name I did not recognize, and with some misgivings I asked them to come and give me the details.

The following Friday the parents, plain Irish working people, were waiting bleakly for me in my old grey office at the Civil Liberties Union. Their story was not encouraging. Their son, then twenty years old, had been free on bail for several charges when he was arrested once again for burglary. Some hours after his arrival at the precinct, he was dead by hanging. There were no witnesses. Those few short sentences were all they knew, and I was pervaded by the unhappy sense that it was all any of us was ever likely to know about the boy's death. Under my working rules, I could not accept complaints of police abuse for investigation if there was no corroboration, or at least a fair likelihood of finding some. In my then short experience, this had already excluded the possibility of investigating most of the complaints arising solely in the station house; for most of them, I had simply no means at all of authentication. I occasionally made an exception to my rule for a case like this one, when there was a death, but I usually regretted it.

I was regretting now that I had asked the parents to come in, not because I had any reason to doubt their story, but because I could not see what I might contribute. I began at last to draw up the dismal papers to obtain a copy of the autopsy in the hope that it might offer a clue, while the mother went on with the story. Slowly I began to come awake and realize that we might be at the edge of another case that could be successfully investigated. The mother said that a Puerto Rican boy in the neighborhood had been threatened "with the same thing that my son got." Other boys had been punched and arrested, and Mr. Franklin, she said, had witnesses to all of it.

That night I gave Franklin a call. He was the vice-president of a union local in the shop where Victor Badillo, one of the neighborhood boys, was working. Badillo had been in Seward Park when two other Puerto Rican boys were assaulted and one arrested by the police. In search of help outside the neighborhood, he had turned to Franklin. He reported that after the hanging and then the assaults, the young men were in the mood for a riot, and Franklin had undertaken to talk to the police and organize a community meeting. He was uncertain whether the boy arrested had a lawyer, but he was sure that his name was Jose Rivera and that he was in Polyclinic Hospital with a broken jaw. On Sunday, I went down to the park to talk to the witnesses.

Seward Park is a small square of trees and ball fields at Essex Street and East Broadway. Its south side faces the Folksbiene Playhouse and the offices of the *Jewish Daily Forward,* two of the few remaining bastions of the old Yiddish culture on the East Side. It sits in the center of a small island of old tenements, now largely occupied by Spanish-speaking people, surrounded by middle-income and low-income housing projects. On fine summer afternoons and evenings it is filled with older people resting on benches and young men playing games.

It was on such an afternoon that I walked down Jefferson Street south from the park, looking for Victor Badillo and his friends. I found them sitting on a broken doorstep, surrounded by a litter of soda cans. Badillo introduced me to Ismael Gonzalez; both were rather alike, slight and dark-haired, very polite. Gonzalez had been a witness to the arrest of Jose Rivera, as well as himself the recipient of a little rough treatment. We strolled through the south entrance into the park and sat in the shade while I took affidavits from them. It was slow work, because Gonzalez' English was halting and I knew no Spanish.

Presently we walked west across the park to get a look at the scene. The incident had apparently started the previous Sunday at about 8:30 P.M. when two policemen drove their squad car through the west entrance to the park and began ordering everyone to leave. Those who protested, or left too slowly, had been shoved or hit. In some way that was still not clear, Jose Rivera had been arrested. As we talked about the incident, the boys pointing out the places where the car had stopped, other witnesses to the incident began to gather around. They were all about the same age as Badillo and Gonzalez, between eighteen and twenty-two, and most were of the same slight build.

I asked them a question to which I was never to have a really satisfactory answer: Why did the police happen to drive into the park that evening and chase everyone out? The ex-

planations were various. Victor Badillo thought the hanging in
jail had something to do with the incursion; it had made the
community suspicious and the police tense. Another boy, Jose
Cruz, said that the police seemed to think the youths were
members of a gang, even though the local gang had not existed
for years. He pointed with some contempt to the name "Im-
perial Dragons" stenciled in faded paint on the stone fence,
together with the war slogan "DTKLAMF."

I asked whether there had been some disturbance nearby
that night. They were a little vague about this, but one of the
boys said he thought there had been some people raising hell
on the opposite side of East Broadway. That was some time
before the incident, however, and none of them had paid much
attention to it. The officers were later to testify in court that a
crowd had thrown stones at them from the park, but on the
Sunday I was there, no one so much as mentioned any provocative acts from the park. The short of it was that the boys
were, or seemed to be, completely in the dark about the reasons
for the incursion; as far as they were concerned, it was just one
more incomprehensible police action.

I was surprised to find that no one knew Rivera well. He was
then living in Hoboken, though he had once lived in the neighborhood, and had been merely visiting the park for a ball
game. Victor Badillo said that his attorney was Jacob Fishman,
with offices near the Manhattan Criminal Court, and the case
was to be called the following day.

In Criminal Court the next morning, I found Rivera and his
mother talking with Mr. Fishman. Rivera was, if possible, even
more slightly built than his friends. He was later to testify that
he weighed 109 pounds, though when I first saw him he
scarcely said a word, on account of the wires in his jaw. He was
charged with third-degree assault (that is, assault without a
weapon), a misdemeanor. Mr. Fishman had the case adjourned
to June 30 for trial, and after the adjournment I asked him if
there was anything I could do to help. It seemed such a simple
case that he could recommend nothing, except that I might
gather the witnesses for the trial. With organizers like Franklin
and Badillo, I knew that meant I had nothing to do.

Curiously, the case which led me to Rivera, the death in the precinct, vanished in the month before Rivera's trial. When I called the dead boy's mother to find out why I had not received a completed copy of the form requesting the autopsy report, she said that the family had retained a private attorney for their action against the city. He had directed her to discuss it with no one. That, except for a single grisly line at Rivera's trial, was the last I was ever to hear about the matter.

For more than a hundred years, the Men's House of Detention in Manhattan has been called The Tombs. The original building was actually modeled after a mausoleum, and the huge edifice that has replaced it might easily have been a tomb as well, while the adjacent Criminal Court at 100 Centre Street presents an aspect even more repellently funereal. Through this building pass substantially all the criminal cases in New York County. On the upper floors, felonies are tried by the State Supreme Court, and all lesser offenses, including misdemeanors, are tried in the parts assigned to the City Criminal Court. Actually, relatively few cases are "tried," perhaps as few as 5 percent, because almost all cases, misdemeanors as well as felonies, are disposed of by a plea of guilty.

Although it is next to impossible to obtain a jury trial in New York City for a crime less than a felony, a misdemeanor defendant like Jose Rivera does have a right to be tried by a panel of three judges, and Mr. Fishman had elected such a trial in preference to a summary trial before one judge. The calendar of cases for the three judges is first called before a single judge in a separate room. The calendar, posted in a box outside the door, often extends to some fifty-odd cases, more than the three judges could possibly handle. The calendar judge vociferously disposes of most of them, postponing some, accepting pleas of guilty in others, and himself trying those few cases in which the Assistant District Attorney and the defense attorney agree to waive the three-judge bench. It is at best an unceremonious and sometimes a ferocious performance, created by the shocking congestion of the calendar. When I arrived, the calendar judge was vehemently sending Mr. Fishman upstairs to trial before the three judges. It was almost exactly a month since Rivera had been arrested—an unusually short time from arraignment to trial, when the defendant is not in jail.

Three-judge trials, in Manhattan, are conducted in a small wood-paneled room on the fifth floor. To the left of the bench sits the clerk, receiving and stamping papers, under a strong desk lamp necessitated by the inexplicably dim light in the rest of the room. Before the bench is a long table where the defendant and the lawyers sit, and between the table and the judges' dais the court stenographer is perched. In deciding simple cases, the judges simply wheel their swivel chairs about, so their backs are to the public, and put their heads together for a few moments. In weightier cases, they step into the back room to confer.

Behind the bar are a few rows of benches for the public. At least half the section on the right is always filled with aged pensioners in clean sport shirts, their hands folded quietly over the heads of their canes. These old court buffs are called "the jury" by some lawyers, and they are occasionally asked their opinion of the outcome when the judges go into the back room to deliberate over a decision. In the Rivera case, since I had almost nothing to do, I sat down in the front row of the "jury" and waited for a few small matters to be disposed of before the case was called. Sitting next to me was a white-haired man, apparently a pensioner, with a heavily bandaged foot, and crutches propped against the bench beside him.

A misdemeanor trial is not usually prepared with as much thoroughness, by either the defense or the prosecution, as a felony case. Defense lawyers occasionally go to the scene and interview witnesses, and in extraordinary cases the District Attorney's investigators do the same. It is customary, however, because of the length of the calendar, for the assistant to whom the case falls for trial to prepare it in the hallway outside the courtroom by interviewing the witnesses. It is up to the police to subpoena such witnesses as they need.

There is nothing radically wrong with this system; most misdemeanors are simple enough to prepare in a short time, and the police are experienced in collecting and marshalling the evidence. If an unexpected complexity should develop, the case can be adjourned. However, the prosecution system in the Criminal Court does give a slight opportunity for a careful defense lawyer to drop a well-prepared case on the prosecution without warning. In felony cases, which are much more carefully prepared, such an opportunity does not often arise. It is for this reason that most defense lawyers dread publicity for an apparently minor case, lest the police magically produce a throng of prosecution witnesses.

Rivera's case seemed just such a humdrum misdemeanor case, utterly routine on its face, and the rapidity with which it had been pushed on for trial only strengthened that impression. When the case was called, late in the morning, neither the District Attorney nor the judges could have predicted that it would take more than the hour or so that is allotted to the average misdemeanor trial. But a moment after the first prosecution witness, the arresting officer, was sworn, no one could possibly have made a mistake about the strength of the defense. In all trials it is customary, at the start of testimony, to exclude the other witnesses, so that they cannot tailor their stories to corroborate or refute the stories of others. When the motion to exclude was made in this case, a veritable platoon of young Puerto Rican men stalked out into the hall, there to smoke and talk, and occasionally to squat down in a circle when they grew tired of standing. The face of the presiding judge fell visibly as he saw the length of the trial ahead of him.

It began. The arresting officer testified that on the evening of May 29 he was in a squad car with his partner when rocks were thrown at them by a group assembled in Seward Park. The officers drove into the park and ordered the group to leave. They all straggled out, except for Jose Rivera, who leaned on the hood of the car and made an obscene remark. The officer got out of the car and attempted to arrest the defendant, who kicked him. He then threw Rivera up against the car, and was kicked again. Rivera refused to get into the car, and the officer said that he did punch him once in getting him into the back seat. He described himself, finally, as six feet tall and weighing over two hundred pounds.

The second officer from the squad car recollected that Rivera leaned on the passenger door of the car and "refused to move on." The obscene remark did not reappear. The first officer got out of the car by the passenger door, but when Mr. Fishman asked whether the door hit Rivera when it was opened, the second officer said that he thought Rivera had already moved away. This odd twist in the testimony raised, and left un-answered, a crucial question: Why was Rivera being arrested in the first place?

The second officer saw the assault, the kick, by Rivera, but he testified that he did not see a punch from the first officer. After the first officer had admitted punching Rivera, while claiming it was justifiable, the testimony of the second that he did not see the punch was not helpful. It cast some doubt as to whether or not he had actually seen any kicks at all by Rivera.

During the testimony of the first policeman, the old pensioner next to me shook his head and muttered, "He's lying. I was there, I saw the whole thing and I know he's lying." I said that if he had seen the whole thing he ought not to be in the courtroom; he should be waiting outside to testify. "What do they need me for?" he replied. "They got plenty of witnesses without me." He went on muttering and shaking his head all morning, and I doubted his story until the court broke for lunch and I saw him skipping out of the courthouse on his crutches and his one good leg, conversing with some of the boys. I asked if he had in fact been in Seward Park, and the boys said he was a regular there.

This was my only experience with a man who had observed an event and then quietly appeared in court to see whether the authorities could find the truth about it. I wondered how he would react if the court found Jose Rivera guilty—whether he would be indignant or whether he would laugh at the help-lessness of the court. His desire to watch others struggle with the truth about events to which he had the key was to be only an exotic breeze from all the future problems we were to ex-perience with witnesses.

So many witnesses for the defense were present that Mr. Fishman did not exhaust the supply. He called four, in addition

to Jose Rivera himself and his doctor, and still there were more
waiting in the hall. Some of their testimony, as revealed in the
stenographer's minutes, is difficult to follow because the English is faulty, or because it is Spanish filtered through an
interpreter.

Jose Rivera's doctor first testified to the injuries. He related
that Rivera had been in Polyclinic Hospital from May 31, two
days after the incident, until June 4, with a broken jaw and
"contusions and abrasions" on his back. His testimony was but
the prelude to the defense, because, as he himself said under
cross-examination, he could not testify to the origin of the
injuries.

Like the blind men with the elephant, each of the eyewitnesses who followed the doctor to the stand had a piece of the
puzzle over how the dispute arose between Rivera and the
officers, and how the injuries occurred. The first two, Alfred
Suarez and Ismael Gonzalez, who had been sitting together in
the park, testified at length and were questioned closely by
the presiding judge in the effort to establish a rough picture
of the events of that evening. They both recounted how the
officers had driven into Seward Park over the curb and ordered
everyone to leave. Gonzalez was thrown to the ground by one
officer, and the two boys hurriedly left together. They were
some distance ahead of Rivera when he passed near the squad
car, walking out of the park. Alfred Suarez heard him say,
"Well, looks like we can't stay in the park any more," before
one of the officers snapped, "Take him in." Ismael Gonzalez
made an even odder observation: he thought that Rivera
stopped and looked into the car at the telephone-radio. He
did not have the key to what had happened between Rivera
and the officers, however. He testified on cross-examination: [1]

> Q. Patrolman H—— was in the car at that time, is
> that correct?
> A. Yeah; he was driving the car away, but he came
> off to get me.
> Q. He came out of the car to get you?
> A. Yes.
> Q. To throw you to the ground?

A. Yes.

Q. And—

A. Grabbed me right here and throw me down (indicating).

Q. And then he went back to the car?

A. And then he told me to get the blank off of this park.

Q. And then, he went back to the car, after telling you to get the blank off?

A. Then, he went to the car.

Q. Now in going to the car, he walked away from you towards the car, is that correct?

A. Yes.

Q. And isn't it a fact, that the defendant was walking in your direction, at that time?

A. Well, he was—he was going already because the officer chase him out.

Q. Was he coming in your direction, was he walking the same direction as you were, at that time, this defendant?

A. Yeah, he was walking straight down out of the park because the man told me to get off the park, so I got off.

Q. That's correct, that's right and he was walking behind you, is that correct?

A. Yes.

Q. And when Patrolman H—— left you, did he walk past the defendant back to the car?

A. Excuse me, sir? Say that again?

[PRESIDING JUDGE]. When H——, the fella whom you say threw you down, when he was going to the car, he went back to the car, didn't he?

THE WITNESS. He went back to the car and stand over there.

[PRESIDING JUDGE]. And then he passed the defendant, when he went back to the car from you?

THE WITNESS. Yeah, he passed the defendant but then he scream and tell him, take him in.

[PRESIDING JUDGE]. First, he passed him by and then he screamed, "Let's take him in!"

THE WITNESS. Yes.

DISTRICT ATTORNEY. I have no further questions.

After that testimony the big question was, what had passed between Rivera and the officers. Raul Nazario, who had been sitting with Rivera in the park, had a little more of the story:

THE WITNESS. Jose Rivera and we were discussing about, you know, baseball and stuff like that and when a police car drove through the sidewalk and in the park, you know, which is two steps down and I was surprised, you know—I never seen this before. So the car stopped and two officers got out and one, you know, started—the one that was driving—got out on that side and started—

Q. Which one was driving?

A. Him (indicating).

Q. Pointing to officer H——?

A. Yes, sir. He started telling everybody to move, you know, when I noticed—when I heard the noise, you know, I was looking towards the direction where the noise came from and he started telling everybody to move and everybody started getting up moving and we just stood there, you know, and we figured nothing will happen to us, you know. So then he took the other direction and started—

Q. He? Are you pointing to the other officer, S——?

A. Yes. And he started telling everybody to move and when he got to a bench, you know, he says, you know, to get the hell out of the park. So we got up and—and started walking out of the park. As we walked past the car, he made believe that he was going to go into the car and open the door, which struck Jose, with the door.

[PRESIDING JUDGE]. Say that, again, please?

THE WITNESS. As we were walking past the car—

[PRESIDING JUDGE]. Yes?

THE WITNESS. —this officer made believe he was going to go in the car and open the front door.

[PRESIDING JUDGE]. Yes?

THE WITNESS. Which struck him.

[PRESIDING JUDGE]. The door of the car?

THE WITNESS. Yes.

[PRESIDING JUDGE]. Struck Jose?

THE WITNESS. Yes.

[PRESIDING JUDGE]. I see.

Q. Then, what happened?

A. So I didn't pay no mind, we just kept on walking and before we even reached the next door of the car—that's the rear door—Jose said to me, "You can't even stay in the park any more." So then this officer—

Q. Pointing to officer H——?

A. Yes, sir. Shouted to this other officer, "Put him in!" So this officer grabbed Jose by an arm.

Q. Which officer, S——?

A. Yes and, you know, changed his mind about putting him in and pushing him—

[PRESIDING JUDGE]. Wait a minute! Wait a minute! Don't tell us about his mind, Just tell us what he did, please?

THE WITNESS. So he grabbed—he grabbed Jose by his arm.

[PRESIDING JUDGE]. Yes?

THE WITNESS. And pushed him and Jose said there was no need for the pushing, "I'm walking."

[PRESIDING JUDGE]. He pushed him?

THE WITNESS. He grabbed him by an arm and pushed him.

[PRESIDING JUDGE]. And pushed him away?

THE WITNESS. Yes.

[PRESIDING JUDGE]. From him?

THE WITNESS. Yes.

[PRESIDING JUDGE]. Towards the outside?

THE WITNESS. Yes, towards the outside, the park, you know.

[PRESIDING JUDGE]. I see.

THE WITNESS. And he said there was nothing for the pushing, "I'm walking." So he said, "What was that?" He grabbed him, again, and opened the rear door of the car and struck him, giving him a good sock.

[PRESIDING JUDGE]. What?

THE WITNESS. He gave him a good punch in the jaw, which put Jose down in a sitting position on the back seat of the car and then he gave him another one which laid him down on the back seat of the car and then he climbed on top of him, like he was holding one arm. I stood there, you know, because I was shocked. So he grabbed Jose one arm and he was like—the

knees on his chest, you know—and hitting him with
the other hand, and meanwhile, this officer was opening the other door, the other side and taking out his
handcuffs, you know. So first he put the cuffs on the
arm of this officer was holding and then he grabbed
the other arm and twisted his arms to the rear to his
back and handcuffed both hands and then, they said—
they had a party, the two of them, and they kept hitting him for about three minutes or so and then he
got out, four doors were opened at this time, and then
he started closing the doors and he got into the driver's
seat and started the car and as he drove away, you
know, he was riding in such a position he kept on
hitting him and driving. So that was all I saw.

DISTRICT ATTORNEY. I ask the record to indicate that
the witness sat sideways in his chair looking behind
him at times and holding something with his left hand
and making punching motions.

THE WITNESS. That is the way he pulled out of the park.

Q. Then, what happened?

A. Then we decided to go to the 7th Precinct and find
out some information about Jose, you know, to notify his
parents because he lives out in Jersey City, Hoboken
somewhere and we didn't know—We went to the precinct, two of us, stepped in first.

Q. Who was that, besides yourself?

A. That was Alfred Suarez and Adrian Agosto, and
Jose Cruz.

Q. You all went down to the precinct?

A. Yeah, we went down to the precinct.

Q. I see. Did you see the defendant, there?

A. Cop says, "Nobody can see him because he's a
prisoner," and I understand he was—talk of the shape he
was in. So they gave us a hard time but they finally gave
us the address of—Jose's address of his parents. Following day we notified them.

Q. The parents?

A. Yes.

Q. I see. Now, at any time while you were there, were
you drinking?

A. Oh, no.

Q. Did you see Jose drinking?

A. No. We were sitting down.

[PRESIDING JUDGE]. You can't drink sitting down?

THE WITNESS. Oh, you could drink sitting down, yes, but this particular time we were not drinking; we were reading a paper and discussing baseball.

Q. Was Jose drunk?

A. No, he wasn't drunk, he just finished playing this softball game they had before.

DEFENDANT'S ATTORNEY. Your witness.

All the witnesses agreed that there was no assault by Rivera, but they had only a fragmentary idea of the reason for the assault by the police. The pieces did not fit until Jose Rivera himself testified in his own behalf:

[DEFENDANT'S ATTORNEY]. Did you stay in the park or did you leave, at any time?

A. No.

Q. You stayed?

A. Before—yeah, I went to get the newspaper and then I came back.

Q. And then, what did you do?

A. I was sitting down with Raul Nazario.

Q. Well, had you gone out to eat at all?

A. No.

Q. And then, there came a time when something happened, is that right?

A. Yes.

Q. What time did something happen?

A. About quarter to eight, quarter to nine.

Q. Nine. And what happened?

A. I was sitting with Raul Nazario and I heard a cop coming toward us.

Q. Can you all hear him?

A. So—

[PRESIDING JUDGE]. Yes.

THE WITNESS. —so when I saw the car coming, you know, I got up with Raul and I started walking and so I don't know what happened between the other— the other officer and—and Ismael, I don't know what happened over there but I was walking toward the car and I looked inside the car, you know, so the cop—

[PRESIDING JUDGE]. What?

Q. Wait a minute! Why did you look inside the car?

A. I heard some noise, the radio was on, the radio phone was on and I was hearing things.

Q. You wanted to listen to what the radio was saying?

A. Yes.

Q. What was being said, on the radio?

A. Yeah.

Q. All right, what happened?

A. So this officer over here—

Q. Which one?

A. I don't know his name.

Q. S——?

A. Yes. He told me, "What the fuck" I was looking at and I told him, "I was looking at the phone."

Q. Then, what happened?

A. So he wasn't in the car. He opened—he tried to open the door, I thought, to get inside and he hit me with it and I kept walking with Raul. So then, I told— he chased me, you know, after he hit me with the door, he told me, you know, "Get the fuck out of the park!" and I was walking. Then, I told Raul that, "You can't even stand in the park any more." So the driver told him, "Put him in the car!" So I heard the words, "Put him in the car!" So I was walking to the policeman, so he grabbed me and he pushed me. I told him there was no need for pushing, "I can walk." So he opened the door and he punched me (indicating).

Q. Then, what happened?

A. Then, you know, the other one got into—through the other door and they both started hitting me for a couple of minutes and then before that they handcuffed me, you know.

Q. How did they handcuff you?

A. I was like this (indicating). They forced me like that (indicating) and I was laying almost down with my head down and—

Q. You had your hands behind your back, is that what you're saying?

A. Yes.

Q. What else?

A. So they kept hitting me for a couple of minutes.

Q. When you say "they," are you referring to both police officers?

A. Both of them, yes.

Q. What, exactly, did they do?

A. Well, they were punching me in the face; I know this one was hitting me in the face (indicating). I was telling him, "Stop it! Stop it!" and he told me, "Shut up!" and kept hitting me. I didn't have no—you know—so the other one was in back and putting the handcuffs on me. So he got in the front, he got behind the wheel.

Q. Who got behind the wheel?

A. This one over here.

Q. Pointing to officer H——?

A. Yes. So by the time he was driving, he was driving with one hand and punching me with the other one.

Q. Who was doing that, officer H——?

A. Yes.

Q. What was the other officer doing?

A. They were hitting me and then he told—

Q. Go ahead.

A. He told the driver, "Take it easy." I don't know what he meant by that, "Take it easy." So he made the turn and went to the—the other guy kept hitting me, the other officer, until they got there.

Q. Until where?

A. Until they got to the police station.

Q. Incidentally, how much do you weigh?

A. One hundred and nine pounds.

Q. One hundred and nine pounds?

A. Yes.

Q. How tall are you?

A. Five-four.

Q. What happened, when you got to the police station?

A. Well, they sat me on a chair.

Q. I want to ask you one question. Did you, at any time, kick the police officer?

A. No, I didn't.

Q. Any of them?

A. No, I didn't.

Q. Did you ever try to kick them?

A. No, I never did.

Q. Did you, at any time, use an expression—did you use any bad language towards them?

A. No; the only thing I told them, "There was no need for the pushing." So—"I can walk," you know I told him.

Q. Did you ever use a four-letter word following the word mother, to them?

A. No, I never did.

[PRESIDING JUDGE]. Happens to be a six-letter word.

DEFENDANT'S ATTORNEY. Well, that's another tense.

[PRESIDING JUDGE]. Anything else?

Q. What happened, at the police station?

A. I was asking for my newspaper, you know, I was asking this officer because he took it and put it in his pocket and I told him that was my paper. He didn't want to give it to me. I had my handcuffs on and I told him to take them off and he was punching me and he told me, "Shut up!" and he hit me, you know. So I kept quiet for a couple of minutes and then they came back and they took me to a small room they had where there was a colored cop there and I asked—and then they left and then I asked that policeman, I told him, "Do I have a chance to go to Court tonight?" and then he said, "I find out." He made a call and he told me that I had time. Then, about thirty minutes later they came and they—

Q. "They," meaning the two police officers?

A. Yes.

Q. Who arrested you?

A. They were—they took me upstairs and then I told him, "Are we going to Court tonight?" So this one over here—

Q. Pointing to S——?

A. —he told me, "Well, when—when we finish with you, you ain't going to be able to go to Court."

Q. Then, what happened?

A. So he took me upstairs and this one over here walked behind—ahead of me.

Q. H——?

A. Yes, he walked ahead of us and he opened—he went inside—I don't know what was happening over there. So I sat down—until they opened the door. When I was sitting down, this one showed me—he pull up his pants, you know, and he told me, "You see what you did?"

Q. Which one was that?

A. This one here.

Q. Officer S——?

A. And then I told him, "I didn't do nothing." So he kicked me in the stomach, you know.

Q. He kicked you in the stomach?

A. And knocked me down on the floor. So he kicked me again and then he picks me up and open the door and pushed me in.

Q. Then, what happened?

A. So there was—there was a detective there and another one that took my fingerprints and then another detective, he asked me, "Did you kick the policeman?" and I said, "No." And then he asked me again, "Are you calling the policeman a liar?" And I said, "Yes," because I didn't kick him. So they both grabbed me by—one by each arm.

Q. The police officers sitting here?

A. Yes and they kicked me all over the floor.

Q. Then, what happened?

A. Until I give up. I said, "All right, all right," and then they sat me on a chair where there were three papers and they made me sign them. This one told me, "If you don't sign them, we're going to finish with you!" So I said, "All right," and I signed them and then they—this one told me if I wanted to have myself—hang myself like my friend.

Q. If you wanted to hang yourself, like your friend. Did you know what he was talking about?

A. Yes. He said they were going to help me.

Q. Yes. Then, what happened?

A. So they made me sign the three papers and they took me downstairs again. When they was opening—this one was walking in front of me.

Q. Pointing to S——?

A. This one was punching me.

Q. Who was punching you?

A. This one over here.

Q. Officer H—— was punching you while officer S—— was walking in front of you and you were between them?

A. Yes.

Q. Then, what happened?

A. They took me downstairs to the same room I was before and there was about five, ten officers or seven and they asked him what I did and he told me, "He's a wise guy," and he kept punching me and I was walking around the table, there was a table in the middle and I was walking around. Suddenly, I told him, "Stop it, I had enough already!" So they took me down and they kept watching me all night.

Q. And they what?

A. They kept watching me all night. I don't know.

Q. Then, what finally happened?

A. Then they took me—in the morning they took me down the station.

Q. Did you stay in jail, in a cell in the police precinct, overnight?

A. Yes.

Q. What happened, after that?

A. Well, in the morning—

Q. Did anybody bring you any food?

A. That was—yes, a friend of mine brought me some coffee and sandwich but I left it there.

Q. When was that?

A. That night.

Q. Do you know what time it was?

A. No.

Q. Were you able to eat anything?

A. No. I only drank the coffee and I left the sandwich over there.

Q. Were you in pain, during that period of time?

A. Yes, I was.

Q. Where did you have the pain?

A. I had pains all over my body and my face and I couldn't open my mouth, you know.

Q. And were you unconscious, at any time, if you know?

A. Oh, yes. In the car. You know, in—one was hitting me and—

[PRESIDING JUDGE]. How would he know whether he was unconscious? He's ready to answer anything, even to tell you he was unconscious. How would any human being know he was unconscious?

DEFENDANT'S ATTORNEY. I've heard that question asked very frequently and I've heard it answered and I know what the common consensus is but I maintain that anybody who has been unconscious knows that he has been. I think common experience will attest to it, despite the scorn that I hear from some sources.

Q. Were you to appear in Court the next day?

DISTRICT ATTORNEY. I don't know what counsel is referring to?

[PRESIDING JUDGE]. I don't know.

A. First, they took me to headquarters and took pictures of me.

Q. Then, were you taken to Court, eventually?

A. Yes.

Q. I see and then you were bailed out?

A. I think Tuesday morning.

Q. On Tuesday?

A. On Tuesday morning.

Q. The following Tuesday?

A. Right.

Q. Then after you got out, did you see a doctor?

A. Yes.

At the close of Jose Rivera's testimony, the three-judge court found him not guilty of the assault, by a majority vote, with one judge dissenting. In the course of the dismissal, the presiding judge remarked that he did not fully believe Rivera's story. If his story had been true, he said, "this doctor who testified here would not have been able to describe a single spot on his body that was unbruised." He went on to say he believed an incident did happen "which justified the officers in dispersing the crowd; the crowd, with the exception of this defendant, moved without any trouble." The judges simply found a reasonable doubt as to the assault by Rivera, not that the officers had no right to order Rivera or the others to move.

Both of these remarks are fascinating and instructive. Rivera's testimony, and the judge's comments upon it, reveal especially difficult problems, endemic to all police abuse cases. Abuses which occur in the street often have observers and sometimes a large number of quite credible witnesses, while abuses in the precinct remain shadowy tales. In *People v. Jose Rivera,* although the boys had some difficulty in testifying, they were really very believable witnesses. The fact that they saw only fragments of what occurred, from different points of view, and could not adequately explain it all either to themselves or to the court, in the long run added to rather than detracted from their credibility. A manufactured story would have been more likely to be uniform among all the witnesses, rather than the broken pieces of a puzzle.

The occurrences in the park were heavily authenticated, and Rivera's story about the park was corroborated, but his story about the events in the precinct was scarcely corroborated at all. I at least had some reason to believe his story about fearing a hanging, because of what had happened to the other boy, but the judges had not even that much to go on. After he was taken out of the park, the eyewitnesses did not see him again. All of the injuries diagnosed by the doctor *could* have occurred at the scene of the arrest, and as the presiding judge pointed out, there was only Rivera's word for what had happened afterward. This is ever the way with stories about the precinct, as compared with incidents in the street. In general, the only incidents we have any hope of authenticating are those in the street. Except for the rare case when there is a witness in the precinct, or in the slightly more common event that someone arrives at the precinct and sees the injuries, there is no way to establish any actions by the police after a defendant has been taken away. Even in the case where injuries are visible at the precinct or later in court, it is usually impossible to prove that they are not the result of resisting arrest, or of some even more remote fracas before the arrival of the police. Without thorough corroboration, judges will never accept a macabre story of deliberate injuries by the authorities. The presiding judge in Rivera's case accepted the story of the incident in the park as authentic enough for an acquittal, but did not at all accept the story of the events in the precinct. This was a standard which we were grudgingly forced to apply in hundreds of cases, even when we had particular reason to be convinced of the complainant's veracity. Many complaints from the streets are "true," in the legal sense, because they can be proved, but many more, like Rivera's account of his treatment in the precinct or the death of the boy which led me to Rivera's case, are not "true" only because they cannot be proved. Often the most serious and brutal complaints are the hardest to verify.

The presiding judge's remarks concerning the justification for the police order to Rivera and the others to move also have a special significance that is easiest to grasp from the officers' reaction to the trial. When they were asked what they thought of the outcome, one of them replied that they had "goofed"—they should have charged the defendant with disorderly conduct and resisting arrest as well as with assault. This remark, which seems astonishing, is in fact a perfectly logical reaction from the policeman's point of view, and would evoke only a bored nod from a criminal lawyer. But to anyone who has not spent his time scuffling in the criminal courts, the entire system of arrests to cover police errors must seem mysterious.

The New York disorderly conduct law, as it was at the time of the Rivera trial, was a complex statute penalizing eleven different acts, ranging from abusive language to soliciting a man for a crime against nature, whenever any of them was done "with intent to provoke a breach of the peace, or whereby a breach of the peace may be occasioned." Disorderly conduct was not a crime but an "offense," falling somewhere between a traffic violation and a misdemeanor.

The statute presented an impenetrable forest of constitutional issues, centering about its exasperating vagueness, and most of them were never settled because the charge was rarely serious enough to warrant an appeal. The rather puzzling phrases requiring an intent or a threat of a breach of the peace were generally interpreted according to rule of thumb which required the presence of a crowd, or at least some members of the public, at the scene. Without them, there could be no breach of the peace, but with them, judges often found that there not only could be but was.

The first subsection of the statute penalized abusive language; the third forbade congregating on a street and failing to move on when ordered to by the police. When the presiding judge expressed the opinion that the police had the right to disperse the crowd and make the defendant move on, he apparently felt there had been some basis for a charge of disorderly conduct. If Jose Rivera could have been convicted of that, a charge of resisting arrest might also have been successful. But it was asking too much to attempt to convict him of a naked assault without any explanation of how the police came to arrest him. The failure to charge Rivera with disorderly conduct in fact cast considerable doubt upon the testimony of the officers about his conduct, and that of the others in the park, in throwing rocks, making an obscene remark, and refusing to move on. It seemed strange that if all those things occurred, a charge of disorderly conduct did not result, particularly in view of the fact that the first officer said he got out of the car to arrest Rivera.

The charges of disorderly conduct, resisting arrest, and assault became a familiar refrain in my office in cases of false arrest and brutality. They are the standard "cover charges" for such abuses, and we greeted with amazement the rare case of a police abuse where these charges were not made. In a sophisticated police department like New York City's, police abuses do not usually occur without criminal charges to cover them, and nothing can be done about abuses unless something is done about the cover charges. These charges stand directly in the way of every avenue of redress. If an acquittal cannot be had on a charge of resisting arrest, there is certainly no use complaining of police brutality. Thus nearly every police abuse case is first and foremost a criminal case.

The charges arising out of the cover arrest are as classic as a bid in bridge, and like a bid, they are understood through a kind of code. Each of the charges is designed to account for an action by the police, in order to protect them from a lawsuit or from disciplinary action by the Department. The disorderly conduct charge accounts for the arrest. If the defendant has not been injured in the arrest, that charge may be enough. If there are any injuries, then charges of assault and resisting arrest will be added. The charges themselves tell us much of

what has happened at the arrest; they are carefully keyed to
the seriousness of the arrest, not of the crime.

So deeply ingrained is this system that the police themselves
occasionally use it to explain their actions. In the winter of
1966, a Negro postman, whom we may call Edward Thompson
(a fictitious name), was arrested at a bar in Chelsea. He was
charged solely with disorderly conduct—being drunk and
abusive to other people in the bar. Thompson claimed that the
arrest was in fact a vengeful act by the police, that he was
sober, and that he had been beaten by the police. The police
brought to court a witness from the Vera Foundation,* who
had interviewed Mr. Thompson the day he was arrested to see
whether he was eligible for release with a summons instead
of being placed under arrest. The interviewer had rejected
Thompson for possible eligibility because he seemed too intoxicated to understand the charges. This testimony just about
destroyed any effective defense to the disorderly conduct
charge, but it did not quite dispose of the accusation of beating.
"Counselor," said the arresting officer in an injured tone, "we
never laid a hand on him. You can tell that. If we had, he
would have been charged with resisting arrest, isn't that right?"
The logic was irresistible, and I believed him.

Although the charges in a police abuse case are generally
keyed to the events of the arrest, charges of resisting arrest or
assault may be included even when there are no injuries, in
order to increase the bargaining power of the police. In such
a case the charges are a "bid" in the literal sense: a bid for a
plea of guilty to a lesser offense, in this case disorderly conduct,
in return for dropping the assault and resisting-arrest charges.
Under the "plea-bargaining" system which exists in New York
and most other cities with congested court calendars, such a
plea of guilty is a standard response in criminal cases. Disorderly conduct thus acts as the coin of exchange in the criminal courts for almost all minor charges involving disputes with
the police. Disorderly conduct not being a crime, conviction

---

* The Vera Foundation, a privately supported institution, works with
the New York City police on a number of problems, including the sub-
stitution of summonses for arrest.

results in comparatively little injury to the defendant, while it covers the policeman in all but the most egregious cases. If the defendant can be induced to plead guilty to the offense in return for a dismissal of other charges, that is the most satisfactory arrangement. But even at a trial, if the judges are faced with a scale of charges from assault down to disorderly conduct and feel that the defendant is at least partly responsible for the fracas, they can acquit him of the misdemeanors and produce a kind of standoff by a conviction for the offense. We were confronted by this pattern repeatedly at the project, as other lawyers have been. Many lawyers automatically recommend a plea of guilty to disorderly conduct when they are faced with a charge of resisting arrest.

By the rules of the game, then, the officers in the Rivera case certainly did "goof," as they said they did. By charging Rivera solely with assault, they made the problem more difficult for everyone. They made it difficult to understand by what authority they had him in custody in the first place, they injured their own credibility, and they made the choice more difficult for the judges.

The remarks of the judge and the reaction of the police to them were extremely illuminating. Our first hope, in taking on such cases, had been to "beat the system," at least in cases with particularly strong witnesses. We hoped to be able to clear all criminal charges and go on to some affirmative remedy. Because of the effectiveness of the police in obtaining convictions, we were frequently unable to do so. We learned, a hundred times over, the first principle in attempting to deal with the police: arrest is an immensely powerful tool, and for the most part it renders all remedies useless. We were doing well if we could have the charges dismissed; it was the rare case where we could actually gain an advantage.

Jose Rivera, as it turned out, understood this better than we. A claim for damages for him against New York City was planned, and my office was asked to file a complaint against the police officers. There was still plenty of time to file the claim for damages. It had to be filed within ninety days, and the criminal trial was over within a month after the incident

had occurred. But within a few weeks after the trial, Jose
Rivera was gone. I called Victor Badillo to ask what had happened to him, and Victor said he had heard that Jose had
found a job in Canada. "He didn't see why he shouldn't go,"
said Badillo tersely. Rivera perhaps felt that the most he could
expect was to stay "even" with the law, to stay away from a
criminal record and jail.

It would be a mistake to call the case of *People v. Jose
Rivera* "typical." Every case involving a police abuse raises
some special problem, usually one of proof or a mystery of
motivation. Still, as an assault by the police arising out of a
community conflict, the Rivera case fits a familiar pattern. Most
of the dozens of complaints like it in our files can never be
authenticated one way or the other for lack of witnesses, but
eighteen were verified in the same way that Rivera's case was,
and many of these will be described in succeeding chapters.
They may differ in detail, they may not involve broken bones,
but basically they all describe violent police reactions to sullen
hostility. More important, each one gave rise to a set of criminal charges which were uniquely difficult to clear away, because they involved a direct denial of eyewitness testimony
from the police.

In one way, the Rivera case was unlike any other police case
I can remember: the defense was uniquely easy to prepare.
The witnesses all but followed Victor Badillo around in their
eagerness to testify. Community solidarity is certainly the key
at least to the criminal charges arising out of police abuses. As
long as his witnesses will stick by the defendant, he will at
least keep his liberty, if nothing else. The most basic ingredients for redress of police abuses are a good defense lawyer
and good community organization.

At the close of the case, there remained one conundrum
that was never satisfactorily answered: What provocation did
Rivera give? It was simple to theorize that after the officers
had ordered the young men to leave the park, it was annoying
to see one lingering and peering into their car; when they
hustled him on, he showed a little defiance by saying that he
guessed he could not stay in the park any more and that they

did not have to push him. In the scale of police values, however, a simple arrest, like the ones described in the next chapter, is usually considered sufficient punishment for such mild impudence. A brutal assault such as the one that followed in this case is usually the punishment for some open and flagrant defiance of authority. Here, there seemed to be none. This only emphasized the mystery of motive that lies at the bottom of all cases of police abuse. It is nearly as difficult (or as easy) to understand why the police react as they do as it is to understand why citizens defy them. If the defiance seemed slight here, it rarely seems great enough for the results it often provokes.

Motive is the root question of this entire study. Why did these men commit police abuses? Were they poorly trained? Were they unintelligent? Did they come to the Department with some special streak of authoritarianism? Were their abuses somehow the result of the extreme pressures of life in New York? As we shall have occasion to observe in more detail, the answer to these questions for the most part is no. The truth is that police abuses are the product of the police role as an instrument of authority in society, the traditions of police work, and the attitude of society toward the police. It is these factors which tend to produce in every city a set of problems similar to those in New York.

2

BITTERNESS ON SUGAR HILL

NINE DAYS AFTER JOSE RIVERA was arrested, James Meredith began his famous pilgrimage down highway 51 in Mississippi, accompanied intermittently by dozens of other civil rights leaders. On June 7, 1966, the papers carried banner headlines that Meredith had been shot from ambush, and the first reports left it uncertain whether he would live.

The same night, 1,200 miles from Mississippi, the shooting of Meredith provoked a strange arrest. Mr. Franklin, the organizer in the Rivera case, called to report that two acquaintances of his, Harold Bell and Sam Johnson, had been arrested coming out of a bar at 162nd Street and Amsterdam Avenue, on the edge of Harlem. Johnson had been bitterly telling Bell what he thought of Meredith's assailants, when the two were suddenly stopped by a policeman.

It did not sound like a promising case for the Police Practices Project, but if I had learned nothing else from the Rivera case, I now knew enough at least to pay attention to unpromising complaints from Buddy Franklin. When Mr. Johnson called, I asked him to come in with Mr. Bell and whatever witnesses he could find.

Harold Bell was a cab driver in his early forties, and Samuel

Johnson, then a clerk, was some ten years younger. Mr. Bell, a mild-mannered man with light brown skin, was quite apprehensive about the case. Johnson, a dapper fellow with a mustache, was volubly determined to fight. They were accused of resisting arrest and of simple assault, both misdemeanors, as well as of the offense of disorderly conduct. Neither had ever been arrested before.

At their arraignment, the two had been exposed to the plea-bargaining system. The prosecution had offered to dismiss the misdemeanor charges in exchange for a plea of guilty to disorderly conduct. Bell speculated about whether they ought to accept the offer. He recognized that disorderly conduct was not a crime, and that such a conviction would not mean a criminal record, whereas if he were convicted of the misdemeanors he might lose his job. Johnson scoffed; after all, they had not done anything wrong. Bell agreed, but seemed doubtful. It looked as though Johnson wanted justice at all costs and Bell wanted to survive. Survival is often preferable to justice, and I wondered whether they ought to get separate attorneys. Before I advised them, I wanted to talk to their witnesses.

They had brought a witness with them, but he was reluctant to testify because he had been twice convicted for narcotics crimes. I was nearly as hesitant to have him appear as he was to do so, but I took a few notes of what he said:

> Saw Bell and Johnson come out of bar from 100 or 75 feet away. With [two] girls. Could not hear them. Saw a policeman pass them. Witness walked on, saw nothing until he heard a commotion. Turned back, saw them handcuffed, being pulled across street. Put in car.

This left us nowhere, and I told Bell and Johnson that I could not take the case unless we could do better. They thought there were other witnesses who had gone to the precinct after the arrest, and they agreed to look for them around the neighborhood.

In the next few days my enterprising summer law student, Clift Johnson, took a long statement from an extremely credible witness, Mr. Sanderson, a hospital orderly. Bell and Johnson decided to stick together and fight the case, and I accepted it. It was to be tried in the three-judge courtroom on the fifth floor of Manhattan Criminal Court, where Jose Rivera's case had been tried, though before a different panel of judges. This time, instead of being a relaxed observer, I was going to defend them myself.

On the trial day, the calendar was called, once again before a single judge on the fourth floor. It was a refreshingly good day in my increasingly sad experience of the courts; all the witnesses had showed up. Mr. Bell looked tense and unhappy. I thought of what a cruel ordeal a criminal trial is for the defendants, no matter what the charges. Bell looked a little antagonistically at Johnson, who confidently predicted that they would be acquitted. There were several cases on trial ahead of us, and we sat in the courtroom or stood nervously about the hall during the hours until the case was finally called and the officer sworn.

My Bar is a small place with a glass-brick front, reminiscent of more elegant days in the thirties. It is at a busy corner in the neighborhood that was once famous as Sugar Hill, the upper-class ghetto of Harlem. In the words of a local real estate lawyer, the neighborhood is a casualty of integration; many of its well-to-do residents have moved away. Harold Bell and Samuel Johnson each lived within a few blocks of the corner, and on the evening of Tuesday, June 7, they were sitting in the bar having a few drinks and waiting to meet their wives. A heated discussion of the Meredith shooting was in progress, and Johnson, as Bell ruefully observed, was doing most of the talking. The angry talk continued after the women arrived and all four walked out to Johnson's Thunderbird parked at the curb.

According to the affidavit of the white officer who arrested them, the two men:

> did become loud and boisterous and did shout "the white motherfuckers that shot Meredith." Defendants refused to quiet down and leave and by their actions did cause a crowd to collect, to the annoyance of persons in the vi-

cinity. Defendants were told on three occasions to desist
and leave, which they refused to do.

This constituted the charge of disorderly conduct, and the
testimony at the trial expanded on it very little.

The officer went on to say that when he arrested Johnson,
Bell cried, "You are not going to take him to jail." Bell grabbed
for the nightstick as the officer arrested him, and Johnson
backed into the crowd. They were finally handcuffed together,
and as he took them to a cab for transportation to the precinct,
the officer claimed that they scratched his wrists.

Although this seemed a minor incident, the events described by the officer did supply the technical elements of the
charges of resisting arrest and assault if they withstood the
testimony of the defense witnesses. We had subpoenaed two
witnesses, but one of them had seen relatively little of the
arrest, and it was Mr. Sanderson on whom we had to rely.
Under a cross-examination which was unusually thorough for
this sort of case, he proved to be a solid, self-confident witness.[1]

Q. You saw the two defendants here, Johnson and
Bell, talking about James Meredith?
A. That's correct.
Q. Where were you standing when you first heard
them talking about James Meredith?
A. The Officer was proceeding north and I was behind
him, about 15 feet. We both was walking north. I was
direct behind him and the two men there was talking
their conversation about James Meredith.
Q. How far were you from these two men when you
first heard them talking about James Meredith?
A. About 35 feet.
Q. About 35 feet. And you—you could hear them
talking about James Meredith?
A. We could hear them, yes.
Q. Would you say their voices were loud?
A. They were louder than normal.
Q. Louder than normal?
A. Yes.
Q. And you were going up towards 163rd St.?

A. That's correct.

Q. And did you see the Officer come over to them?

A. The Officer was in front of me.

Q. And you saw the Officer stop where they were?

A. The Officer walked past them, turned his head and [p]roceeded north. He walked about 10 feet and then turned around and came back to the car, and I proceeded past him going north.

Q. In other words, the Officer walked past them and then you walked past them?

A. That's right.

Q. Then you saw the Officer come back?

A. That's right.

Q. What did you do then?

A. I proceeded north to the corner and I turned around.

Q. You continued up to 163rd St.?

A. That's correct.

Q. And did you see where the Officer stopped then in the [block]?

A. Well, the car was parked at—he stopped at the car and walked back to the car.

Q. How far south was the car from 163rd St. and Amsterdam Ave.?

A. About 50 feet.

Q. 50 feet. What did you do when you got to 163rd and Amsterdam?

A. I—I turned around to see what was happening, going on. I heard this—I heard this commotion.

Q. You heard this commotion?

A. Yes.

Q. Did you hear shouting?

A. Yes.

Q. Did you hear Johnson and Bell shouting?

A. They were shouting—they were shouting back at each other, talking among themselves.

Q. Were they shouting about white mother fuckers?

A. I didn't hear that.

Q. You did—did you hear any curse words or words you consider curse words?

A. Heard "it's a damn shame the man got shot like he was, unarmed."

Q. You didn't hear any words that you would consider curse words?

A. No.

Q. You hear the word "coward"?

A. I heard "coward".

Q. Did you hear the word "bastard"?

A. I heard that.

Q. Would you consider that a curse word?

A. I hear it all the time.

Q. Now, did you come back to where the Officer
was with these two defendants?

A. No, I didn't.

Q. You stayed there?

A. I stayed there.

Q. And did a crowd gather around—

A. The—

Q. —this commotion?

A. A crowd didn't gather until the Officer placed the
handcuffs on to the men, took them out into the middle
of St. Nicholas Avenue.

As the cross-examination went on it became evident that
these arrests were a neighborhood sensation.

Q. When the Officer went down, you say, the area
of St. Nicholas Ave. and Amsterdam Ave., the crowd
stayed where it was?

A. That's correct.

Q. Where was that?

A. In front of the subway, which is 162nd St. and
the Supermarket. All in the general section, about 200
feet; one section all stayed there.

Q. And they didn't follow him down to where he was
getting in the cab?

A. No.

Q. Sir, on your direct testimony, did you say that
when the Officer had these two, and when he was going
to take them to the cab, that he raised his night stick
and the crowd said, "you can't hit an unarmed man"?

A. That's correct; that's what he did.

Q. Was the crowd right there when the Officer was
trying to get in the cab?

A. He was in the street, about 25 feet in the middle of the street where the cab stopped.

Q. And was the crowd where the Officer was trying to put these two men in the cab?

A. On the sidewalk.

Q. Nobody on the street?

A. Nobody on the street. All the crowd stayed on the sidewalk.

Q. On the east or west side of the street?

A. That was on the west side of the street.

Q. That's across the street from where he first stopped them?

A. Across the street from the restaurant, from the restaurant. Took them directly across the street.

Q. So, the cro[w]d didn't stay where the Officer first stopped them? They accu[m]ulated on the other side of the street?

A. They was accu[m]ulating on both sides of the street.

Q. And they followed the Officer to where he tried to put them in the cab at St. Nicholas and Amsterdam Ave., you say?

A. The cro[w]d didn't follow him. The crowd on the other side of the street where he was going. One was on one side of the street and one on the other.

Q. The crowd on the other side said, "don't strike them. They are unarmed"?

A. That's correct.

Q. How many people were in both these crowds now?

A. I guess about 75 on the west side of the street; about 150 on the east side.

Q. Some 225 people out there in the crowds now, and you said that nobody was in the street?

A. They weren't on the street. The Officer wasn't in no danger at any time.

We were making progress. But once again, as in the Rivera case, we were in the dark as to how the altercation actually arose. The judges were not likely to acquit the defendants unless they could come to some understanding of why all this had happened. Bell's brief, direct testimony opened the door to the problem.

Q. Will you tell the Court what transpired after the time you left that bar, if you please?

A. Well, we walked out of the bar. Johnson and I had had a discussion in there about Meredith. So somebody said—it came over the television that he died, and it—they started arguing about it in the bar. We walked out of the bar. Mr. Johnson was telling me about—I don't know his exact words. I didn't hear the exact words he said, but he was just—Meredith—

[ASSOCIATE JUDGE]. Where? In the bar or out?

THE WITNESS. Out on the sidewalk.

[ASSOCIATE JUDGE]. Outside the bar?

THE WITNESS. Yes, sidewalk, yes. We proceeded to the car, the Officer passed us. I didn't even know he was there. We getting in the car. He came over to the car and he told Johnson he could arrest him.

[PRESIDING JUDGE]. Keep your voice up.

THE WITNESS. We wanted to know: arrest us for what. We hadn't did anything. So at this time, he told me to shut up and I said, "why should I shut up? I haven't did anything." So he told me to get out of the car. He put handcuffs on us and took us across the street in the square.

Q. And then what happened?

A. Got in the cab, took us down to the Precinct.

Q. All right. Now, will you describe to the Court the appearance of the street at the time you came out of the bar in the company of Mr. Johnson.

A. Well, it wasn't very many people on the street. It was people in the street.

Q. Did you see any of these people stop when Mr. Johnson spoke about Meredith?

A. No.

MR. CHEVIGNY. All right, that's all.

The cross-examination was astonishing. The first question and answer were:

Q. Mr. Bell, what did Mr. Johnson have to say about Meredith?

A. He said, "It's a shame how these white bastards do us colored people down south and something should be done about it."

Then the District Attorney asked Bell what he himself had said. He seemed even more unhappy than he had before trial; there was an interminable pause as he looked at the three white judges. He finally replied:

"I said, 'I can't see why a white motherfucker would shoot a man in the back.'"

There were a few more questions, but the defense was essentially complete. The defense rested, the prosecution rested, and I made the expected motion to dismiss on the ground that the People had failed to prove their case beyond a reasonable doubt. The judges reserved their decision until the following morning. I hoped that Bell's testimony had finally given them a clear idea of the genesis of the incident.

Although the allegations of resisting arrest and assault were the most serious charges against the defendants, the issue facing the judges as they considered the case that evening really centered around the charge of disorderly conduct. If Bell and Johnson were not lawfully taken into custody for that, under New York law they had a right to make a verbal uproar and even to use "reasonable force" to resist the arrest. Such an action is never wise, but if the arrest was unlawful, resisting it was not then a crime.* The acts of resistance and assault alleged by the policeman were minor enough so that it was likely that the judges would find them to be reasonable if the disorderly conduct arrest was rejected. While it was important to me whether the charges of resisting arrest and assault were made in good faith, from a technical point of view the issue was much narrower.

The issue in the disorderly conduct charge, as usual, turned upon the question of whether the defendants disturbed or intended to disturb the public by their actions before they were arrested. From a legal point of view the most important piece of testimony in the entire trial was a small fragment of the cross-examination of the policeman near the beginning of the proceedings.

---

* This law was changed on March 21, 1968, by a law making it a crime to resist any arrest, whether lawful or not.

Q. Now, I'm going back to the time you first spoke to them. Tell me, how many people you perceived in the street at the time you first heard them yelling?

A. At the first time I stopped—when I stopped, they continued to walk, there were four people standing off to the side, and there were two more standing on the other side of them, six people.

Q. Now, let me go to the first time you spoke to the defendants. What did you say to them?

A. I said, "Excuse me, but you can't use that kind of language and that tone in the street. This is a public street."

Q. Now, after you said that, did you notice how many people were on the street?

A. No, I didn't turn my backs to the defendants after I began speaking to them.

Q. When was the next time you noticed how many people were on the street?

A. As I backed up a little bit away from the defendants, a crowd of about 15 to 20 people had gathered by that time. This was after the second warning. We stood there for a few minutes.

Q. So that at the time you first spoke to them, there were only six people there, at the most; is that right?

A. Yes.

Q. Did you consider that to be a crowd?

A. More than three persons in one place, I would say is a crowd.

Q. But they weren't standing together, were they?

A. No; four was standing in one crowd and two were standing further down.

Q. Did you see where the four came from?

A. I—I think they came out of a restaurant. There are two restaurants right around 2063 Amsterdam Ave.

This testimony made the issue an extremely narrow one. If the judges wanted to acquit the defendants they could do so simply on the basis that the public did not appear to have been disturbed by their conduct. It really depended upon how well disposed the judges were toward them.

The following afternoon, I appeared with the defendants

before the three judges. Without the slightest comment, or
intimation of the reason, the presiding judge said, "The motion is granted." They were acquitted.

A few minutes later we were sitting in the bar on the corner across from the courthouse. Harold Bell's face was the
picture of beatific relief. I asked them whether they wanted
to make a complaint; they said they would get in touch with
me. We shook hands and parted, and I waited for the call.
Some weeks later I left a message for Johnson, but he never
called me.

I felt that this was a just end to the matter, in a rough sort
of way. The officer had made a bad mistake by arresting Bell
and Johnson, but he had showed real presence of mind when
the crowd warned him not to hit them. Sanderson testified at
one point that the policeman actually told the crowd he was
not going to hit the two, and he probably avoided a worse
disturbance by doing so. An arrest like this one is the stuff
of which riots are made, and with the crowd at St. Nicholas
Avenue, there might easily have been a violent end to the
episode. Perhaps it was best to do what Bell and Johnson
obviously wanted to do and forget the whole thing.

The last question in my mind was why the charges of
resisting arrest and assault came into the case at all. I guessed
that this had been a bid for a plea of guilty to the lesser
offense of disorderly conduct, and my conviction was strengthened by Mr. Sanderson's report of what had occurred when
he followed Bell and Johnson to the station house in a taxi
with another witness. He asked the sergeant why Bell and
Johnson had been arrested, and was told that it was for disorderly conduct. Nevertheless, they turned up at Criminal
Court charged with two misdemeanors besides. That seemed
quite a lot for such a minor incident, and I suspected that the
bid had gone up because the witnesses appeared at the precinct. There were no injuries on either side, but there was
an obvious public outcry at the arrest, and under such circumstances the chances are that the charges will be drawn so as
to cover every contingency, including publicity, a lawsuit, or
a civilian complaint. In other complaints which came to us,

allegations were made that charges had been increased after
witnesses came to the precinct, and in one case an observer
said the police *told* him they were going to add the charge
of resisting arrest because he was making life so difficult for
them. Unfortunately, that complaint was one of the many in
which the witness "moved, left no address," and it remained
unsubstantiated.

It is somewhat unusual for bystanders to show enough interest in a case to appear at a precinct station. When they
do so, it is frequently to complain about the conduct of a
policeman, and they inevitably make it clear that a contest in
Criminal Court, and possibly a civilian complaint, is in the
offing. The same effect is produced when the defendant is
foolhardy enough to threaten an officer in the precinct with a
civilian complaint. In one of the complaints we received, a
woman who fitted the description of a murder suspect was
being released after a routine investigation when she was rash
enough to announce that she was going to complain of the
way she had been treated. According to her story, she was
promptly charged with assault. The judges believed her suffi-
ciently to acquit her of the charge, but her complaint about
the way the charges arose in the police station, though perfectly plausible, remained unsubstantiated.

In short, the pattern seems to show that any action which
raises the threat of a major case will cause the police to take
steps to protect themselves. Defense lawyers generally regret
the appearance of witnesses or the threat of a complaint before the trial in routine criminal cases, for the same reason
that they dread publicity. All of these tend to make the
charges more serious and the opposition more persistent.

The importance of the obscure case of Bell and Johnson
does not lie in the charges; the misdemeanors of resisting arrest
and assault merely clouded the issues. The point is that a
policeman reacted to an inflammatory racial remark by making
an arrest. Offended by what he heard, he attempted to cast
the damage to his sense of fitness in a legal form. As it so
often is in street situations, the legal form was a charge of
disturbing the peace. In short, an encounter between police-

man and citizens was followed by defiance and an argument resulting in an arrest.

What little systematic research there has been on police behavior, in New York and elsewhere, shows that some variation of this pattern of conflict is nearly always at the root of police abuses in the street. An appallingly large number of arrests are made because of "fighting words" between police and citizens. A study of disorderly conduct arrests in Washington, D.C., for example, found that a fifth of them were made solely for loud or obscene words to the police.[2] The legal status of such arrests, as it stands in New York and most other states, has been well expressed by Orlando Wilson, now Police Commissioner of Chicago: [3]

> The officer . . . must remember that there is no law against making a policeman angry and that he cannot charge a man with offending him. Until the citizen acts overtly in violation of the law, he should take no action against him, least of all lower himself to the level of the citizen by berating and demeaning him in a loud and angry voice. The officer who withstands angry verbal assaults builds his own character and raises the standard of the department.

Actual practice is quite different, as students of the problems of juvenile offenders have frequently observed. Most of them appear to agree with the proposition that "defiance on the part of a boy will lead to juvenile court quicker than anything else."[4]

The petty conflicts with the police which give rise to defiance are not restricted to juveniles. Kenneth Clark, in his interviews for Dark Ghetto, collected stories of the resentment in Harlem against arrests for failure to move on.[5]

> Last night, for instance, the officer stopped some fellas on 125th Street . . . [T]he officer said, "All right, everybody get off the street or inside!" Now, it's very hot. We don't have air conditioned apartments in most of these houses up here, so where are we going if we get off the streets? We can't go back in the house because we almost

suffocate. So we sit down on the curb, or stand on the sidewalk, or on the steps, things like that, till the wee hours of the morning, especially in the summer when it's too hot to go up. Now where are we going? But he came out with his nightstick and wants to beat people on the head, and wanted to—he arrested one fellow. The other fellow said, "Well, I'll move, but you don't have to talk to me like a dog."

Complaints of arrest on account of a personal conflict—where no offense is committed, but where, because of some real or imagined threat to authority, an argument arises and an arrest is made—were among the most frequent which came across my desk during my work on the project. Mr. Goldman's famous dictum about juveniles may be paraphrased to cover everyone in the city, young and old alike: "Defiance will lead to court quicker than anything else."

The Bell and Johnson case had an interesting twist because it did not begin with any obvious act of defiance. There was no crowd of sullen juveniles, no insult, none of the customary catalysts for the conflict. There was simply a private conversation which the policeman perhaps found threatening or offensive. His ensuing reactions, while interesting because of the special circumstances of the case, still resemble police reactions in any threatening situation. Jerome Skolnick, in a sketch of the "working personality" of the policeman, based on research in Oakland, California, has attempted an explanation: [6]

The policeman, because his work requires him to be occupied continually with potential violence, develops a perceptual shorthand to identify certain kinds of people as symbolic assailants, that is, as persons who use gesture, language, and attire that the policeman has come to recognize as a prelude to violence. This does not mean that violence by the symbolic assailant is necessarily predictable. On the contrary, the policeman responds to the vague indication of danger suggested by appearance. Like the animals of the experimental psychologist, the policeman finds the threat of random damage more compelling than a predetermined and inevitable punishment.

He quotes Colin MacInnes' description of the English police-man to much the same effect: [7]

> The true copper's dominant characteristic, if the truth
> be known, is neither those daring nor vicious qualities
> that are sometimes attributed to him by friend or enemy,
> but an ingrained conservatism, and almost desperate love
> of the conventional. It is untidiness, disorder, the un-
> usual, that a copper disapproves of most of all: far more,
> even than of crime which is merely a professional mat-
> ter. Hence his profound dislike of people loitering in
> streets, dressing extravagantly, speaking with exotic ac-
> cents, being strange, weak, eccentric, or simply any rare
> minority—of their doing, in fact, anything that cannot
> be safely predicted.

It is not hard to see why the words of Bell and Johnson could
have been those of a symbolic assailant to a policeman in
Oakland or in London as well as in New York.

Few conflict-arrest cases demand an explanation as sophisticated as the Bell and Johnson incident. Straightforward
arguments leading to arrest are much more common. Another
arrest, that of a young man whom we shall call (fictitiously)
Carlos Caulaincourt, for disorderly conduct in May 1966, fits
the classic design for street incidents.

Late in the evening of Wednesday, May 25, my phone rang
at home. It was one of the members of the Du Bois Club, a
radical student group concerned with peace and civil rights.
I had come to know him well in my investigation of the riot
case in Brooklyn. Now he was telling me about an arrest
in front of a schoolyard across the street from the Lower
East Side office of the Club. The defendant was being taken
to night court, and a troop of neighborhood kids was on its
way downtown to meet him. If I wanted to talk to the witnesses, that was the place to do it.

Night court is conducted in a cavernous, ill-lit room on the
second floor of Manhattan Criminal Court. In the spring of
1966, a single courtroom in Manhattan served the entire city
after the criminal courts had closed for the afternoon. After
5:00 P.M. it was the only arm of the judiciary acting to get

defendants out of the police station and before a judge. Vital
though the court's work was, the function of a lawyer who
appeared before it was minimal. It was impossible to accom-
plish anything there except to have bail set or to plead guilty.
After expressing my despair about night court, I agreed to
meet my caller there. When I arrived, at about ten thirty, a
procession of drunks and disorderly men was being shunted
before the bench and back to The Tombs. Assorted friends and
witnesses for the defendant were occupying the back benches.
I spoke to them briefly, to get an idea of the case. They were
all Puerto Rican teen-agers, except for one middle-aged Irish-
man named Frank, who had been sitting on the doorstep
across from the schoolyard. He looked as though he regretted
coming to court. "I didn't like the way that kid was pushed
around," he said, "but they don't need me, do they? I don't
even live around here. I was at my sister's." I urged him to
stay with the case and asked for his last name. He said he
would think about it, and looked down. I knew I was never
going to see him again.

By this time it was nearly twelve, and the defendant
Caulaincourt, a cool, wiry young man, was finally brought in.
I made the customary plea for low bail, emphasizing that he
had a job and a wife and family; the judge barked, "Good for
him," and paroled him without bail in my custody. I agreed
to meet the witnesses for an extended interview the following
week, and went home to bed.

At that time the Du Bois Club had an office across from a
public school, at 13 Norfolk Street, in the most dilapidated and
crowded part of the old Lower East Side and some three
blocks north of Seward Park, where Jose Rivera had been
arrested. The clubhouse was crowded when I arrived. I recognized a number of witnesses from the Brooklyn case trading
political gossip, and an owlish young man was lecturing to a
group in the back of the room on the history of jazz. Caulaincourt and his witnesses were sitting quietly near the front
door. I interviewed three of them, together with Caulaincourt
himself; they all told substantially the same story.

May 25 had been a hot night and all of them had been out

in the street. Caulaincourt's cousin was sitting on a bench at the edge of the schoolyard, playing the bongos with two boys he did not know by name, while Caulaincourt was standing by and listening. A policeman passed on a motor scooter, then turned back and stopped by the fence. He came into the yard, and one of the boys, Angel Muñoz as I shall call him here, a bundle of curiosity, followed close behind. Everyone else stayed in the street. The officer told them to stop playing the drums because he had had a complaint from one of the tenements. The boys took up their drums and began to walk out of the yard, while Caulaincourt hit his cousin's bongo a few times, reminiscently. The policeman told him that if he wanted to play the drums, he could go home to do it. Two of the boys recollected that Caulaincourt replied, "I can play in my house anytime. That's why I pay rent." They disagreed only about whether he had said it before or after the boys got out of the yard. Everyone agreed that the officer went back to the scooter, while other boys drifted over to the scene. The officer came back and blamed them for a flat tire; he said he was going to make it tough for them. He told them again to move, and Caulaincourt replied that they were moving. The policeman said he had a big mouth. Two witnesses remembered Caulaincourt saying that he paid taxes, and one thought that he added, "I am even paying for your work." At this point, they said, the policeman pushed him and asked if he wanted to be arrested. Caulaincourt told him not to push, and the officer pushed him again and grabbed him by the arm. He pushed him over to the scooter, while Caulaincourt spoke the same words that Jose Rivera was to use a few days later in Seward Park under similar circumstances: "I can walk." The officer called for the patrol car, and Caulaincourt was taken away. Charges were brought under Section 3 of the eternal disorderly conduct statute, which penalized congregating with others and failing to move on when a breach of the peace might be occasioned.

As I talked to the witnesses, I tried to find out a little about their character. Angel Muñoz, at eighteen, was the youngest, a short, mercurial fellow with a slight mustache who seemed to be the neighborhood clown. He was then working for the Parks Department and awaiting a letter from his draft board. I was sure he would make a good, happy-go-lucky soldier, but I was doubtful about him as a witness. The credibility of one of the others was limited by the fact that he was Caulaincourt's cousin, and the third, as it turned out, was never to show up in court.

On the adjourned day of the case, June 23, we were determined to get to trial because Angel Muñoz was crowing over the draft notice he had already received. Clift Johnson and I arrived in Part 1C of the Criminal Court, where petty offenses are tried, armed with a brief attacking the constitutionality of Section 3 of the disorderly conduct statute. We sat waiting miserably through a long calendar call and half a dozen depressing trials for jostling in the subway, pandering, and solicitation to commit an unnatural act.

Angel Muñoz had begun the day with antics. He told jokes, then went out into the hall to smoke and dance romantically to an inaudible rhythm. As time wore on, he fell silent. I had promised him a trial after lunch, at two o'clock, and when it did not immediately develop, he said he was going out into the hall for a smoke. I paid no attention, but within the next thirty seconds one of those funny feelings one reads about in books came over me. I sent Clift to keep an eye on him. He returned with a sheepish Angel Muñoz. "I just grabbed him at the elevator," he said.

Toward four o'clock an extra judge became available, and we were sent out into the hall to wait for our case to be called in a small room in the back. An assistant district attorney began to prepare the case with the policeman at the other end of the hall. I heard him say, "But it's not an offense to refuse to move." Presently he came over and asked me if I would consider accepting a dismissal of the charges in return for a waiver of claims for damages against the city and the officer. I agreed, we stepped into the room before the judge, and the case was dismissed. We all went out to the elevator, and Muñoz started talking to the policeman. "Next week I'm going in the Army, man." He imitated a machine gun. "You're

going in the service?" the officer replied. "That's great. I wish
I was back in."

We had run up against one of the chief problems in criminal charges arising out of police abuses: the waiver of claims
for damages. Although its legality is doubtful, such a waiver
is almost always extracted in return for a dismissal without a
trial by prosecutors in New York, as well as in some other
jurisdictions.[8] Some district attorneys, as I was later to find,
consider that the waiver covers a disciplinary complaint against
the police officer as well as a civil action for damages. "If this
case is dismissed," one said to me, "then it is forgotten." In
any case, the question was undoubtedly moot for Caulaincourt,
for he was unlikely to want to make a complaint. The Du Bois
Club office reported that he and the other people in the neighborhood were relieved and delighted with the result of the
case. In later cases, however, the waiver was to present a
serious issue. On the one hand, if the state wants to drop the
charges against a defendant, it is extremely awkward to refuse; the only possible reason for rejecting the offer would be
to preserve one's rights for a civil action. Once the District
Attorney's office understands that a civil action is threatened,
it is likely to redouble efforts to get a conviction. The chances
of a defendant being convicted in a trial before a magistrate
are always high, no matter how strong his defense may be, and
the effectiveness of his civil remedies is considerably reduced,
if not annihilated, by a conviction. If a lawyer refuses a dismissal in return for dropping his civil remedies, he is likely
to be faced with a criminal conviction and the collapse of his
civil remedies to boot. At least in cases where no permanent
physical injury has been done to the defendant, it is foolish
to risk a criminal conviction for an individual on the slim
hope of the recovery of civil damages or of disciplinary action
against a policeman.

Most lawyers and judges consider such a waiver unenforce-
able [9] because of the coercion used to get it. Theoretically, this
is a way out of the dilemma, but to bring suit after giving a
waiver, the lawyer must in effect break his promise to the
judge and the prosecutor. For the individual lawyer who has

to keep on representing criminal clients, this is not a practical alternative. The waiver continues to be the first of many hurdles along the route to redress for police abuses. The better the case for the defense, the more important the hurdle becomes, because it is usually in cases where the defense is nearly airtight that the prosecution will consider a dismissal.

It is a little easier to understand why Carlos Caulaincourt was arrested than to see why Bell and Johnson were picked up, but the workings of the arrest process are similar in both cases. In Caulaincourt's case, it was his failure to cooperate, his challenge to the authority of the policeman, that got him arrested. The policeman sees the defiant person as a troublemaker and a legitimate subject for the discipline of the law. Piliavin and Briar, in their study of a "major Western police department," found, for example, that 60 percent of the arrests of juveniles were based on demeanor.[10] The defiant man is guilty of a crime at least in intent, by threatening the authority of the law. He is, in Skolnick's convenient phrase, a "symbolic assailant." Many policemen apparently believe that a defiant demeanor literally shows a propensity toward crime.[11]

By the ethics of police work, the symbolic assailant is fair game, just as a criminal is, because he presents the same threat to society. In the Bell and Johnson case, as we have seen, the defiance was not, at least initially, a defiance of the police; but it was quite as much defiance, in the broader sense, of the authority of society as a whole.

The incident which generated the arrest in Caulaincourt's case is nearly identical with the incident in the Rivera case. In both, there is an affront to the policeman's authority from a young man, in a public place. The conflict is exacerbated by more protest from the citizen, ending in an arrest. The obvious difference, of course, is that the issue was not settled by violence in the Caulaincourt case. In the Bell and Johnson case, it appears that the officer actually had the presence of mind not only to refrain from using his club but to tell the crowd that he was not going to use it.

But the similarities among all these cases are more striking than their differences. Personal conflicts like these are the tinder from which street-corner abuses of power are invariably ignited. Whenever an incident occurs which seems threatening to a policeman, there is an attempt to "break it up." Acceptance of authority marks the end of the incident, but defiance results in an arrest. An extra modicum of defiance (and sometimes none, as we saw in the Rivera case) may be the occasion for summary corporal punishment on the street in addition to arrest. The genesis of false arrest and the genesis of police brutality lie in the same conflict.

3

DEFIANCE
AND FORCE

DURING THE FALL and winter of 1966, we had received a
number of complaints through the Brooklyn affiliate of CORE,
then on Nostrand Avenue in the Bedford-Stuyvesant ghetto.
We had found that most of them could not be authenticated
for lack of witnesses, until finally, on a Friday in December,
I had a telephone call from one of the volunteers manning the
CORE office. He reported that an officer had beaten a young
Negro man the previous Monday, at Nostrand and Fulton, the
neighborhood's main intersection, in front of several witnesses,
including a schoolteacher and a minister. A schoolteacher and
a minister! My caller made them sound like the dream defense
witnesses—to hear him tell it, the officer might as well have
made an affidavit of his misdeeds. The volunteer went on to
say that the man was in jail and that CORE was trying to
locate his father to bail him out.

A little later I had a call from the father of the injured
man, who we shall call (fictitiously) Isaiah Green. The son
was charged with disorderly conduct and resisting arrest, and
his case was due to come up later in the week. The schoolteacher had filed a complaint with the Police Department on
the night of the incident, and investigators from the Depart-

ment's Civilian Complaint Review Board—which we will describe in detail shortly—had immediately come to the scene.
Green's father said he was going to raise money for bail as
soon as he could.

The case was on the calendar in Brooklyn Criminal Court
for the following Wednesday, and when his case was called,
Isaiah Green had been in jail for a week. Still no bail. When
I interviewed him at the side of the courtroom, I found him
to be a soft-spoken, consistent sort of man. But he had had
experience with jail and the courts before; he had been arrested a few times and once convicted of a misdemeanor. Like
many ghetto victims of force by the police, he seemed less
shocked by the policeman's actions than the observers were.
He expected no better from the police, and besides, his chief
concern at that moment was to get out of jail. He was in a
frame of mind to accept the District Attorney's offer to permit
him to plead guilty to disorderly conduct in return for a dismissal of the charge of resisting arrest. There is no better
remedy for the determination of a defendant to prove his
innocence than a lengthy incarceration under a bail he cannot
meet. At this point, however, the judge asked the police officer
if Green had "given him any trouble," and when the officer
said yes, he ruled that the charge of resisting arrest had to
stand; Green was not to be permitted to "cop out" that day.
It is relatively rare in a case like this for a judge to refuse to
"take the plea" when the District Attorney is willing, particularly when the charges are drawn in such a way as to permit
the defendant to cop out. But from the words of the policeman, the decision was technically justifiable. The result was
that Green would lie in jail until we could collect witnesses
for a trial or until his father could find the bail money.

Fortunately, within a few days he did raise the money, and
we were able to begin preparing the case in a sensible way.
The following Sunday my assistant, Eve Cary, and I went to
an address on Fulton Street, a few doors down from the scene
of the arrest. On the second floor we found Reverend William
Baltimore at home. A dignified man in his fifties, he preached
evenings and weekends in a local Baptist church and worked
by day as a barber.

There were two restaurants at the corner of Fulton and Nostrand, a Chock Full o' Nuts and a tiny café known as Corbee's. The incident had started in Corbee's at about 10:00 P.M., shortly before Reverend Baltimore walked in. His sworn statement took up from there (only the names are changed or deleted):

. . . I walked into Corbee's Restaurant, the officer was saying, "I told you to shut up." I heard Isaiah Green say, "Am I supposed to be under arrest?" The officer said, "if you think I'm bull-shitting, you'll go out of here head first." The officer was sitting on a stool between Green and the door, and Green was in the back. The restaurant is very narrow. The officer stood up off the stool and raised his gun up out of his holster about two inches. Green was leaning on the counter, and did not make a move toward the officer. The officer turned from Green and ordered a glass of orange juice. I was standing by the door about six feet from the officer.

After he ordered the orange juice, the officer sat down and as Green came by, the officer backed up on the stool to block his path. Green stood back. The officer straightened up, Green went by, and the officer hit him with his elbow. I said I was Reverend Baltimore, and I would take the man out. I opened the door and pushed Green out.

Green started across the street, and the officer pushed by. Green was crossing Fulton and as he stepped off the curb the officer hit him on the head with his hand and grabbed him with the other hand by the collar. He said, "I told you to go home." He backed Green across the street by his collar and a hand on his shoulder to a police car. The driver opened the back door on the sidewalk side. Each policeman grabbed him by an arm and a leg and threw him in the back seat. The first officer got in and put a knee on Green's chest or stomach. The officer began to hit him. I heard the schoolteacher trying to get the driver to stop the beating, and I began to cross the street. Before I reached the other side, Green was hit about six or eight times. I asked the driver, "Can't you make him stop? Does he have to beat him like that?"

Green's feet were hanging out. The driver was sitting

in the front with the door open and his feet on the sidewalk. He got out and pushed Green's feet in. The first officer pulled a leather blackjack out of his hip pocket and began to hit Green. The driver shut the door and jumped back in the front and drove off.

The schoolteacher said we should go investigate. We went with a man from the Youth Board who knew her, and another lady, in a cab to the precinct. The schoolteacher spoke to the desk sergeant and said we wanted to make a complaint. The schoolteacher filled out the complaint. A captain took a statement from her. We saw Green with a broom handle behind his back locked through his elbows, and his hands in front. He was seated in a back room with the door open. His jaw was swollen and his eyes were swollen. One was red. An ambulance arrived. I talked to a doctor who said his jaw might be fractured. The captain told me that Green said he had drunk three quarts, and I asked permission to speak to Green. Green said that he and three others had drunk together, not three quarts, but one. The ambulance arrived at 1:40 A.M. After they took Green away, we left the precinct. The captain and sergeant shook hands and said they were glad I came down. I said I hoped the officer would be taken off that corner.

The abuse was clear from this statement, but its origins were still obscure. The schoolteacher, whom we were to interview later in the day, was able to confirm much of this story, but she could not shed any more light on the cause of the conflict. She had been in front of Chock Full o' Nuts when the policeman first grabbed Green, but she had not heard the altercation in Corbee's. That story we could only get from Green.

On December 5, 1966, at 10:00 P.M. I was in Corbee's Restaurant at Fulton and Nostrand with my friend George. I had walked in alone, and I met George there. I had been drinking a 4/5 quart of Old Taylor with three friends. George and I were talking, when Officer ———— came in and sat down. I asked him what he would do "if someone would take your pistol." He replied, "I would bust their ass." I said, "But if he got it first, then he would shoot your ass." He said, "Shut up and leave me alone." There was some conversation, but I saw he was angry, and I went back to talk to George.

Green's account had some slight corroboration. On the night of the arrest, Reverend Baltimore heard the girl who worked in Corbee's telling an investigator from the Review Board that Green had threatened to take the officer's gun. But essentially, Green himself and the policeman were the only available witnesses to all that had occurred in Corbee's. Our prospects for the disorderly conduct part of the case were dim. Green's own account of what had happened was not likely to endear him to the judges, and his credibility was low because he had a criminal record. The policeman could be expected to make the episode sound more like a disturbance than even the defendant had (as a matter of fact, he did claim that Green had threatened to take his gun and "shoot his ass").

So the situation remained until April, when Green pleaded guilty to disorderly conduct before a second judge and was sentenced to a fine. There was no question in my mind that Green was innocent of resisting arrest. As for disorderly conduct, however, the facts even as he gave them might sustain a conviction, and considering his provocative words and his previous conviction, it was very easy to imagine a magistrate convicting him of that charge and of resisting arrest as well.

The violence by the officer presented a case of Doric simplicity: summary punishment in the street for a minor offense. The affront to the officer's authority was clear enough; the case hardly required any explanation beyond what Green and his witnesses had already said. The rest was up to the Police Department's disciplinary procedures.

At the time Isaiah Green's case came up, those procedures were formidable indeed. Complaints were investigated and formal hearings held by a review board, which determined whether a complaint was substantiated or not. Before discipline could be imposed, however, the strictures of the state civil service law required a second trial in front of the Commissioner

or his deputy. Many voters who either favored or opposed
Mayor Lindsay's Civilian Review Board for the New York
City police, during the ferocious referendum campaign over
the issue in 1966, imagined that this board would eliminate
internal review by the Department. No action of the Mayor,
however, could have changed state law, and the civilian-
dominated board actually affected only the first, or investigative, stage of review of police complaints. The Review Board,
whether dominated by police or civilians, has for fifteen years
been able to recommend that the Commissioner prefer charges
and hold a trial, but it has never been able to bypass him. The
Commissioner can bypass the Review Board and prefer charges
on his own initiative, and in special cases he does so, but the
ordinary case can end in discipline only if the charges are
found substantiated after a hearing and then sustained at the
departmental trial. The presumption is naturally in favor of
the civil servant in both proceedings. Although policemen
fear and resent the Review Board, the truth is that the entire
disciplinary process is an extremely fine sieve through which
relatively few complaints are pure enough to pass.

The Review Board that was to consider the teacher's complaint was to some extent a holdover from the civilian-domi-
nated board of the summer and fall of 1966, though the voters
had already approved the referendum forbidding civilian review. The Board members drawn from outside the Police Department had been dismissed, but the organizational reforms
had survived. The result was a curious mixture. The members
were long-time employees of the Department, but not members
of the force. The investigators were policemen especially assigned to the Board, while the staff at the middle level in charge
of investigations and hearings was drawn from outside the Department. Thus the civilian employees working under the
members of the Board, an executive director and two hearing
officers, had been retained, as well as the staff of policemen
working independently as investigators.

The hearing officers were originally expected to take the
testimony of witnesses at hearings on complaints and have a
stenographic transcript prepared on which the members of

the Board could base their decision. The officers, however, were not hearing any cases during the first part of 1967. The Police Department, after protests from the Patrolmen's Benevolent Association, had decided that the terms of the referendum forbade anyone who had not been an employee of the Department for at least a year to hear (that is, take testimony) as well as to decide any case.* The members of the Board, most of whom had been with the Department for many years, were taking turns acting as hearing officers for the cases pending before the Board, while the civilian staff waited for its year of seasoning to pass. This hiatus was to afford us an excellent opportunity to study the relative virtues of police as against civilian hearing examiners.

Since 1965 the Civilian Complaint Review Board, as it is called, whether predominantly civilian or predominantly police, has been located in a studiedly "civilian" office in a business building, away from the ancient green baroque of police precincts. In April 1967, a hearing was held in those offices on the charge made by the schoolteacher against the officer of using excessive force in the arrest of Isaiah Green. The procedure at such a hearing is much like that of a trial. The examiner sits at one end of a large table, with the witness chair and a stenographer on his right. The complainant and his lawyer (when he has one) and the accused officer and his lawyer (supplied by the Patrolmen's Benevolent Association) range themselves around the table. Witnesses are ordinarily excluded until after they have testified, just as they are at any other trial.

The hearing did not start well for the complainant. The witnesses were late, and Isaiah Green was even later. The first witness was one of the schoolteacher's pupils, who had been accompanying her home after class at the time of the incident. She had forgotten some details in the five months since the

* With much justification. The successful referendum abolishing the Civilian Review Board forbade any officer or administrator of the city to authorize any person who had not been an employee of the Department for at least a year to "investigate, hear or to require or recommend action upon civilian complaints against members of the Police Department."

incident; but she gave a fair circumstantial account—except
that she positively identified the wrong policeman.

This was not a terribly important point. It is easy to confuse
the faces of a group of men who are all dressed alike. In civil
disorders and demonstrations, it is sometimes both crucial and
difficult to identify a policeman, but here only one policeman
was accused and only one was involved in the arrest. Identification was not really an issue, but a mistaken identification
always creates a bad impression. The schoolteacher and
Reverend Baltimore told their stories very much as they had
told them to me, and there was no difficulty about their identification. Their testimony was as cruelly matter-of-fact as it
had been when I heard it for the first time. In his cross-examination, the policeman's attorney brought out the fact that the
lady had made complaints about policemen twice before. This
was intended to show that she was a crank, but its effect was
blunted by the fact that the minister, who confirmed her account, had never previously made such a complaint.

After these witnesses—a student, her teacher, and a minister
—the policeman's testimony began. The accused officer related
that Green had asked him in Corbee's what he would do if he
(Green) "took his gun and kicked his ass." The officer told him
to be quiet, and Green presently left. When the officer left,
about twenty seconds later, Green, who was still in the street,
began to curse him and started to strike him. The officer
arrested him and pushed him, struggling all the way, over to
the police car. Green had to be forced into the car and tried
to kick the officer, who got on top of him to keep him under
control. The officer denied that he had punched Green, but he
said that he had hit him in the shins to stop him from kicking.
In fact, he said, the officer driving the car had to hold Green's
legs down.

In view of this story, the testimony of the other officers was a
little strange. The driver of the police car had heard no shouting in the street, but he had seen the arresting officer seize
Green and hustle him across the street. He said that he had
helped the arresting officer put Green in the car, and, far from
holding Green's legs down, had pushed Green's feet in to shut

the back door. He testified that he never saw the arresting officer push Green in the face, but unexpectedly he did say that he had found Green's bridgework on the floor of the car and had given it back to him. A third policeman, who had been standing on the corner, saw no resistance from Green before he was put in the car, but thought he saw him struggling inside the car.

At 12:15, after all the witnesses had testified, Isaiah Green finally appeared. He said he had got a new job the previous Friday (the hearing was on a Tuesday), and in order not to offend his boss, he had agreed to work a half day on the date of the hearing. He too told the same story he had told before of his provocative remark in Corbee's followed by the arrest in the street and the beating in the car.

On June 15, a little over two months later, I received a carbon copy of a letter addressed to the schoolteacher. The important paragraphs read as follows:

> After due deliberation, the Hearing Officer filed his final report together with a complete stenographic transcript of the testimony taken at the hearing and the exhibits. The matter received careful study and review by the Board, which filed an advisory recommendation with the Police Commissioner to the effect that the evidence adduced is insufficient to sustain the complaint and it should be filed as unsubstantiated. The Police Commissioner approved the Board's recommendation.
>
> It must be remembered that disciplinary action may be initiated only after showing of substantial evidence of misconduct. After a full hearing and impartial evaluation of the testimony, the necessary amount of evidence was not present.
>
> This letter is written to you by and under the authority of the Police Commissioner who, along with the Board, has asked me to thank you for your cooperation in this matter.

In effect, the Board had found that there was not even enough evidence to warrant a departmental trial of the issues in the case. On September 7, I wrote a letter to the Commissioner asking him to reconsider, but he reaffirmed the judgment.

The Green case is a paradigm of street-corner brutality. Provocation of the policeman by a challenge to his authority is invariably the key, and all the research into the attitudes of policemen toward the use of force centers around that problem. One of the earliest important studies of violence and the police, published in 1953 by William A. Westley, concerned "a municipal police department in an industrial city of approximately one hundred and fifty thousand inhabitants." Westley found that 37 percent of the patrolmen he interviewed gave "disrespect for the police" as a justification for the use of force ("roughing a guy up"), and that this justification was given much more frequently than any other.[1]

Understandable doubts have been expressed as to whether these findings, now fifteen years old and drawn from a small city, can be applied to an enormous metropolitan department like the New York City Police. It is clear from later research, however, that the challenge to police authority continues as a chief cause of the use of force in all urban police departments. A task force of the President's Commission on Law Enforcement, in reporting twenty instances of the unjustified or excessive use of force actually observed by its investigators, said of the victims that "most appeared to contest verbally the police officer's authority."[2] Whether the situation with respect to the abuse of force is better or worse in New York than in other cities remains an open question. It may well be worse in other communities. The twenty instances observed by the Task Force occurred in a total of 5,339 encounters with citizens in slum or high-crime areas outside New York. This seems a rather large number, especially in view of the fact that the officers knew they were being observed. The percentage of encounters involving excessive force is small, but the total number of encounters (only a few thousand) is also small by comparison with the millions of police-citizen contacts which occur each year. The figures suggest that the absolute number of such police abuses may be very large.

The most important work on the attitudes of New York

City policemen in the sixties toward the use and misuse of force has been done by John McNamara, in the course of three years' work with trainees at the Police Academy. Mc-Namara tested, with recruits and experienced men, this proposition: "Most officers agree that some force is necessary and justified when a citizen unjustly insults and curses a police officer." The percentage of men who agreed with this statement rose from 25 percent at the start of training in 1962 to 34 percent after one year in the field. A correlative proposition was: "A patrolman who frequently ignores challenges to fight from citizens will probably make it harder for other patrolmen to work his post or sector." The percentage of men who agreed or strongly agreed with this proposition rose from 21 percent at the beginning of training to 42 percent after two years in the field.[3]

The most interesting thing about these findings, meager though they are, is that they were made at all. They indicate that policemen themselves feel, regardless of the legal strictures, that defiance justifies the use of force. Westley remarked: [4]

> Since all the men were conscious of the chief's policy [critical of the use of violence] and of public criticisms, it seems likely that those who did justify the use of violence for illegal and personal ends no longer recognized the illegality involved. They probably believed that such ends fully represented a moral legitimation for their use of violence.

Those words are true to this day. Judging by the decision in Green's case, and as we shall have occasion to observe in other cases, the statement is true to some extent even of senior officers in the New York City Department, and of members of the Review Board.

In the light of these police attitudes, a case like Isaiah Green's becomes a stereotype. In dozens of cases a verbal act of defiance is followed by summary punishment and an arrest, and the charges against the offender, of course, are drawn so as to account for the events in the street as well as

for any injuries to the defendant. Sometimes those who protest the actions of the police are drawn into the orbit of defiance and are arrested as well. The arrest not only punishes
their defiance but eliminates them as effective witnesses. The
only problem with this procedure is that as the arrests increase, the charges become progressively more difficult to
explain to the courts. One such act of defiance, followed by
a chain of arrests, occurred on the Lower East Side in the
spring of 1966.

The Lower East Side Action Project (LEAP) occupies an
old slum tenement building on East Third Street. The staff
works intensively with a small group of youths, educating
them, counseling them, and trying to extricate them from
occasional conflicts with the law. On the night of March 5,
1966, two Puerto Rican teen-agers were at the project, talking to their teachers Susan Ribner, a social worker, and
Charles Allen Lingo, awaiting ordination as a minister. Presently the two boys wandered downstairs to the street.

The origin of the ensuing conflict is a little obscure. It is
clear at least that plainclothes officers of the Police Department and the Federal Bureau of Narcotics had just searched
a nearby apartment under a warrant. They had arrested the
tenant and were walking down Third Street with their prisoner.
In order not to be conspicuous, they had not handcuffed the
man. The two boys were out on the sidewalk as they passed
by, and the smaller one, Angel Hernandez, uttered the words
"fucking flatfoot." Both of the boys claimed that he said it
not to the plainclothesman but as an opinion about a passing
police car. The words were not intended to be audible in the
car, but they were audible on the street. This story is just
credible because the plainclothesmen probably did not appear
to be policemen; on the other hand, the coincidence of utter-
ing those words *sotto voce* just as plainclothesmen were passing does seem a little fantastic. In any case, the precise
intention of the boy who spoke the words matters very little;
everyone agreed that he had said them and that the plainclothesmen had heard him.

The only witnesses to the events of the next few instants
were the officers, their prisoner, and the two boys. The bigger

boy, Leonardo Negron, testified at Hernandez' trial to the events: [5]

> [OFFICER C——] grabbed Hernandez, threw him against the car, said, "What did you say to us? What did you call us?" Excuse me. He said, "What did you call us, fucking flatfoot?" and then he hit him. I said, "Wait a minute. What do you think you are—" I said, "Who do you think you are?" He said, "I'm a cop." I said, "Well, prove it." And a big husky one of them hit me in the mouth and said, "Shut up." So, instead of fighting, I ran to get help. . . .
>
> When they hit me in the mouth, I fell back. I got up to see [Detective A——] dragging Angel into a hallway. I didn't decide to go in after—to help him, but to get help to stop it. So I called Allen Lingo at the Lower East Side Project. By the time I came down, we saw Angel Hernandez coming down the steps, staggering across the sidewalk, and they were already crossing the street.

The original prisoner, in his testimony, generally confirmed this account, even though it would have been to his interest to corroborate the police story in the hope of a more lenient sentence.

Up in the LEAP office, Miss Ribner and Mr. Lingo heard Negron yell, "Allen, help. Guys are beating up Angel." Lingo ran downstairs, with Miss Ribner close behind. This is how he described the scene in the street at the trial:

> As I walked around the exit of LEAP to the right, three doorways down, the three men I have already mentioned came by me and became five men and crossed the street. At the point that they got by me, I looked at them, and I cannot remember them saying anything, and the man I later learned to be [Detective A——] said to me, "The kid called me a motherfucker," and then I went on over to Angel Hernandez with Leonardo Negron.
>
> ❊ ❊ ❊
>
> Angel Hernandez was dazed and staggering, and I supported him and asked what had happened to him. He indicated, as Leonardo Negron had indicated,

that he had been beaten, and I asked where, and I
noticed that his face was reddish, the back of his neck
was reddish, and he pulled up his pants leg to show
me his skinned shins. I asked him what happened,
and he told me he had been beaten in the street and
beaten in the hallway. He said, "There go the
guys that beat me up." He said, "Let's get them." I
said, "Surely. We will follow them and find a patrolman."

They did find a patrolman on Second Avenue, under the
marquee of a Yiddish theater, and Mr. Lingo, Miss Ribner,
and the two boys asked him to arrest the men. When he refused, Negron, his mouth still bleeding from the blow he had
received on Third Street, ran to the precinct, while Angel
Hernandez was arrested. Miss Ribner went back to the
LEAP office to get help, and Mr. Lingo followed the group.
The plainclothesmen tried to make him leave, but he refused.
At his trial he told what happened when the party reached
a station house:

> As we approached the precinct, [Officer C——] said
> to me, "I am telling you for the last time, get out of
> here, go home." I said, "No, I'm going into the pre-
> cinct." As we approached the entrance to the precinct,
> he bodily blocked me out of the door and said, "You
> are under arrest. If you want to go in here, you are
> under arrest for interfering with an arrest." I was
> taken in the precinct house, searched, taken upstairs
> and generally verbally abused there.

Inside the precinct, Negron had already arrived to make
a complaint against the men; when they came in they found
him there and arrested him as well. The circle of evidence was
apparently closed when all three were charged with interfering with an officer, a misdemeanor.

The case of Hernandez and Lingo* was tried some six
months later, before a bench of three judges in the small
courtroom on the fifth floor of the Criminal Court. For a

---

* Negron was charged separately as a youthful offender.

misdemeanor trial, this one was unusually long and dramatic, consuming the better part of three days of the judges' time. Just before the start of the trial, and six months after the arrest, the Assistant District Attorney suddenly added a charge of assault to that of interfering with an arrest.

The story told by the plainclothesmen was that Angel Hernandez had not only cursed in their presence, as he admitted, but had grabbed at the shoulder of one of the officers, trying to get him away from his prisoner. Negron had run up and attempted to contribute to this interference, but was stopped by a blow from one of the federal agents. He ran away, presently to return with Lingo, and Hernandez was arrested then and there, in front of LEAP, for interfering with an officer. One of the plainclothesmen admitted that he took Hernandez into a hallway, but he said that it was to search him, not to beat him up.

The officers said that they were taking away their original prisoner and their new one, Angel Hernandez, when Mr. Lingo came up with Negron. Negron then ran away, while one of the officers shouted after him that he was under arrest. Lingo pestered them all the way down Second Avenue, tried to have a uniformed man arrest them, and finally interfered physically with the arrest of Hernandez. Lingo was then arrested, and Negron, all agreed, was afterwards found and taken into custody in the station house.

This testimony roughly tracked the sequence of events as we knew them, with a few significant changes. The officers tried to eliminate as many of the problems in their case as they could, but too many simply could not be hidden. Everyone agreed that neither of the boys knew the original prisoner the police had in custody, and it was somewhat difficult to see why either of them would want to interfere physically with the arrest of a man he had never seen before. Furthermore, though the officers denied participation, it was obvious that someone had beaten up Hernandez. The medical records of that night from Bellevue Hospital showed "multiple contusions," including an apparent blow to the head. The plainclothesmen's original prisoner testified that Hernandez had not interfered physically, but that his arresting officer had beaten up Hernandez.

More important for the defense of the criminal charges was the problem of the sequence of the arrests. If the officers did not arrest Hernandez immediately outside the LEAP office, as they said they did, then it was hard to believe that he had actually committed an interference. Several witnesses had Hernandez staggering about in a daze while the plain-clothesmen crossed Third Street. Even the patrolman who was stopped by the group at the theater saw someone (he was not sure who it was) being handcuffed at that time. It looked very much as though the officers had not meant to arrest Hernandez at all until he and Lingo caught and accused them at the Yiddish theater.

It was difficult to believe that Hernandez and Negron had been conscious of committing a crime when Hernandez deliberately followed the men and tried to have them arrested and Negron then ran to the precinct. Finally, it was difficult to believe that Mr. Lingo was guilty of a crime at all. At the time of his trial he had left LEAP to become an instructor in contemporary theology at the Ecumenical Institute in Chicago. It was plain that his purpose on the evening of the arrest had been to go along and protect his pupils. Cross-examination at the trial showed that he had had long experience working for civil rights in the South. He had been arrested in Alabama and Florida, and it was easy to see that he expected the worst of the police and that he was quite capable of staying with the boys even up to the point of arrest. His courage probably made the difference in the case, for without him it would simply have been the word of two ghetto teen-agers against the police. By Mr. Lingo's persistence, the ultimate in middle-class respectability, a man of God, had at least momentarily joined forces with the youths.

Strong emotions, for the usually sedate three-judge court, were exposed at the trial. A visiting jurist from Australia was invited by the court to listen to the trial, and one of the things he heard was the cross-examination of the officer who had arrested Hernandez. The officer testified that he took the young man into a hallway to search him. When I asked him why he did not search him in the street, he said that the light was better in the hallway. In reply to the question whether he had ever been in the hallway, he snapped ferociously, "No, but if I don't know what a light looks like I'd be a damned fool." This produced consternation from the bench, and the visiting jurist looked as though he could not believe his ears. Lawyers emphasize the value of cross-examination, but I have never found it particularly useful with policemen, who are hardened to the courtroom; this flash of anger constituted one of the most valuable bits of testimony I ever obtained from the examination of an officer.

Each of the boys had filed a claim for $25,000 damages against the city before the case came to trial, and the District Attorney made much of the fact in his summation. He said of Hernandez, "That is more money than he has [ever] seen, because he had a part-time job for fifteen dollars a week." He reverted to this line later, causing one of the judges to ask testily, "You think there should be a conviction because of a civil suit?"

In the end, the teacher and the teen-ager were acquitted unanimously of the assault charge added at the last minute, and, by a two-to-one vote, of the interfering charge as well. The majority said that they did not approve the words used by Hernandez, but they could not see how they were an interference with an officer. One judge said he thought "the wrong charge was brought." Again, as in the case of Jose Rivera, it was a hint that a disorderly conduct charge might have been sustained, but not an assault.

In the last analysis, the LEAP case was one in which an insult by a citizen set off a chain reaction. The police, who could not have been identified in plainclothes, tried to avoid arresting the two after they were summarily punished. However, partly because they were members of LEAP, the boys would not let the matter rest. When they and Mr. Lingo pressed for justice, the plainclothesmen were no longer cloaked with anonymity, and they tried to eliminate all the meddlers they could. But for once, the boys and their mentor were

successful in enforcing their rights. It is a risky course to
follow, but when people with as much courage as Mr. Lingo
take it, it is sometimes the right one.

Most lawyers will be surprised that the civil damage claims
had been filed before the criminal trial, and indeed almost
everyone predicted that the claims would make it harder to
win the criminal case. The claims had been filed ahead of trial
because it appeared that under state law, at least some of the
claims against the city might have to be filed within ninety
days after the assault, and the case could not be reached for
trial within ninety days. It was a risky experiment, though not
as catastrophic as it might have been, because the District
Attorney had tried to make too much of the claims. In the end,
however, the results were disappointing. After the first trial,
the District Attorney agreed to dismiss the youthful-offender
charges pending against the other boy in return for the customary waiver of claims against the city and the officers. I
could not see a sufficient reason to run the risk of a conviction
for this claim, and I reluctantly agreed. Hernandez, who had
already been acquitted, had not shown any interest in his
claim, and after hounding him for a while, the private attorney who represented him in his civil case gave it up. From the
course of the trial in this case, it appears that the pendency of
claims against the city can be enormously prejudicial to the
defense of criminal cover charges. Except where there is a
serious or permanent injury, damage claims probably should
not be brought before the criminal case is completed, because
the risk is too great and the chance of success too small.

Not every word of defiance by a citizen is as offensive
as those in the Green and LEAP cases. Citizens are sometimes
subjected to summary punishment simply for asserting their
rights. One such case occurred in the Bronx on the evening
of April 6, 1966.

Two Negro men, who worked in adjacent shops as auto
repairmen, had been out bowling together that night. They
drove to a restaurant near a rather rough corner on their way
home, and, as people will, they had become so absorbed in

talking about the game that they did not immediately get out of the car. Three plainclothesmen drove by, stopped, and got out of their car to investigate. They told the driver that they were detectives and ordered him out of the car. When he complied, they asked for his registration, and he demanded to see some official identification. One of the officers, who was a Negro, snapped, "What are you, a wise guy?" and another detective slapped the driver repeatedly. He then produced his registration, while the detectives searched the glove compartment. The driver was given a summons for the traffic violation of failing to comply with a lawful order (refusing to show his registration). At his trial the passenger testified for the defense, and the driver was acquitted of the charge on June 28, 1966, in the Bronx Criminal Court.[6]

From this case it is apparent that, from the officer's point of view, the essence of the offense that provokes punishment is defiance, and the justifiability of that defiance has little to do with his reaction. It is easy to imagine that in many cases an assertion of right may be seen as more of a threat even than an out-and-out insult.

It was not hard for me to see why the detectives chose to interrogate the two men in the Bronx case. The neighborhood was known for drugs and prostitution, and I had once previously received a complaint that the police had a practice of stopping men seen traveling alone there in a car. The summons was apparently an excuse for the stop, made up after the driver objected. I made no complaint against the officers in this case. It had been sent to me by a private attorney after he had successfully represented the driver in the traffic case. I sought the defendant and his witnesses, but they never responded; apparently they were satisfied with the acquittal, or did not want to be bothered with a complaint.

Policemen often take the speaking of a foreign language to be a form of defiance. A policeman told one of the staff lawyers at the NYCLU that he had once spoken to a Puerto Rican boy; when the fellow answered in Spanish, he could not understand, and the other boys laughed. The officer slapped him to maintain his authority. Fantastic as it may seem in a polyglot city like New York, this is not a rare occurrence.

On the evening of June 2, 1967, five teen-age boys from Haiti, driving across a West Side street, were stopped by two policemen for a "routine car check," as one of the officers phrased it. The radio in the car was blaring, and the officer asked the driver to turn it down and get out of the car. The young man complied and the two stood on the sidewalk while the officer examined the license and registration. One of the boys in the car spoke up in Haitian creole; he later said he was asking what the officer wanted, but the second policeman said that the other boys laughed. In any case, the first policeman told the boy to shut up, and when he said, "I was not talking to you, I was talking to my friend," the officer punched him in the mouth. The policemen then simply began to walk away, but like Angel Hernandez, the Haitian youth was too incensed to let it go. He jumped out of the car and ran after the policeman who had struck him, demanding that the officer go with him to the precinct. Naturally, he was promptly arrested and charged with disorderly conduct. He was tried and acquitted of the offense in Manhattan Criminal Court on August 24, 1967. A complaint was made to the Review Board and three of the Haitian youths appeared to testify. After they endured lengthy cross-examination on the facts without faltering, the complaint was found substantiated, and sent up for a departmental trial.

The complaints to my office concerning brutality bear out the hypothesis that most such acts arise out of defiance of authority, or what the police take to be such defiance. A majority of the complaints about force (55 percent), whether authenticated or not, appeared on their face to involve defiance, and the overwhelming majority of the authenticated complaints were shown to involve such defiance (71 percent). Predictably, nearly all acts of brutality were followed by arrest. Only 20 percent of all the complaints, whether authenticated or not, and 24 percent of the authenticated complaints occurred without arrest. It is plain that people who have been arrested are more likely to complain, especially to a defense organization like the Civil Liberties Union. Nevertheless, the figure does demonstrate that scarcely any complaint of the use of force can be authenticated without a previous attempt to clear the victim of the criminal charges. It confirms our estimate at the end of the Rivera case that the criminal charge is the first and by far the most important hurdle to be cleared in obtaining redress for abuses.

"Defiance," up to this point, has implied no more than speech, and in most cases (61 percent) nothing more than the use of speech is involved. In some cases, however, acts of defiance, rather than words, are at the root of the use of force, and this presents a complex problem because such acts range in seriousness from a simple failure to move on to taking a policeman's weapon away. In one complaint, for example, it was claimed that tearing up a traffic ticket had provoked the use of force. The less serious acts of defiance, such as a failure to move on, do not usually lead to violence except when policemen are acting in a mass against a crowd (see Chapter 10), or when the refusal comes from some pariah, like a petty criminal or a derelict. Against these outcasts, the police feel a particular animosity, and they know they can act on it with impunity (see Chapter 7). Other acts of defiance, such as recording an officer's badge number, imply a criticism by the citizen and these provoke special reactions, to be discussed in Chapter 6.

Sometimes citizens engage in physical fights with policemen that are astonishing, considering the fact that the officers are armed. In at least four cases which came to us, the complainant had taken a nightstick away from a policeman, and, as can be imagined, the action usually provoked violent retribution. Some of these fights seemed to be inexcusable attacks by citizens, and some to be justifiable acts of resistance to an unlawful arrest; but in either case, I was always surprised to find the complainant still standing up and able to walk to my office.

In one notorious case from Queens, two policemen came into a ghetto bar on Christmas Eve, 1965, to look into a complaint of assault. They tried to push the Negro manager out of the way, and he objected that he worked there. When one of the policemen raised his club, the manager, who is paid for being "good with his hands" as the euphemism has it, took away the club, as well as the blackjack which was then produced by the officer. The fight escalated to the next logical step when the policeman drew his pistol. Here the manager yielded, and was forced at gunpoint onto a bench in one of the bar booths and struck in the head. When the patrons began to move in, murmuring angrily, one of the officers pointed his pistol around at the crowd, telling them to get back or he would kill them. Then he fired into the ceiling. The customers used every available exit. The manager, and an unfortunate musician from the band who simply went to the precinct to complain, were arrested for assault. As the officers did not fail to point out to the manager, he was lucky to be alive.

The Department charged the officers with making false statements in connection with the case, but no charges were made concerning the shot fired or the blow in the face. The most interesting thing about the charges in this case is that they were drawn entirely by the Commissioner's investigators and without the intervention of the Review Board at all; the Commissioner exercised his prerogative to bypass the Review Board. At this writing, the case has never been resolved because the manager jumped bail on the assault charge. However, a full description of the events is preserved on tapes taken by Stephen Nagler, a lawyer then at the Scholarship, Education, and Defense Fund for Racial Equality. Made in the bar two days after the incident, they record the statements of eleven witnesses, including two soldiers who had been free that night on a pass, while Fontella Bass's "Rescue Me," then at the height of its popularity, plays on the jukebox.

This case, and others investigated by my office in which a policeman's weapon was taken, have one striking thing in common: in every one it was a black man who took the weapon. Only ghetto people are experienced and daring enough in street fighting, or feel enough animosity toward the police, even to consider running the risk entailed.

Some complaints of the use of force do not at first appear

to concern police retaliation against an act of defiance so much as summary punishment for a crime that is not directed against the police. For example, it is frequently charged that the police kick or slap people when they find them to be in possession of narcotics. And in one case, it was claimed that the police clubbed a man who was found in possession of a pistol. Curiously, this is the only use of force that officers with whom I have discussed the problem define as brutality. They talk disapprovingly, for example, about the tendency of some officers to punish sex criminals summarily. Retaliation to an insult is perceived by the police as qualitatively different from punishing a man for a crime that does not directly affect the policeman. In fact, many of the cases in which the nonretaliatory sort of punishment was alleged are found to have involved some element of threat to the officer. In the case of the punishment for possessing the pistol, it turned out that the complainant had pointed the weapon at the police.[7]

Most people, if they think about it at all, conceive "police brutality" to be a deliberate and cold-blooded act of violence, and it appears that policemen themselves share this notion. The truth is that many incidents of the use of force by policemen bear an unfortunate resemblance to assaults by private citizens; they are hotheaded reactions to a real or imagined insult. While policemen may be quicker to take umbrage than private citizens, it is plain that their reactions are no more premeditated than those of a civilian misdemeanant. This is shown, if in no other way, by the fact that so many police abuses take place in front of a crowd of witnesses, and no real attempt is made to conceal the act until criminal charges are filed after it is over. The false criminal charges are a more serious offense by a patrolman and constitute a greater evil than the act of violence itself. The unjustified use of force in front of witnesses, when public feeling about police brutality is running as high as it has for the last few years, must be an act performed in a flash of anger; the premeditated act is filing the cover charge.

Some acts of violent retribution for defiance of the police do seem deliberate, when an effort is made to conceal the

fact that force is being used even while it is in progress. A
common device for hiding the use of force is to push the victim down a flight of stairs. It is difficult to prove that a man
actually has been pushed, because it is simple to claim that he
tripped, particularly when he is handcuffed and cannot keep
his balance properly. In two cases referred to our office, the
act of pushing seemed well authenticated, but the problem
of proving the complaint was still frustrating.

The first case is so much in the classic pattern of police
abuses as we have followed it here that it is unnecessary to
explain it at length. A young man with a history of mental
illness refused a summons from a transit policeman and called
him a "fascist cop." Four reliable bystanders (two welfare investigators, a college student, and a secretary) testified that
after the man was handcuffed they saw the officer, with a
gesture they identified as an unmistakable push, throw him
downstairs. The Transit Authority found a complaint against
the officer "unfounded."

The second case, involving city policemen, is not so simple,
but it better illustrates the difficulty of proving this sort of
complaint. An odd chance found a *New York Times* reporter
outside his apartment on the afternoon of July 22, 1966, when
he saw policemen running into a nearby house. Thinking there
might be a story, he ran in after them. On the top floor, he
found a young Puerto Rican under arrest for breaking and
entering. The man was handcuffed, and when he asked to have
the cuffs taken off so that the neighbors would not see them,
the reporter heard one of the policemen say, "If you give me
any more trouble I will push you downstairs." The two then
went down one flight while the reporter remained on the
landing. He heard someone falling and ran down to see the
Puerto Rican man crumpled on the floor of the next flight and
still handcuffed, crying, "Why did you push me?" The policeman said, "You must have tripped."

The first difficulty with this case was that the reporter had
not seen the victim pushed. There was no compelling evi-
dentiary reason to conclude that the young man had not in
fact tripped. One of our volunteer lawyers, William Erlbaum,

under the repeated urging of the reporter, finally undertook
to break through this central problem in the case. He went to
the building and began his work by interviewing the superintendent. Instant success. The man had been on one of the
landings and had looked down the stairwell, where he saw the
shadow of the policeman throwing the young man down
the stairs.

The *Times* reporter made a complaint to the Police Review
Board, which was found unsubstantiated after a hearing. Three
officers testified that the young man fell when he tried to
twist out of his arresting officer's grasp. This result illustrates
the problem in relation to complaints of pushing on the stairs.
The witnesses may be quite sure that they can distinguish a
push from a stumble; they may even be able to picture the
push to themselves. But in the description of it after the fact
to a hearing officer, the difference may seem extremely speculative. With one witness who heard the threat and another
who saw the shadow image of the push, I should have thought
there was at least enough to make out a case for a departmental trial. The fact that there was an especially convincing
bit of evidence in this case, however, only serves to emphasize
that there is an ambiguity inherent in cases where pushing is
alleged which often defies the standards of legal proof.

Any complaint of pushing presents a special problem of
proof because the act is subject to misinterpretation, but many
other, more ordinary complaints that are not so ambiguous
present equally difficult problems. The complainant and his
witnesses may not be able to identify the officer, and perhaps
most common of all, there may be no witnesses other than the
complainant and the officers.

The lack of witnesses is endemic, though as we have seen,
witnesses are available in such a large number of street-corner
incidents as to eliminate almost entirely the presumption that
such police abuses are calculated acts. In complaints about
actions in the precinct, on the other hand, a witness who is
not a policeman is a rare find indeed. It is possible and even
probable that abuses in the precinct are more deliberate than
those in the street. If a confession is coerced by physical force,

for example, it must be done through a course of conduct quite different from the policeman's indignant street reaction to a threat to his authority.

The truth is that I have very little reliable information about precinct incidents during the period of this study. There is little doubt that, until recently at least, confessions were coerced at the station house by the New York City police. In 1965 alone, a total of six murder charges were dismissed when the prosecution conceded that each defendant was in fact innocent; yet all the suspects had given detailed confessions.[8] I received several complaints of coerced confession in 1966 and 1967, but I cannot describe any of them as authenticated, because of the secret conditions under which police interrogation is conducted.

Even in cases where it can be shown that a confession is false, because someone else appears as the guilty party or the defendant has an airtight alibi, it is usually impossible to know whether physical rather than mental duress was used to get the confession. Westley found that 19 percent of the officers he interviewed in 1951 said they would use force "to obtain information,"[9] but it is impossible to know whether this is true of New York City police at the present time. I suspect that it is not. During the period of this study the Supreme Court, amid great public controversy, changed the ground rules for interrogation. The Vera Foundation, which has worked with the Police Department on many aspects of the administration of criminal justice, undertook a project to study interrogations through constant tape recordings and, in one precinct, the presence of a lawyer twenty-four hours a day.[10] When the methods of interrogation are undergoing such rapid change and intense study, it seems likely that the number of attempts to coerce a confession by violence must decrease. Quite apart from these changes in law and practice, the fact is now widely accepted that it is possible to obtain, without violence and by approved methods of interrogation, many of the confessions which were formerly obtained by violence. Physical coercion is not necessary. The standard texts for criminal interrogation describe methods which, if used for long enough or against a susceptible subject, apparently can produce a false confession.[11] This disturbing fact implies that skilled interrogators can and undoubtedly have obtained false confessions, not only without physical violence, but without being aware that they were false.

While our information on confessions during 1966 and 1967 is largely speculative, at least one authenticated case gives us a momentary glimpse into precinct abuses. They appear to be surprisingly like street incidents.

The defendant, Melvyn Harris (a fictitious name), seventeen years old, was attending Queensborough Community College at night and working as a clerk by day. He was living with his parents (his father is a cab driver) in a quiet neighborhood in Queens. On the night of Friday, November 11, 1966, he went with his friend, whom we shall call Leonard Schwarz, to a dance sponsored by the college.

Late in the evening a brawl broke out when some local toughs tried to get into the dance. The guests began to leave, and the fight started again in the street. The boys from the dance, including Harris, defended themselves as best they could, until the police arrived and chased their assailants. A good friend of Harris and Schwarz's had been knocked out, and they waited with him until the police came back, bringing a boy they had arrested fleeing from the scene. Restrained by several officers, Harris was asked if he could identify the boy, and when he said he could, he was taken with Schwarz to the precinct as a complaining witness. The police took them to the clerical office to fill out the complaint, where an argument ensued that ended with Harris' arrest for assaulting an officer. Schwarz testified at the trial about what had happened (only the names have been changed): [12]

> . . . there was two Policemen sitting at the table and there was one man in a green uniform and me and the Defendant and Patrolman L——. And, going in there to make a Complaint against that boy for assaulting another boy. So, we went through the procedures of, you know, in other words, we were going to press charges and all the papers were getting ready and then Mr. Harris asked me

for a cigarette. And, I said, "I didn't have any." And, then he asked Patrolman L—— if there was a cigarette machine inside the Police Station. And, he said he didn't know. And, he wanted me to go out, Mr. Harris wanted me to go outside, to find a candy store and I wouldn't leave the Police Station because—

Q. Don't tell us "Because" tell us what happened.

A. Well, I stayed at the Police Station and a period of ten minutes elapsed and Mr. Harris asked the man in the green uniform for a cigarette and another man that was—Patrolman that was sitting at the desk said, "Don't give him a cigarette, he's nothing to you." So he got a little discouraged and, you know, he wanted to get a cigarette so then Patrolman L—— said to the other guy—to the other—to the man in the green uniform, "Give him a cigarette, he's been a hard on all night." And then Mr. Harris took the cigarette and he broke it after the Officer had given it to him and then by this time he wanted to go up—go out, leave the building, and get his own cigarettes. At that time the Patrolman stepped in front of him and wouldn't let him leave the building.

So, he started to walk, you know, Melvyn, Mr. Harris said, "I'm not a prisoner, I could go," you know, "I'm here making a Complaint. If I want a cigarette I could get one." So at that time he started to walk to the door and the Officer had pushed him back in his seat. And, he stumbled to the seat and—

And, at that time he fell back in the seat in such a way that he had to grab something and when he went back he held, you know, went to support on something and so he held with one hand on the chair and he accidentally touched the Patrolman at which time the Officer smacked him twice in the face and then hit him over the head repeatedly with a little black club and said, "Now [you're] my prisoner."

THE COURT. You were present when all this happened.

A. I was five feet away.

THE COURT. Where were you?

A. I was near the desk.

THE COURT. What room?
A. It was the big room that we were all in.
THE COURT. All right.

There was no doubt that Schwarz was present during the incident, because the officers admitted that he was, though they told a rather different version of the facts. They claimed that Melvyn Harris had been trying to get at the accused assailant in the next room and had grappled with one of the policemen who tried to prevent him from leaving the clerical office.

The history of this case was long and exasperating. At the beginning Melvyn Harris' case and that of the assailant he originally accused outside the dance were accepted for consideration by the Youth Counsel Bureau, an arm of the District Attorney's office, which handles cases of youths with clean records arrested on minor charges. The cases are customarily dismissed after a number of months, if the boy cooperates with the Bureau. Unfortunately, during the three months that the Bureau was studying the cases, a new, more inflexible district attorney was elected in Queens, and when Harris' case came up again, the assistant in charge refused to dismiss it. He exhibited virtuous horror at the charge of assaulting an officer; the District Attorney's office could not be expected to move for the dismissal of any such heinous offense. The truth was, of course, that the DA's office was wary of a complaint against the policeman in case of a dismissal. The result was that the assailant in the street fight, who was apparently guilty, had his case dismissed, while Harris, who was apparently innocent, had to go to trial as a youthful offender.

The trial was held in the youth part of the Queens Criminal Court on a hot July afternoon some eight months after the episode. Three police officers told their story of Melvyn Harris' attempt to leave the clerical office, and Leonard Schwarz told his story for the defense.

When the police had called the members of Melvyn Harris' family on the night of his arrest, they had all put on their clothes and driven down to the precinct. His sister, Madeleine, testified that she had had a talk with the officer, and he had told her, "I had to arrest your brother, I hit him."

Shortly after this testimony, the judge called all parties into his chambers for a conference. After a discussion lasting the remainder of the afternoon, the case was dismissed in return for a promise not to sue the city or the officer for damages, or make a complaint to the Department. Melvyn Harris was technically unable to waive anything because he was a minor, but the District Attorney put him on the witness stand to swear to his promise. A little old-fashioned, perhaps, but nevertheless effective.

The most surprising thing about this case was that the police made so little effort to conceal the abuse, even though it occurred in the precinct. From my previous experience of such cases, the only unusual event in Schwarz's account was that he had not been arrested. From one point of view, that even made his story a little hard to believe. Easier to accept, curiously, was Madeleine Harris' testimony about her conversation with the officer. She was so captivating that I think she could have extracted a full confession from a Mafia chieftain. She was evidently telling the truth, and it was apparent that the police had made a botch of Harris' case. The only way to explain it is that the police must have assumed they had done the logical thing in arresting the youth. The officer's classic statement of the rationale of such arrests undoubtedly was an honest expression of his own views; he did think he "had to arrest" Melvyn Harris.

In this chapter we have discussed the predominant pattern of street incidents which give rise to summary punishment by the use of force. The point has been that it is the defiance of authority that provides the rationalization for such punishment in each individual incident. The provocation tends to lead to the use of force and then to its concealment by arrest on a criminal charge, regardless of the class or status of the person who offers it (though as we shall see, force is used more frequently against ghetto people). The middle-class youth Melvyn Harris suffered an assault for his defiance in the same way as a ghetto youth. Indeed, after the case was dismissed, the Assistant District Attorney who had prosecuted it muttered, "There, but for the grace of God, go I." I doubt that he had ever said that about any of the poor, black defendants he had prosecuted. The pattern shows that the justification for the defiance has no effect on the police action. The man who asserts his constitutional rights is just as likely to be treated as a "wise guy" as the man who openly insults a policeman. To the policeman it is his authority that counts, not the legality of his authority.

Many incidents of brutality, particularly those alleged to have occurred in the precinct, defied analysis by our crude tools of investigation. Those incidents which we were able to authenticate generally failed to survive the review procedures. Some, like Melvyn Harris' case, did not reach the Review Board at all, because of the prosecutor's intervention, but those that reached the Board often did not fare much better.

This result is at first puzzling. The Board, as we have seen, is well organized and ably staffed. It has a centralized investigating unit which works only on civilian complaints. It affords a hearing before an examiner who is not a police officer. The Board, of course, does not have the power to discipline an officer, and in fact it appears that no review board in the country has that power. Even in Philadelphia and Rochester, both of which have civilian review boards, it is the police commissioner who makes the decision. All in all, the chief procedural failing of the New York Board, as it appears from the cases in this chapter, is that it is not required to give any reasons for its decisions; it simply mails a letter stating whether or not the complaint has been found substantiated. And ,when a solid complaint is found unsubstantiated, a curt letter is just not a satisfactory explanation.

A comparison with the complaint procedures of the Transit Authority shows that the Police Department's procedures are relatively consistent and unbiased. No regulations which govern the Transit Authority's disciplinary actions are available to the public. This is not to say that there are no disciplinary procedures, but rather that they may vary a good deal from case to case. Until April 1967, it was not even customary for the

Authority to inform the complainant of the results of an investigation. After criticism from my office, the procedure was changed just enough to let the citizen know the outcome of his case. The entire thrust of the Transit Authority's methods is toward keeping all internal problems out of the public eye, and this secretiveness carries some attendant abuses. Investigators have been known to discourage citizens from making complaints. Similar abuses used to occur at the Police Department's Review Board a few years ago, before it began to operate under such intense public scrutiny, but I have not heard of them since the middle of 1966.

The Transit Authority's procedures are a sorry excuse for a system of review, but unfortunately they are not very different from those prevailing in most departments throughout the country. In a general survey of review methods, the *Harvard Law Review* found in 1963 that only 5 percent of the 191 departments responding to its questions relied exclusively on special units to investigate complaints. Thirty percent had no formal hearing procedures.[13] A field survey of the President's Commission on Law Enforcement observed that officers receiving complaints were attempting to discourage and intimidate the complainants.[14]

From a procedural standpoint, then, New York City's Review Board is relatively successful. Why, then, doesn't it get more results? I have no choice but to think the Board makes the decisions that it does because the senior officers in the Department tend to sympathize with the reactions of police officers in the field. For the Department, summary punishment for defiance is an assertion of authority, perhaps even an expression of excessive zeal on the part of the officer, but when that officer hits somebody, he is at least on duty and exhibiting some of the initiative the Department values in an officer. Senior officers take a less serious view of excessive zeal, even when it results in violence, than they do of corruption or avoidance of duty. Taking a bribe or being off one's post are much more likely to be punished by the Department than reacting to an insult with violence because, essentially, the Department agrees with its men that the latter is a less serious abuse, if indeed it is an abuse at all.

In some cases, the pattern of assault followed by a cover charge is used by a police officer for purely personal purposes, as for example in an act of revenge. Predictably, there is a significant difference in the Department's view of such cases, and that problem is the subject of the next chapter.

4

FORCE AND
REVENGE

ON THE EVENING of July 6, 1966, a group of teen-age boys
were gathered in a pizza parlor near their homes in Queens.
One of them, Dennis Iannitti, had brought a car, and at about
nine o'clock a man began to back his Ford station wagon into
the space ahead of Iannitti's, bumping against the auto. No
particular damage was done, but when the man bumped the
car again, an argument began. The man's wife went to a sidewalk telephone booth a few steps away, saying she would call
the police. There was a long lull in the argument, until finally
another man, menacingly attired in a black shirt and a garrison
belt, showed up with an enormous German shepherd on a
leash. Presently a third man, the brother of the second, appeared. Witnesses later testified that he and the original driver
suddenly grabbed Iannitti, threw him up against his car, and
began to punch him. A crowd gathered, shouting angrily, but
the brother with the dog stood in the way, saying, "If anybody
wants to get in there, he has to go through me." One boy did
get "in there," however, by slipping behind the telephone
booth. The witnesses recalled that the latest comer then drew
a pistol and whipped the second boy over the head. As he
began to bleed profusely, the man with the dog finally

walked with him away and around the corner. At about this
time, the man with the pistol announced that he was a policeman, and Iannitti was arrested, together with another boy who
was standing nearby. A truck driver, Joseph Mimmo, who
knew the second boy, stepped in. He later testified to his
conversation with the policeman.[1]

> I said to the officer, "What are you doing to this kid?"
> He said "He is my prisoner," and I said, "For what? He
> didn't do anything. He wasn't even involved." I said,
> "Furthermore, if you are a police officer, just show your
> badge," and with that he said, "You are under arrest."

The boy with the bleeding head was arrested near the hospital, after seven stitches had been taken, and all three teen-
agers were charged with felonious assault. Mr. Mimmo was
charged with interfering with their arrest and spent five or
six days in jail before he was able to make bail.

On July 8, an extraordinary version of the facts, derived from
the account given out by the police, appeared in the Queens
edition of the New York *Daily News*.[2] The story was that the
teen-agers had set upon the driver of the station wagon and
then upon the off-duty patrolman when he attempted to stop
the fight. The boy who had gone to the hospital had received
his injuries, it was claimed, by falling against a parking meter.
The closing sentence in the story was, "The driver whose parking started it all disappeared."

The sentence implied that the arresting officer had not
known who that driver was, and in fact, in an affidavit and at
two trials, he swore that he did not know. Fortunately, someone had had the presence of mind to write down the license
number of the station wagon. Mimmo's attorney, who was almost certain from the way the fight had arisen that there had
to be some connection between the three assailants, checked
the number with the Motor Vehicles Bureau. The car belonged
to the patrolman's brother-in-law. Police Review Board investigators arranged a lineup, and one witness picked the
brother-in-law out as the driver.

The Department was faced with an overwhelming case

against the policeman. Seven eyewitnesses to the assault gave their names to the Review Board on behalf of the defendants, and I myself interviewed five of them. The teen-agers were tried as youthful offenders and acquitted, and Mimmo was acquitted by a three-judge court of interfering with their arrest. Finally, charges against the policeman were preferred by the Department for trial.

This was the second stage in the two-tier process of discipline for policemen, after the complaint has been heard, and when it is found substantiated, by the Review Board. Departmental trials are conducted in an ornate courtroom in the ancient police headquarters on Centre Street. All the punctilio of due process is observed, but the acoustics are so bad that witnesses are barely audible. A policeman trained as a lawyer acts as prosecutor, defense counsel cross-examines, and a deputy commissioner takes the evidence and makes findings of fact to present to the Police Commissioner. In this case all the many witnesses appeared for the Department, and the officer was found guilty of the charge of concealing the fact that his brother-in-law was the driver, although he was acquitted of other charges.

Many of the incidents in this case are familiar from the last chapter. An assault by a policeman, followed by a chain of cover arrests, is the essence of the matter. Bystanders, drawn into the vortex of the dispute by friendship or a sense of justice, were arrested, as they were in the LEAP case in Chapter 3. The difference is that in this case there was no defiance of, no threat to authority; rather, an obviously personal dispute was at the heart of the incident. This appeared to have been purely an act of family revenge against some supposedly "wise" teen-agers. No conceivable element of race or class conflict was involved; the patrolman as well as two of the defendants were Italians, and in fact, the defendants themselves were related to policemen. This was not far different from the typical assault case between private citizens, in which each side charges the other with assault; the difference once again was that one party was a policeman. Some of the teen-agers followed through the logic of the situation by filing a cross-complaint in Criminal Court against the officer for assault, but the court refused to entertain it.

The most significant thing about the case is that the Department, from the Review Board up to the Commissioner, took a much dimmer view of the policeman's actions than it had in cases where a policeman on duty had summarily punished an act of defiance to his authority and covered the punishment by a criminal charge.

There is a fair distinction between a policeman's actions taken on duty, in response to a threat to him as an officer, and actions taken off duty and for personal reasons, but the difference is not so great that the first ought to be ignored. Both are abuses, though the second is more serious and perhaps ought to be more severely punished. But the Department tends to dismiss the first as insignificant, because it is justified by departmental customs and administrative needs. The Department seems to have made a decision, poorly articulated to be sure, that an officer is not to be disciplined for acts performed in the line of duty if those acts show initiative and an effort to maintain order. An angry reaction to defiance is thus felt to be one of the more minor of a policeman's failings. The effort to convict a prisoner is likewise to be commended, and shaving the facts a little to bring about that conviction is less reprehensible than avoiding the arrest altogether. The officer is at least showing initiative and the will to make arrests and obtain convictions—as far as the Department is concerned, virtues of a "good cop."

5

DEFIANCE
AND ARREST

ON THE AFTERNOON of October 12, 1966, Gerald Zuckerman, a twenty-four-year-old biology teacher, was out for a Sunday drive with his father and Albert Amato, an old friend
from school days. As their car passed the corner of Lydig and
Cruger Avenues in the Bronx, a few minutes from the Zuckerman residence, they saw a large crowd gathered around a man
being arrested. They got out of the car, and Zuckerman recognized an acquaintance, one Stuart Klein, among the young men
in the crowd. He went up to speak to Klein, and Albert Amato
was later to testify in court about what happened during the
next few minutes: [1]

> As soon as I got out of the car we were confronted
> by someone named Stuart who said there was a Steven
> Handler who was being arrested, being held by a police-
> man. I don't know Steven Handler. Jerry did, so we
> walked over to the crowd. We walked over near the edge
> of the crowd. I stood there. I didn't say anything to the
> prisoner Steven Handler or anyone else around there. . . .
> Gerald asked the prisoner what had happened, why was
> he arrested. The prisoner wasn't very coherent. He made
> a few rather incoherent statements to the crowd at that
> time such as "pot is here to stay" and other incoherent

statements. The crowd was speaking back to the prisoner
from time to time saying such things as "you should be
ashamed of yourself," and "a young man like you should
be working." At this time Gerald Zuckerman said to the
crowd words such as "Don't you people have anything
better to do than just stand here." At this time the policeman told Gerald Zuckerman to shut up. He didn't say
anything further to the crowd or to the prisoner. As the
policeman told him to shut up, right after that Gerald
Zuckerman said to the policeman, "Isn't this a free country, don't I have a right to stay here and speak?" Well,
the policeman didn't say anything after that and neither
did Gerald Zuckerman. I would say about five to ten minutes passed when a patrol car pulled up and the prisoner
was thrown into the patrol car, and I was standing right
behind Gerald Zuckerman and the policeman right after
that walked up to Gerald Zuckerman and said—I don't
remember the exact words—he said, "I am going to show
you what kind of free country this is," and he just
grabbed him around the collar and he threw him towards
the police car and with the help of the other policeman
he was thrown into the police car and he was taken away.

Zuckerman was charged with interfering with an officer, a
misdemeanor familiar to us from earlier cases. Some two weeks
after his arrest, his family came to the office to ask me to take
the case. They had lived most of their lives in that neighborhood of the Bronx, the father, Nathan, quietly practicing as a
podiatrist near their home. Their son, a mild-mannered young
man with a sandy red mustache, was understandably nervous
about the charges. It was a serious matter for him because he
might lose his job as a teacher in the city's public school system if he should be convicted. I agreed to defend him after I
had confirmed the story in interviews with Albert Amato and
Stuart Klein.

At the next adjourned day of the case, one of our volunteer
attorneys, Henry Salitan, went with the Zuckermans to the
ancient Bronx County Criminal Courts Building, nearly an
hour away from my office. He conferred with the Assistant
District Attorney assigned to the trial part of the court, and

tried his best to persuade him to drop the case. No luck. Mr.
Salitan took the matter on to a preliminary hearing, and as
usual there was a long wait until late in the afternoon before
the magistrate could get to the hearing. In theory, a hearing
is intended to determine whether there is enough evidence to
sustain the charges against a defendant, but Mr. Salitan, like
most criminal lawyers, was also making use of it to glean an
idea of the prosecution's case so as to avoid surprise at the
trial. In practice, a preliminary hearing does not look very
different from a trial. The prosecution introduces its witness
before a judge, usually the same judge who is conducting trials,
and the witness presents some of the prosecution's case. Because it is only necessary to establish that the prosecution has
some evidence against the defendant, it is customary for the
prosecution to put on just one witness and the defense none.
In this case, the District Attorney presented part of the policeman's story, and the judge naturally found that there was a
basis for the charges against Gerald Zuckerman.

I ordered a transcript of the hearing, to learn just what that
basis was. The heart of the People's case was in these words: [2]

> At the time and date in question, I had already placed
> Stephen Handlergutter under arrest . . . for disorderly
> conduct and assaulting me, and I had brought him to that
> corner waiting for my relief, my car to come up and pick
> me up. At that time a crowd of about 150 people had
> gathered because it was a holiday. The defendant here
> came up and he asked what I was arresting his friend
> for, and I said, "For disorderly conduct," and then he
> turned to the crowd and he was telling the crowd then
> this is another illegal arrest and an uncalled for arrest.
> I didn't say anything to him at that time. I let it pass.
> He then gave the defendant a cigarette, and I told him to
> stay away from the guy, to stay away from my prisoner.
> At that time he grabbed my prisoner's arm and he was
> pulling on my prisoner's arm who was handcuffed at the
> time. My prisoner was handcuffed at the time. . . .
> I pulled him back and I said at that time to go away
> and not interfere with this and stay away from me. Then
> he turned to about six or seven of his friends and said to

them, "Come on, help me get Steve out of here," meaning the defendant, my prisoner rather. At that time a car came to pick me up. I gave my prisoner to him, to the car, and the defendant had disappeared into the crowd. I found the defendant and placed him under arrest.

We had no other alternative than to go to trial.

On a rainy Wednesday in January, the case was called for trial before a panel of three judges in a dim, stuffy Bronx courtroom. Ours was the first case called, and I barely had time to observe that Stuart Klein had come to court in a grubby white shirt and no tie, before the policeman was on the stand. He testified substantially as he had at the preliminary hearing, and the presiding judge denied our motion to dismiss the case at the close of the officer's testimony. It was now in the hands of the defense.

Albert Amato was an excellent witness, telling the story of his arrival at the scene with the Zuckermans, Gerald's attempt to get the crowd to let the prisoner alone, and his question to the policeman, "Isn't this a free country?" together with his arrest and the policeman's reply, "I am going to show you what kind of free country this is."

Stuart Klein was at first a disturbing witness. One of the judges remarked that he ought to be wearing a jacket and tie, and he was several times reproved for vague and inaudible answers. As sometimes happens, however, he improved under cross-examination. He said that he had been standing some distance away from the arrest and could not testify to any conversation, but he was sure that Zuckerman had stood there for five or ten minutes without physically interfering with the policeman or his prisoner. Gerald Zuckerman and his father gave testimony which substantially corroborated Albert Amato and Stuart Klein. The defense rested after Gerald Zuckerman's testimony, and the judges acquitted him after a few moments' deliberation.

It is perhaps hard to see at first why the few words which had been uttered to the policeman would be enough to provoke an arrest, but Albert Amato and Gerald Zuckerman told me something of what had happened after the arrest, which helped to explain it. Zuckerman remembered that as he was being taken to court for arraignment, the arresting officer told him, "If I let you get away with it, other people might think I'm an easy mark and jump me."

John McNamara's work on the attitudes of New York City policemen suggests that this rationalization for arrest is very common. In Chapter 3, in connection with defiance and force, we saw that many officers believe that an officer who "ignores challenges to fight from citizens will probably make it harder for other patrolmen to work his post or sector." Similarly, Mc-Namara found that 55 percent of the men who had been in the field for two years agreed with the proposition that "Respect for the police in a tough neighborhood depends on the willingness to use force frequently and effectively." [3] Zuckerman of course did not offer any challenge to fight, and his arrest did not take place in a particularly tough neighborhood. The arrest suggests that *any* challenge to a policeman, when the public is present, even if the challenge is legally justified, will be considered a dangerous threat to his authority. The policeman's remark, "I am going to show you what kind of free country this is," is significant; there is no right, as the policeman sees it, to defy his authority in public. Whether he reacts by violence and an arrest, or by an arrest alone as in Zuckerman's case, is not so important as the fact that the two reactions are in essence the same.

Albert Amato recalled that when he went to the precinct the afternoon of his friend's arrest, an officer in plainclothes told him that Zuckerman was "some sort of civil rights person"* and that the police intended to call up the Board of Education about him. This complaint remains unsubstantiated because Amato unfortunately was not able to identify the speaker, but it perhaps sheds some further light on the motivation for the charges against Zuckerman. By telling the policeman that this was a "free country," Zuckerman had marked himself as a troublemaker. He was at least a potential offender, and fair game for an arrest.

---

* There is not the slightest evidence that the allegation was true, apart from Zuckerman's words at the scene of his arrest.

On January 19, 1967, I wrote a letter to the Review Board containing the facts of the Zuckerman case as I understood them, including the names of the witnesses. In July, some six months later, I received a reply, the key sentence of which read: "Although every effort was made in this case to find objective proof, such as other witnesses, etc. the investigation failed to substantiate the allegations in your complaint." In short, the Board did not even consider the matter worth hearing.

Sometimes a threat to the officer's authority amounts to little more than a personal affront to the officer as an individual, but because he is in uniform it is taken as an attack upon authority. A photographer and a public relations man learned this to their sorrow on the night of November 3, 1966. George Howard, as we shall call him (fictitiously), and Robert Gore were walking out of a large office building in midtown Manhattan together after an evening meeting. Both men are Negroes.

The two hailed a taxi outside the building. An argument ensued about whether the driver would take them or not, and a mounted policeman intervened. He took the two aside to ask them what the trouble was, and the driver seized the opportunity to drive off. The two men were left without their cab. Even though Gore and Howard both agreed that Gore had been doing all the shouting at the driver, Howard was suddenly arrested for his comments to the officer and charged with disorderly conduct. The officer's affidavit charged, in boilerplate language, that:

> with intent to provoke a breach of the peace and under circumstances whereby a breach of the peace might be occasioned, the defendant did become loud and boisterous, refuse to quiet down and leave and by his actions did cause a crowd to collect to the annoyance of persons in the vicinity.

After George Howard had called my office about his arrest, I did the obvious, which was to call Robert Gore, the only person not directly involved in the arrest, to hear his version of

the facts. A veteran of many civil rights campaigns, Mr. Gore
was not likely to accept an insult from a cab driver in silence.
His manner, on the other hand, was precise and reserved, and
it was repugnant to him to recount the curses and racial
epithets of that evening. His account, as he told it then and
later at the trial, was a vignette of the ills of the city: [4]

> A young lady was getting out of the cab and when she got
> out I got in. At that point where I got in the cab the
> driver turned back to me and told me to get out of the
> cab and he used a number of racial epithets at the time
> and it sort of shocked me, and I asked him to repeat what
> he said, and he did at which point I got out of the cab.

The District Attorney demanded to hear the driver's exact
words. Mr. Gore quoted, with as much distaste as if he were
picking up a rat by the tail, "Get out of this cab, you black
son of a bitch," and went on with his story (only the names
have been changed):

> . . . I kept suggesting to the cab driver that there are
> certain laws in the State of New York, in the City of New
> York, which said that if he had an empty cab he had to
> take me where I wanted to go, at which point, if I recall
> correctly, Mr. Howard, who was with me at that time,
> then called a mounted police office[r], who came up and
> asked what was going on, and I explained to him what
> was going on.
>   While we were talking the cab left and he suggested
> that we move over to the side, to the sidewalk, so that we
> wouldn't obstruct the traffic, and we did, and we dis-
> cussed it a little further and when the—I am not sure of
> the sequence of events right here, but, after the cab
> pulled away, then Mr. Howard suggested that the officer
> should have stopped the cab because he was the one who
> was causing the disturbance, and the officer then got off
> the horse and arrested Mr. Howard.

Mr. Gore was a little reluctant to repeat Mr. Howard's
exact words. However, to give the judge a clear idea of the
source of the arrest, I insisted that he do so.

A. After the cab driver had left, to the best of my recollection Mr. Howard said to the officer, "You should have got your fat ass off the horse and said something to the cab driver."

Q. Did the officer get off the horse?

A. Yes, sir, he did.

Q. Will you tell the court what tone of voice Mr. Howard used to the police officer F——? Was it loud, soft or medium?

A. I would say it was medium.

To anyone who knew Howard, this account was easy to believe. He was a reporter who had worked in many difficult situations, and he was not excitable, though he was likely to express his opinion clearly at any place and any time.

At the trial, held in the petty-offense division of Manhattan Criminal Court, where we had once waited so long for Carlos Caulaincourt's case to be dismissed, the policeman's account was just a bit different from Gore's:

A. His friend kept trying to calm him down. I told him to quiet down also. He said, "You let him go." I said, "I didn't." He said, "You didn't do what you should have done." He said, "You get your big white ass off your horse and I'll show you what I'll do." I said, "I have a better idea. I will stay on my horse and place you under arrest. Let me have your two hands."

Q. Was this in front of the crowd?

A. Yes.

Q. How many times did he tell you that you let the cab driver go because he was white and he was black?

A. At least three times.

Q. You say he made this statement in a loud tone of voice?

A. Yes.

The judge heard this account, and then listened to the testimony of Gore and Howard. He reserved decision, and we sat in the audience while he thought it over through a number of other short trials. Finally, at the end of the day, he acquitted George Howard.

Neither Zuckerman nor George Howard had a terribly important or dramatic case for the State of New York. These cases may have been the most interesting tried that day in their respective trial parts, but by the following day they were forgotten. They are important for us, however, for other reasons. A citizen does not have to be poor or black or even to live in the ghetto to be summarily arrested in a street dispute with a policeman. Just a little defiance will suffice. These complaints, moreover, are representative of over sixty we received from March 1966 to June 1967 from within and outside ghetto communities, alleging an arbitrary arrest. Seventeen of them, including the Zuckerman and Howard cases, as well as the cases of Bell and Johnson and Carlos Caulaincourt, were so strongly corroborated that we considered the facts established. The twenty-odd which are not "authenticated" by our standards are nevertheless so much like the ones in which the facts are established that it is difficult to escape the conclusion that there is a strong tendency to arrest for defiance.

There is an enormous variety of circumstances in which the policeman sees a threat to his authority, which then must be asserted by arrest. Many are like those we have already discussed, involving a failure to move on when ordered or an argument over some trivial legal matter. Three of our complaints, including George Howard's, arose out of disputes over taxicabs and three out of disputes over traffic tickets. A rude reply to a policeman, not to speak of a refusal to obey, even when it is given in response to an unlawful order, or to rudeness on the part of the police, is an invitation to arrest. Whether the incident starts with a provocative remark from the citizen or from the policeman, it makes no difference to the result, as one of the cases which arose over a traffic violation showed.

Early one morning in April 1966, two policemen pulled a car occupied by seven Negroes over to a curb in Harlem. They asked the driver to get out of the car, a procedure occasionally followed as a step in determining whether the driver is intoxicated. Up to this point, none of the passengers in the car seemed to take offense, but after the policemen received a negative answer to the question whether the driver had taken

anything to drink, they asked him if he had a knife and com-
menced to frisk him. The driver began to protest, and all the
other six in the car promptly got out and demanded to know
why the police were so suspicious. One of the witnesses told
me that she demanded to be told why they had asked such a
"stupid" question. The driver was finally arrested for disorderly
conduct and failure to obey a signal, apparently as a way to
end the row.

The kindest word to describe the conduct of the police in
this case is foolish. Quite apart from the fact that their questions and the frisk were of doubtful legality, it is remarkable
how they could have failed to recognize that questioning a
Negro, stopped for a routine traffic violation, about a knife, in
the presence of six of his friends, was an extremely provocative
act. The point for our present purposes is that the officers felt
that the driver's defiance, and his friends' protests, demanded
the assertion of police authority by arrest, regardless of the
fact that the provocation was offered by the police.

The driver was acquitted after a trial, and I later wrote to
him asking whether he wanted to go further with the case. He
had been threatening throughout the criminal proceedings to
"leave this country where they treat a black man worse than
a dog," and to go home to his native British West Indies. I
assume that, like Jose Rivera, he did just that, because my
certified letter was returned marked "unclaimed."

Ten of our sixty-odd complaints of arbitrary arrest occurred
in the subway and involved transit patrolmen.* No doubt this
percentage is as high as it is because the transit regulations
govern behavior on the train rather strictly (forbidding spitting,
smoking, playing music, and the like) and because, as a result
of violence in the subway, there are a large number of patrolmen at work there. The complaints, like those against city
policemen, typically begin with minor infractions of the subway regulations, followed by an order to leave the train.
Sleeping in the subway, playing a radio or a record player

* The Transit Authority has its own policemen, who wear police uniforms, receive police training, and have the powers of peace officers.
There are 3,000 of them, as compared with 28,000 city policemen.

too loudly, smoking or spitting, and putting feet up on the seats have all resulted in persons being ordered off the train. A refusal to leave, or an argument, generally results in an arrest.

Our sixty-odd complaints of arbitrary arrest, spread out over a period of fifteen months, may not seem like a large number, taken by themselves. It is by now obvious, however, that the genesis of these complaints is the same as that of complaints of unlawful use of force. Complaints of arrest must be considered together with the much more numerous (164) complaints of force.* In fact, the most vicious aspect of the unlawful use of force is often not the blow itself—blows are common enough—but the arrest which follows. The ultimate abuse of authority lies in the power to arrest and cover up the assault.

The genesis of nearly all street abuses is defiance of authority, real or imagined, regardless of whether the reaction is arrest alone or arrest and summary punishment. These abuses are in essence the same, and they will be treated as the same in succeeding chapters. The sanction chosen depends on the victim, the place, and the individual officer. For example, my records show arrests for defiance from every race and neighborhood, but force seems usually (though by no means always) to be used against Negroes or Puerto Ricans. An arrest, or in rare cases a summons, is usually the least sanction available for disobedience; the use of any other sanction, such as violence, without an arrest is rare, because of the risk of a lawsuit or a civilian complaint when criminal charges are not filed.

---

* It does not follow that force is used more often than arrest without force. It is self-evident that people who are physically abused are more likely to complain than those who are simply arrested.

6

CRITICISM OF THE POLICE

THERE ARE A NUMBER of acts by citizens which the police in-
terpret as indirect threats to authority. Criticism of a policeman's handling of a situation, for example, is interpreted as
an extremely offensive challenge to the officer personally, as
well as to his authority. George Howard's case is a rather
special example, but similar occurrences—questions about the
policeman's methods or his honesty, or even threats to report
him to the Department—are very frequent, and they are always an invitation to arrest. Typically, such an arrest is made
on the charge of interfering with an officer, although in some
cases the charge may be that old catchall, disorderly conduct.

The classic example of street-corner criticism is noting down
an officer's shield number, and the arrest that often follows
this act is among the most time-honored of police abuses. As
long ago as 1930, a lawyer who had noted down a policeman's
badge number was cleared by appeal of a conviction for disorderly conduct,[1] and as recently as December 1967, the Department had to issue a special order about press relations
because some officers had confiscated the notes of a *New York
Post* reporter, apparently supposing him to be a demonstrator
who was recording shield numbers. In my office we received

eight complaints of arrest, accompanied in some cases by assault, because of an attempt to take the shield number, the license number, or the photograph of a policeman. Some of them are unsubstantiated for lack of witnesses, but they are all so much alike that it seems safe to assume at least a tendency to react to such impliedly critical acts by arrest.

A most memorable case of arrest and assault on account of recording badge numbers occurred at the Spring Mobilization for Peace on April 15, 1967. Hundreds of thousands of people marched some twenty-five blocks from Central Park to the United Nations at the East River. It took many hours just for the demonstrators to march into the UN Plaza and out. There were a number of incidents of harassment by hecklers, and policemen were frequently criticized by demonstrators. Apparently under orders to avoid conflict with the marchers, most policemen stared stoically ahead through such incidents, though sometimes scarlet with anger; but in the case of George Fischer, they finally lost their patience.

Mr. Fischer, a noted student of Soviet society, was at that time an associate professor of sociology at Columbia. He was marching with his wife and some friends away from the Plaza, late in the afternoon, when they passed a particularly vituperative group of hecklers. Mr. Fischer and some others went back along the line of march to ask the police to keep the hecklers away from the marchers. When the police refused, Mr. Fischer extracted from his pocket a 3×5 card of the sort upon which one records research, and began to note down shield numbers. The first few officers accepted his actions without comment, but as he continued, some of them grabbed at him. John Cowley, a young British psychologist who was slightly acquainted with Mr. Fischer, narrated the events of the next few moments at a pretrial examination: [2]

> I saw George Fis[c]her standing close to a few feet away from this group that were on the pavement. There was also a number of policemen and they were pushing some passersby along, clearing them away, and George Fis[c]her was writing on a small card, piece of paper, in his hand. It wasn't immediately clear to me what he was writing.

THE COURT. How far away was he from you at that time approximately?

THE WITNESS. I can't measure it in feet.

THE COURT. Give us your best approximation.

THE WITNESS. I would say he was a little bit further away than the policeman sitting to the left there, a little bit say in the row behind that.

MR. CHEVIGNY. Indicating about 20 feet.

THE COURT. About 20 feet. Is that so stipulated?

DISTRICT ATTORNEY. I suppose 20, 25.

THE COURT. All right, 20 to 25 feet. Go ahead. Now what did you see?

THE WITNESS. Then the police started—

THE COURT. What did you see?

THE WITNESS. The police pushed George Fis[c]her.

THE COURT. When you say the police, who in particular, do you know?

THE WITNESS. Three or four policemen.

THE COURT. I see.

THE WITNESS. Pushed George Fis[c]her backwards.

THE COURT. Well did you see George Fis[c]her doing anything?

THE WITNESS. Writing on a piece of paper.

THE COURT. That's all?

THE WITNESS. He wasn't speaking. I couldn't see him speaking.

THE COURT. Well you were 25 feet away, is that right?

THE WITNESS. Yes but one could see his mouth moving.

THE COURT. Go ahead.

THE WITNESS. They began to push him backwards, four or five policemen. It was difficult to tell how many were involved in it. I then broke from the line of march and crossed onto the pavement to discover what was happening. By the time I got to the pavement they had pushed him against the wall.

Q. Mr. Cowley, when you say "the pavement" tell us whether you mean the roadway or the sidewalk. Do you mean the roadway or the sidewalk?

A. I mean the sidewalk.

Q. You are referring to the sidewalk?

A. Yes.

Q. Go on.

A. So once I was on the pavement I became quite close to George Fis[c]her but there were then a number of policemen around him, it is difficult to estimate, seven maybe, and there were four or five who seemed to be pushing him, pummeling him against the wall. I moved close to him but then I was pushed back by a policeman and I was unclear as to why they were pummeling him and then he started to walk down the pavement towards me and we saw each other and, you know, exchanged— Just stated each other's names to each other. We recognized each other. He wasn't under arrest at that time.

Q. Just tell us what happened. Don't characterize the facts.

A. So he was walking on the pavement; walked past me. A policeman was holding me back and pushing me back along the pavement, back towards 46th Street; then the next thing I noticed was George Fis[c]her put his arm out across the barrier with his card in his hand to hand it to somebody that was at the other side of the barrier. At that point eight or nine policemen gathered around him; rushed him backwards a few yards, by this time we were at 46th Street, and threw him onto the roadway, 46th Street and he was—There were eight or nine policemen around him or on top of him and then they pulled him up and took him away to a garage on 46th Street following that.

At some point in this melee Mr. Fischer did release the card. Although John Cowley could not see it, Mr. Fischer reported that his arm was twisted behind him and some unknown person added a touch of the macabre to this otherwise familiar series of events by biting his hand until he let go of the card. A medical record made that night showed that he had indeed been bitten. He was then arrested and charged with disorderly conduct, assault, and resisting arrest. His wife, who had vociferously protested the whole fracas, was charged with interfering in his arrest. After a lengthy investigation by the police, the charges were dismissed through the good offices of the District Attorney.

The hearing at the Review Board on Professor Fischer's case was a short course in the problems attendant upon complaints growing out of demonstrations. There had been so many policemen present that few of the witnesses could positively identify even one of them. Those who could pick out the face of one officer could not recall just what he had done, and of course no one knew who had bitten the professor. The problem of identification is characteristic of civil disturbances, from demonstrations to riots, and it is exacerbated by the fact that all policemen wear the same blue uniform. It was clear that someone had assaulted Mr. Fischer in a unique way, but we were never to find out who it was.

The recording of his shield number is one of the most threatening of all actions to a policeman, because, apart from the fact that he interprets it as an act of defiance, it implies that, justifiable or not, his behavior is about to be called to the attention of his superiors. Verbal criticisms are not such direct threats, but, like the remark of George Howard, they are affronts that seem to many policemen to demand some punishment.

One such officer was on patrol in Times Square on New Year's Day, 1967, near the Cinerama Theater, where the film *Grand Prix* was having a reserved-seat engagement. Peter Hall, as we shall call him (fictitiously), a blond fellow in his twenties, rode up on his red Honda motorcycle, with his girl Linda sitting behind him. He parked directly in front of the theater near a fire hydrant, intending to leave the motorcycle there only a moment while they bought tickets. When he came back, the officer was writing him a ticket. He asked if Hall owned the Honda, and then asked for his license and registration. Hall attempted to explain the situation, but naturally enough, he got the ticket anyway.

Hall moved the motorcycle up the street a short way and parked it at an angle to the curb. According to the girl's account, the officer came up and ordered him to move, or get a ticket for angle parking. Hall asked what he had done, and the policeman demanded his license and registration, which he had already seen by the fire hydrant. By this time Hall had the license in his hand, and when he again asked what he had done, the officer threatened to arrest him if he did not show the papers. Hall made the mistake of once more asking what he had done, and the officer told him he was under arrest. Two other officers had come up by this time, and all three knocked Hall off the motorcycle. A police car drove up, and the driver asked what the trouble was. One policeman said, "Resisting arrest," and all jumped out of the car, seized Hall, and put him in the police car. Hall was still asking what he had done as he was driven off, to be charged with parking by a fire hydrant, angle parking, resisting arrest, and disorderly conduct.

When Hall and his girl came to my office after work three days later to tell me this story, I asked the same question Hall had asked some four times: What *had* he done? The story, as I heard it, seemed literally to have a piece missing, even from the police point of view. Hall is no motorcycle tough. Working on weekdays as an inventory clerk, he races a bicycle on weekends and vacations, and the Amateur Bicycle League considered him a "potential Olympian," as one of its members wrote in a letter to the court. He is invariably well-dressed and well-spoken. The tale of harassment as I have recorded it here and as the girl first told it to me, was simply incomprehensible. I asked her to begin the story again, picturing its progress to herself step by step and leaving nothing out.

To my considerable surprise, the method worked. She recollected, and I recorded in an affidavit, the following episode which seemed to her insignificant, occurring between the time Hall received the ticket in front of the theater and the time he parked again at an angle to the curb up the street:

Mr. [Hall] started the motorcycle, when the policeman walked over and looked at a car, and walked back away from it. We moved up a few feet to the car, and looked in the window. He [Hall] said there was an ID card for the Warner Theater there. We stopped the motorcycle as the doorman came up to [the officer] and said it was the manager's car. [Hall] said, "Are you going to give this man a ticket?" The policeman did not reply, that I can remember.

It was immediately after this that Hall moved his motorcycle up the street, parking at an angle to the curb. Apart from the girl, who was obviously a somewhat interested witness (although her manner in giving the facts convinced me she was telling the truth), Hall's case had some slight corroboration. In the first place, there were those traffic tickets. One had been issued on a summons and the other on an arrest, an odd circumstance in itself. Moreover, a young Negro man who worked in the penny arcade across from the theater said that he had seen the episode, and that Hall appeared to him to be sitting on his motorcycle seat with his hand out when the police knocked him off it. He thought Hall was arguing with the officer, but he could not hear him. Although I subpoenaed this man on two separate occasions, he never appeared in court. It would have been a little surprising if he had. He did not know Hall, and he was working at a job which probably depended partly for its existence upon the indulgence of the police. There was not even the solidarity of common minority status to induce him to come; he was black and Hall was white. Theoretically, of course, the subpoena gave him no choice; a refusal to appear was contempt of court. The trouble is that a witness who is so reluctant that he will run the risk of a citation for contempt is seldom worth having at all. Like most legal sanctions, a subpoena does not work well unless it is obeyed.

Whether that witness came to court or not mattered little in the end. Hall did not want to make an issue of the case; he just wanted to avoid a conviction. After much negotiation, he finally paid the traffic tickets and the other charges were dismissed.

Support for civilian review of police abuses provided a case study in the consequences of criticizing the police. The Civilian Review Board, unique among public agencies during its short life in the summer of 1966, implied such criticism, as well as a threat to police authority. Campaigners who supported the Board on the street ran a distinct danger of suffering the same fate as those who directly criticized an individual policeman.

On July 1, 1966, the Police Commissioner had appointed four civilians unconnected with the Police Department to act with the three existing members of the Civilian Complaint Review Board drawn from the Department, thus creating a nonpolice majority on the Board. The Patrolmen's Benevolent Association, a tightly organized union which, until then, had rarely been heard from on public issues, showed its strength by commencing a successful campaign, first to put a referendum forbidding civilian review on the ballot for November 8, and then to collect an enormous majority of voters in favor of abolishing civilian review.

As the reader will probably recall, the campaign was passionate indeed. The police appealed to the need for order, arguing that if the Board were established, policemen would avoid difficult problems rather than risk the criticism of civilians. The supporters of civilian review appealed to the sense of liberty, arguing that the Review Board would deter police misconduct. The PBA used a now-famous leaflet showing a policeman with his hands tied behind him, while supporters of the Board had a somewhat less provocative broadside listing all the extreme right-wing organizations that opposed it.

This is not the place to argue the merits of that debate; the point for us is that citizens who got into arguments with the police in the heat of the campaign sometimes found themselves in Criminal Court.

The most celebrated of these cases began on Saturday night, October 22, 1966. Toward midnight, Mr. and Mrs. Marshall Kaplan were being driven home by Mrs. Kaplan's father, accompanied by a cousin, Harriet Weingarten. Driving down Henry Street on the Lower East Side, they passed a police car parked in the roadway, with a paper sticker on the back opposing the Civilian Review Board.

The Kaplans had both been teachers in the New York City school system, and they not only favored civilian review but were sensitive to the limitations of political activity imposed on public employees. They agreed that a partisan sticker on a police car was improper, and they got out of the car with Miss Weingarten to walk back and ask the police to remove the sticker. When the two policemen refused, Mrs. Kaplan asked them to write down their badge numbers. They did it, and in turn asked for identification to prepare summonses for jaywalking. Mrs. Kaplan, incensed by this tactic, refused to give her identification. At this point a police sergeant passed in a truck, and the Kaplans appealed to him, asking whether it was right to have a sticker on the car. He agreed that it was not, but drove on, saying that the men were not under his command. Mrs. Kaplan steadfastly refused to give her name, and all three were finally arrested. They were later released from the precinct station without any bail, and late the next day they were sent to me by another attorney. With the vote on the Review Board scarcely two weeks away, the case was bound to make political news. A rumor of the arrest had got out, and all day Sunday the newspapers were calling me to interview the three. I refused to permit this until they were arraigned, for fear of more serious charges. When I met my clients the next morning in court, I was relieved to find that the charges had remained at jaywalking, but with the addition of disorderly conduct.

Harriet Weingarten, pretty and clever as she was, had succeeded in charming the officers while she was at the precinct. The next morning, after I brought her the disorderly conduct affidavit alleging that all three had been "loud and boisterous, causing a crowd to gather," Miss Weingarten gave the younger of the two officers a frosty look and tossed her head. When he asked why she was mad at him, she lisped, "Because you lied." In my office this became the parable of Sweet Naiveté. We had become so cynical about the charges brought in cases like this that it was hard to imagine being disillusioned about discovering a lie. Whether the officers had lied, was, of course, precisely the question. As I saw the matter, the defense did not seem so easy to establish. By my customary standards, the complaint was unsubstantiated. The defendants did not then know of any witnesses to the incident except themselves.

That night we began to walk down the line of houses on Henry Street facing the scene, inquiring of the people lounging on the doorsteps, mostly Puerto Ricans, whether they had seen the incident. They all denied it as I had assumed they probably would; the Kaplans were nothing to them. To my surprise, one man finally hinted that we should ask an old lady in one of the apartments facing the street. We rang her bell and tried to talk to her, but her English was so uncertain that she called in her daughter. The girl came out of the bedroom, her hair in curlers, preparing to go to her job as a barmaid. Yes, she had seen the whole incident from the window. Sure, she would be happy to appear in court. As she said this, a young man in bed in the living room was volubly advising her to tell us to go to hell. I thanked the girl profusely, but she merely smiled the smile of superior knowledge and said, "It is all right. I understand these things. I'm a Puerto Rican."

As it turned out, there were other witnesses: two neighbors, schoolteachers who knew the Kaplans, had passed the police car and seen them standing there. Far from seeing a disturbance of the peace, they had thought so little of the incident that they simply drove on without stopping.

The trial for disorderly conduct was held in the petty-offense part of Criminal Court, scene of the Carlos Caulaincourt and George Howard cases. The three defense witnesses, the schoolteachers and the barmaid, testified that there was no disturbance of the peace. What the barmaid had to say was perhaps most persuasive, because she was utterly disinterested. She knew the defendants so slightly that she did not even get their names straight; she thought "Marshall" was Kaplan's last name.[3]

I saw them and I stayed outside to see what is happening with these people, and my friend said, "No, I am going in, you stay out." So I stayed outside and I heard —I didn't hear much but I heard Mr. Marshall tell his wife—tell the cops, "If you take my wife, I am going too," that's all I heard. And the girl, the young girl, she was a long way. She was on the other side of the car. She was—they are fixing a house there, she was close to the wall. She was close to that, far away from the police officer. I thought the argument was with the two of them. I didn't know she was included.

Q. How far were you standing from the police car at the time?

A. The police car was across the street from 235 and I was in 229, it's three houses from my house.

Q. At the time you saw these three defendants in the street by the police officer, did you see any other persons in the street near them?

A. No.

MR. CHEVIGNY. That's all.

At the end of all the testimony, the judge found all three defendants guilty of disorderly conduct.

There was consternation after the verdict, and the *New York Post* quoted me as saying, "I never had such a strong defense." I probably had said it. The prosecutor told me he would not demand that the defendants be fingerprinted if I would withdraw the complaint against the police officers. I refused, and the defendants were led off to be printed.

The immediate aftermath of the disorderly conduct conviction was even more astonishing. The three defendants were tried some time later upon the jaywalking charge, and were acquitted. The complaint against the officers was found substantiated by the Review Board, and charges were preferred against the men by the Commissioner. The Review Board, at the first level, had sent the matter to the Commissioner without a hearing and recommended that charges be preferred, an indication that they thought the case against the men extremely strong. In my experience it was unprecedented for a case to be sent for a departmental trial when the complainants had been convicted of an offense which would have explained the charge. To be sure, the charges against the officers were very artfully drawn, so as to leave any direct criticism of the disorderly conduct conviction out of the case. They were charged only with having the sticker on the back of the police car and with refusing to remove it when the Kaplans asked them to. On the other hand, it was unlikely that the Department would have bothered with such a minor charge if there had been no arrest.

The case was heard before Aloysius Melia, the Deputy

Commissioner who handled substantially all the departmental trials. The departmental investigators, through a feat of record retrieval I would previously have thought impossible, had located the police sergeant who was passing in a truck at the time of the incident. He testified that he had seen the sticker and that Marshall Kaplan had asked him whether it was right to have it on the back of a police car. He had said no. The two arresting officers claimed, in their own defense, that they did not know about the sticker on the back, but in the light of the sergeant's testimony, that was hard to believe. The Commissioner found the charges substantiated, and the officers were subsequently fined five days' pay.

In January 1967, some fourteen months after the arrest, with the acquiescence of the office of the District Attorney, the disorderly conduct convictions were reversed on appeal by an opinion in the strongest language. The appellate judges said, "The substance and quality of the evidence presented at the trial fairly compels the conclusion that the appellants' convictions were unmerited." It is because of this reversal that the story of the case has been told here; in general, cases from the project which were lost, in the sense that a conviction which will explain the policeman's actions is on the record, are not included in this study, no matter how much I might disagree with the verdict. With its aftermath, which showed that hardly anyone else in the city agreed with the verdict, this case must stand for the myriad others in which I believe the courts made one egregious error and covered up another. In most of them it was not as obvious to others as I felt it to be that a mistake had been made. With all due respect to the Kaplans, they were eminently respectable, and it was easy for the authorities to believe they were innocent. In other cases, I often thought the defendants much more violently abused, but if they came from the ghetto or had criminal records, it was harder for the Police Department and the Criminal Court judges to think they were in the right. In one case in the Bronx, for example, witnesses told me that a Negro had been beaten unmercifully when he refused to get out of a car after the driver was charged with a traffic violation on Fourth of July weekend. The passenger was charged with the usual trio—disorderly conduct, resisting arrest, and assault. I went to the houses of the witnesses repeatedly, and literally got them out of bed in the morning to testify at the trial. The defendant had a discouraging criminal record, and he was convicted by three judges on all counts. The conviction was affirmed on appeal.

After the Kaplan case was all over, the charming Harriet, no longer quite as ebullient, had some telling things to say on the subject. "When they arrested me and took me in the police car, I was thinking, 'It's true, they really can just pick you up for nothing!' Now I see that the whole business is irrational. Anything can happen; you think life is rational, you know, but it's crazy."

Irrational? Yes, but not surprising. These three came up and told the police they were doing something wrong, and that was a direct challenge to authority. In a sense, this is a case which could only have happened to middle-class people. It would never occur to a ghetto Negro or a Puerto Rican that he could with impunity go up to a policeman and tell him how to run his business, even if the policeman *was* in the wrong. To do that, one really must have lived all one's life in a "rational" world.

From this point of view, the most impressive character in the case was the barmaid. She risked what she must have felt to be at least a slight chance of retaliation, to help people from a completely different world, richer but more naive. She had worked until 4 A.M. on the morning she came to court. On the job, she had spilled some scalding water on her leg, and she took the witness stand with her calf bandaged. As she limped out of the court after the trial, I wondered how many girls would have bothered to do for others less fortunate than they what she had done for three who were more fortunate, if less experienced.

It is surely the job of the courts to try to make the world a little more rational rather than less so, yet often they only exacerbate injustices and misfortunes. Sometimes the courts act deliberately to protect the police, sometimes they are reluctant to blame an injustice on the authorities, and sometimes they simply make mistakes. All in all, the likelihood of conviction in Criminal Court is great enough, and in any case unpredictable enough, to make the criminal trial for the cover arrest alone the principal stumbling block in the way of redress for police abuses. The Kaplan case itself became part of an inadvertent experiment in how erratic the system of criminal justice can be. As it happened, the case was tried on the same charge, in the same room, with the same Assistant District Attorney, as the George Howard case, though with a different judge. I think that a neutral observer, comparing the facts before trial, would have concluded that the Kaplans were more likely to be acquitted. They commanded more sympathy. Howard had made quite an offensive remark, and the Kaplans, after all, were only trying to get the police to comply with the law. Nevertheless, the Kaplans were convicted and Howard was acquitted.

The Kaplan case was not the only clash which occurred between citizens and police during the Review Board controversy. The police felt that the entire campaign for the Board showed disrespect and challenged the police authority. Outsiders were telling the police how to conduct their business, as George Howard did when he told the mounted policeman to get his fat ass off his horse, and in the same way it was an insult that seemed to demand an arrest.

Two days after the Kaplans were arrested, a young man was handing out leaflets for civilian review at a main intersection on Broadway across the street from another group opposing civilian review. A police lieutenant came up with some patrolmen and told the young man to keep his voice down and move along. When he repeatedly refused, he was arrested and charged with disorderly conduct and resisting arrest. This action so obviously discriminated in favor of the group that was opposing civilian review that it provoked the sort of chain reaction from bystanders with which we have become familiar. A young woman stepped up to the lieutenant and said angrily, "You have no right to arrest him." She was arrested, along with her escort, who objected to *her* arrest. Both of them were charged with interfering with an arrest.[4] The charges against all three were eventually dismissed with the consent of the District Attorney, in return for a waiver of claims against the city.

In each of the cases in this chapter, there was a hero behind the scene who has not had the credit he deserves: the Manhattan District Attorney. Three of the cases were dismissed before trial, and one was reversed on appeal with the consent of that office. The District Attorney has enormous power to correct police abuses—more power, perhaps, than the courts themselves—by refusing to prosecute when police testimony is doubtful or when the defendant's case is overwhelmingly strong. Nothing can put a stop to abuse more quickly than a refusal to prosecute. However, most district attorneys are concerned only with convictions, and they exercise their discretion to control the police even less often than the courts do. The Manhattan office has been the exception; from a position of cynicism about police abuses in 1965, some assistants moved to a position of concern about the problem during the period of this study and began to exercise their discretion creatively. Even though some of the assistants still extracted waivers of claims, the change in attitude has been one of the most hopeful developments on the horizon. Unfortunately, other offices in New York City (there are four) have so far failed to follow the lead of Manhattan, but I hope that its work is at least a straw in the wind for New York City as well as for the rest of the country.

7

OUTCASTS

THOSE NEW YORKERS who were arrested during their campaign for civilian review of complaints against the police in the summer of 1966 did not realize that they were recapitulating the history of a dozen other groups. They were merely the latest in a long series of minorities which, though they do not all constitute as direct a challenge and criticism as the campaigners did, nevertheless tend to provoke a legal sanction from the police. Bohemians, homosexuals, political activists (particularly of the left), derelicts, prostitutes, and narcotics users all evoke police action. A member of one of these outcast groups will not be harmed if he obeys the orders of the police, unless there is a drive on to round up homosexuals, derelicts, or prostitutes (see Chapter 12). On the other hand, the police do tend to take some action, short of arrest, against a member of such pariah group, even without any verbal challenge or other threat. His mere presence seems to be enough challenge to make the police tell him to move on. Any sort of defiance of the police action in such cases is likely to be answered with violence.

The reasons are many. The police, in common with most other conventional citizens, feel an uncomprehending fear of the deviant, and find it difficult to think of him as an individual. They call deviants "germs," as a policeman was once heard to say of the drifters in Times Square,[1] or "bedbugs" who "should be exterminated," as an officer said of the hippies in one of our cases.

It is significant that as soon as any group ceases to be outcast and is accepted, most police harassment ceases. Sixty-five years ago, Jews on the Lower East Side complained of police discrimination and brutality in a disturbance at the funeral of Rabbi Jacob Joseph, but that incident is now almost forgotten. Thirty years ago and more, unions complained of police brutality during labor disputes. Nowadays, the union simply calls the precinct and warns the desk officer before the pickets go out. Usually a few policemen are present, just to make sure there are no fights. The next group of outcasts to be drawn into the mainstream was the civil rights demonstrators. Up until five or six years ago, there were frequent charges of police brutality at civil rights demonstrations, but they have almost ceased. During the work on our project in 1966 and 1967, peace demonstrators and hippies seemed to be the chief targets of police harassment. Supporters of civilian review probably suffered less serious harassment than other "outcast" groups. Though most people disagreed with them, they were not real pariahs, and the police knew that any abuse was likely to become a political issue.

Relatively few complaints came to us involving deviants or social outcasts, or people whom the police mistook for outcasts. Although it is widely believed that most police abuses are directed against such pariahs, police complaints tend to be made by people who have never had any conflict with the law and have no reason to fear the police. Many deviants are too afraid or too cynical about the problem to complain. Others live a rough life anyhow, and they accept police roughness as part of the game. In a case involving a charge of possessing narcotics, one of the two men accused had a long criminal record. He said that the police searched him, found a "bag" on him, and then "did the Thing on me." He just looked bashful when I asked him what "the Thing" was. The other defendant, who had had no previous contact with the law, angrily said that the police had kicked him in the groin. That was the

Thing. The experienced defendant looked worried. "Don't tell the judge about that, man. He doesn't want to hear about that. We got to get acquitted, that's all."

With a few exceptions, then, complaints about police abuses against deviants come from middle-class people who accidentally witness such abuses, or who themselves become part-time outcasts by demonstrating against the war in Vietnam, for example, or joining the hippie culture. A few come from people who are simply mistaken for outcasts.

In this chapter we shall have occasion to examine police behavior only toward true outcast groups: derelicts, homosexuals, and political dissenters. Police treatment of the hippies we shall consider in later chapters dealing with searches and mass police action (riot), two sanctions which are especially reserved for outcasts.

DERELICTS AND DRIFTERS

The most successful of our cases involving the harassment of drifters and derelicts came from Greenwich Village. Of late years, as more and more tourists have poured into the Village, more police have been assigned to the area. They are working in a fishbowl, because all the local people watch them warily.

In the heart of the Village there is such a mixture of races, classes, and habits, particularly on a summer evening, that any violence directed against a pariah must sometimes spill over onto the middle-class bystander, who frequently has never before seen or imagined misconduct by the police. Such a case occurred on August 16, 1967, in a little playground along Sixth Avenue, only a block from Washington Square. Here small boys play basketball, while parents and idlers sit on the benches beside alcoholic drifters, some of them Negroes. A number of sketchers, also mostly black, sit along the sidewalk trying to make a dollar or two by drawing quick portraits of the tourists. That evening a group of tactical patrol officers came into the park and began to arrest some of the Negro men for drinking in the park. One of them refused to go, denying the charge of drinking. An officer grabbed him and threw him to the ground, while a second handcuffed him. An-

other of the drifters got up and tried to leave the park, when a
third officer, who happened to be cruising along the avenue,
jumped out of his patrol car and, without any inquiry or
comment, clubbed him to his knees. He remained there, bleeding and complaining.

A witness later testified that a large crowd had gathered to
watch this and one of them yelled, "Let's jump the cops and
kick their asses." One of the policemen drew his revolver and
said, "Get back, you motherfuckers." [2] A woman lawyer with
offices in the Village had gone to the park that evening with
her nine-year-old nephew. The boy had chased his basketball
to within a few feet of the police when the incident started,
and he stood there as the gun was drawn. His aunt rushed up,
caught the boy, and left the park as quickly as she could.

I had heard complaints like this from ghetto neighborhoods,
but I had never before heard one from a neighborhood like
the Village. The police apparently thought that the crowd was
menacing them, and they gave them a little taste of what it
was like to be really abused by the police. This was a ghetto
case, transported by the panic of the officers to a place where
the rest of the city could get a look at it.

Because they could not make bail, the derelicts arrested that
night stayed in jail for two weeks awaiting trial on charges
of drinking in the park, resisting arrest, and assault. The woman
lawyer and two other witnesses, still as angry and determined
as ever, went down to Criminal Court and testified in their behalf. Ably defended by a Legal Aid lawyer, the three drifters
were at last acquitted. The one who had been clubbed in the
street left court with a fresh three-inch scar across his forehead.

Similar cases came from Washington Square itself. The fountain in the center of the square draws knots of folk singers, and
a floating population of drifters lounges on the lip of the
stone circle that surrounds the fountain. During the summer,
many of these drifters virtually live in the park, and the police
sometimes try to get rid of them. In June 1966 the police arrested a young Negro for drinking in the park, and when his
friend attempted to intercede, he was also arrested. When he
denied that he had been drinking in the park and refused to

submit, witnesses said that the officer broke a wine bottle over his head and took him away bleeding. These two men, like those arrested at the playground, could not make any bail, and they remained in jail for a week on charges of drinking in the park and resisting arrest. The District Attorney finally agreed to drop the charges against the first man, but the police claimed that the other had "given them trouble." It was apparent that they were determined to punish him for his defiance, and to get some sort of conviction on the record in case a complaint was made. Unfortunately, he had such a long criminal record that he was afraid to go to trial. In the prisoners' area at the side of the courtroom, he whispered to me, "I can't go to trial, man. All the judge has to do is find me guilty of drinking, and then he'll convict me of resisting, too. With my yellow sheet [record] I'll get a year. I *have* to cop out." He ended by pleading guilty to disorderly conduct, and he did thirty days in jail as recompense for having a bottle broken over his head.

From time to time during that summer, I stopped in Washington Square to look for the principals and witnesses in the case. I never saw the injured man again, but I did see the first several times, and I asked him to get in touch with me if he wanted to make a complaint. He had lost my card, so I gave him another, but he never called.

It is interesting to speculate why these cases, and others like them, came from Greenwich Village rather than any other part of the city. Similar abuses have probably occurred in other parts of town, when there were not enough people, or enough concerned people, to bring the abuse out into the open. Yet all the liberal outrage in Greenwich Village was not enough to make complaints in these cases successful. The drifters drifted on, and the complaints were forgotten.

The police sometimes make mistakes and treat as "bums" people who are ordinary citizens. The results are suggested in a surprising case from Harlem. One evening in January 1967, a group of young Puerto Ricans was standing outside a housing project on the west side of Harlem, singing together and talking. Most of them were under age, but one of them, whom we shall call (fictitiously) William DeCristo, was over eighteen, and he had a bottle of wine in a paper bag.

A patrolman came along and, in a style familiar to us, told them to move along because they were making noise. He spotted the bag in DeCristo's hand, and assuming that the older boy was giving wine to the younger ones, he drew his pistol, as all the boys later testified, and took the bottle from DeCristo at gunpoint. He took the cap off, poured most of the contents over DeCristo, and then left, after an avuncular lecture to the younger boys. No one was arrested.

A short time later, all the boys appeared at the precinct to complain, and within an hour and a half after the episode a police lieutenant from the Review Board came up to investigate.

The Review Board sent this case to the Commissioner without a hearing, recommending that charges be preferred. The patrolman was charged with pointing his gun at DeCristo and pouring the wine over him. At the departmental trial in July, the police investigator testified that DeCristo's shirt had been damp when he felt it in the police station, and six witnesses, including DeCristo, recounted the story of the patrolman's actions. Rather absurdly, he was acquitted of the charge of pointing the gun, though he was found guilty of pouring the wine, and he was reprimanded by the Commissioner.

The policeman's contempt for DeCristo was apparent from his actions alone, but the testimony at the trial made it unmistakable. One of the boys testified that after he had poured out the wine, the officer came up to him and said, "Stay away from this bum." The patrolman's defense attorney asked the witness whether he did not think that the policeman was just trying to be friendly. The boy replied, "Probably he was, but I resented it very much."

There are a number of lessons to be learned from this case. One is, simply, the extraordinary vagaries and mischances of proof in police cases. DeCristo's case went all the way up to a successful departmental trial, while nothing was done in the other two cases, which involved more serious abuses. Part of the reason is that the policeman made a mistake about De-

Cristo; he thought him a bum, but he wasn't. DeCristo stayed with the case, and so did his friends. From the policeman's point of view, I am afraid the moral of the story is that he should have made an arrest; this is one of the very rare cases where there was a police abuse, heavily authenticated, without one. If there had been an arrest, the boys might have been unwilling to complain, and if they had, the arrest might have helped to explain their complaint so that departmental charges would not have been preferred. It is for this reason that I think the simple reprimand given by the Commissioner was sufficient punishment. The case could have been a lot more serious, and it would have been a mistake to give the appearance of penalizing an officer because he did not make it so. One of the reasons that there was no arrest, perhaps, is that DeCristo did not make a protest, or refuse to move along at the time he was mistreated. There was little or no defiance of the officer; if there had been, the situation might have been different. DeCristo saved his protests for the Review Board, which is always a wise course of action.

The police feel a kind of disdain for drifters and derelicts that is summed up in breaking a bottle over a man's head or pouring liquor on him. There is a sense here that the pariah is not entitled to the same rights as others because he is so strange as to be hardly human; it is a feeling that the police share with most other citizens. The treatment of derelicts is a perfect example of the way the police reflect the prejudices of the rest of society. One day, for example, we had a complaint from a girl who had been brought up in suburban New Jersey, but was then living on the Lower East Side. She claimed that the police had been surly to her. It seemed hardly worth complaining about, but I began to write down what she said. There had been a man passed out in the entranceway of her house, and fearing that he might be dead, she had called the police. When they finally arrived, she said they called her "girlie" and grumbled over her fears for the man in the hall. I then asked her the next logical question: Did they do anything about the drunk? Well, later he was gone, anyway. Did she see them do anything? Yes, they kicked him.

I sat up. Did they kick him hard? Oh, no. How many times? Oh, about five. Now, did they really kick him, or just stir him with the toes of their shoes? They kicked him, all right, but not very hard.

HOMOSEXUALS

The harassment of homosexuals decreased during the period in which this study was conducted. At the beginning of 1966, there was a drive on to "clean up" homosexual hangouts, including certain bars and Turkish baths. We received a number of complaints that homosexuals had been entrapped into making passes at plainclothes officers who behaved like homosexuals, or that the officers themselves made the proposition, and we campaigned vigorously with the Police Department to put a stop to the practice. The Department denied that entrapments occurred, but on May 11, 1966, the Commissioner did issue an order forbidding the entrapment of homosexuals. The complaints stopped, even though the police continued to patrol some areas of suspected homosexual activity, such as subway washrooms.

This is a good example of the way a firm administrative line can cure certain types of abuses. There are two reasons, perhaps, why it was relatively easy for the Department to stop the complaints of the practice. In the first place, the campaign for arresting homosexuals for solicitation had been assigned chiefly to a small group of officers working directly out of the Commissioner's office. Any orders to them about their conduct were supremely easy to supervise. In the second place, entrapment of homosexuals is a rather artificial practice. It is a classic case of the application of the police doctrine that a defendant should be arrested if he is "guilty at heart"; the wretch who is entrapped is *ipso facto* guilty at heart. Nevertheless, such an entrapment would oblige an officer to behave like a homosexual, and, as compared with collaring someone who talks back, it is probably distasteful work. As the pressure to make arrests as part of the cleanup campaign died down, the practice passed away almost automatically.

None of this implies that the police felt less animus toward

homosexuals after May 11, 1966, then they had felt before. The
cleanup campaign was over, and homosexuals simply assumed
their customary pariah status. There were still police abuses
against some of them, but the problem is that most homosexuals are so afraid of exposure that they will not complain.
Many who did call us refused to give their names, and for the
few cases in which we had an identifiable complainant, we
had trouble getting witnesses. One extraordinary case was
brought to us by a college teacher, who was so exercised by
his arrest that he consented to let us use his name. Nevertheless, his attorney and I agreed that it was the better part of
discretion to change his name here, together with the names
of the witnesses.

The teacher, whom we shall call Gustave Hartman, attended
a party in the East Village (part of the old Lower East Side)
late on a Saturday evening in November 1966. The host later
estimated that there were fifty people in his apartment, and
judging by the camp behavior of the guests we later tried to
interview, it must have been a gathering entirely of inverts.

About 3:00 A.M., when someone opened the door to leave,
the police pushed their way past him into the apartment. The
host was not sure how many officers there were, but he was
sure that at least one had a drawn revolver. Gustave Hartman was near the door, and he stood in the way of one of the
policemen, asking the classic question, "What is the meaning
of this intrusion?" The host remembered that the policemen
seemed to become angry, and when Mr. Hartman continued to
stand in his way, demanding his shield number, the policeman
hit him in the face with a flashlight. The police asked the host
if they could search the place. Under the circumstances, he
was hardly likely to refuse, and the police went through the
apartment. They made seven arrests for loitering and possession
of narcotics, and Hartman was charged with assaulting an
officer.

Mr. Hartman gave us the names and and addresses of several of the guests, and Eve Cary from my office tried systematically to interview them. One was a transvestite affecting
a typically androgynous nickname ("Toni"), who lived with

another of the guests. He categorically refused to talk to us, and all the others said that they had not seen the police when they came in. Apart from Hartman himself, then, the host was the only eyewitness, although a doctor's report made two days after the assault established that there had been a blow to Hartman's left temple.

Mr. Hartman and the others spent the night in jail, and at the arraignment Sunday morning, the judge, the District Attorney, and the Legal Aid lawyer asked the arresting officers the same question that I was to ask Hartman when he later came to see me: Why had the police broken in? The answer was probably not far to seek. Fifty inverts, some dressed as women, could hardly attend a party without attracting notice. The police claimed, rather weakly, that they had come into the house because they heard a shot from the roof, but that (assuming it to be true) would not have justified their breaking into the party. The District Attorney could not see any way around this problem, and the charges against all the defendants were eventually dismissed. Hartman had been charged with pushing a policeman, but since the pushing, if it occurred at all, was in opposition to an unlawful intrusion, it could not be a crime. Hartman sued the city for damages due to the assault and for false arrest; as far as I have been able to tell, the case is still pending.

It is apparent that the explanation for this case was that the police felt less compunction about breaking into a party of obvious homosexuals than they would have felt about intruding upon another party. When outcasts are involved, the restraints on police action begin to weaken, not only those against assault, but those against unlawful entry and search as well. Hartman was assaulted because he belonged to a group from whom the police find it impossible to brook insubordination.

One of the strangest cases I ever encountered concerned an apparent mistake by a policeman in identifying a young man as a "degenerate," to use the policeman's word. I say "apparent" because it was difficult to determine just what the prejudices and motives of the policeman were. I would not have believed the complainant's story (and in fact, I was for

a long time doubtful about it) were it not for the very convincing way it came to me.

I had come to know most of the members of the Du Bois
Club in New York through my investigation of a riot in Brooklyn in March of 1966. One of the members I knew particularly
well, whom we shall call Steven Sellers (a fictitious name),
walked into my office on June 24, 1966, with a long red bruise
down the side of his jaw. He said that a policeman had thrown
a nightstick at him. I took Sellers out to have his photograph
taken while I recorded his story.

Early that morning he had been to Nathan's, a famous sea-
food and hot-dog stand at Coney Island, with three other men
and a girl. They had come in a jeep, and at about 1:30 A.M.,
all five had got back into it with Sellers in the front seat on
the passenger's side. They were waiting for the light to change
when one of the two policemen on the corner said, "Do you
blow?"

At this point in the story I turned incredulously to the witness, one of the other men in the jeep, who had accompanied
Sellers to my office. He had not heard the policeman's words,
but only Sellers' reply, a sarcastic phrase about "New York's
finest, the men in blue." The driver, whom we later interviewed, had also heard only the reply; he must have thought
it audible in the street, because he told Sellers not to make any
trouble.

The light changed and they had turned the corner, when
suddenly they all heard a terrific banging on the frame of the
jeep. They looked around to see one of the policemen running
along and drumming with his nightstick on the jeep. The
driver stepped on the gas in panic, while Sellers continued to
look out of the side. Another policeman, further up the block,
seeing the first one chasing the jeep, ran out into the roadway
and flung his stick, hitting Sellers in the face. The driver
speeded up and ran past a red light. The police caught up with
them in a commandeered car and got them all out of the jeep
at gunpoint to issue a summons for running the light. One of
the officers said that he would have fired his pistol instead of
throwing the stick if there had not been a girl in the car. The

policeman who had been standing at the corner called Sellers a "degenerate."

This fantastic story at first seemed barely plausible. Sellers did have a full-fleshed face and rather long hair; a very conservative observer could have made a mistake about his sexual status. No doubt the whole crowd of them, packed into the jeep, must have looked odd in Coney Island. Still, I could not help but doubt the story, especially since my two other witnesses had not heard the policeman's remark to Sellers. The fourth man and the girl, who were from out of town, had already left New York.

The same day that they came to see me, I sent the men to the Review Board to make a complaint. This complaint was initially investigated under an old system because it was filed in June 1966, just a few weeks before Commissioner Leary appointed a majority of civilians to sit on the Board. The Commissioner had made a rule that complaints filed with the old board had to remain under its jurisdiction, and so the situation stood until some four months later, when the Civilian Review Board was abolished by the voters. The case was finally heard and decided by the Police Review Board established by the Commissioner after the election; all in all, the vicissitudes of this complaint told the history of the Review Board in microcosm.

Under the system of investigation which prevailed before civilians were added to the Review Board, complaints were assigned to the commander of the local police district where the incident occurred. If the local commander was a tough man, the complaint might be thoroughly investigated, but if he chose to protect his men, that was the end of the matter. In short, prior to its reorganization, when the civilian members were appointed, the Board was at the mercy of the divisional commanders because it did not have its own investigative staff. Since the local commanders also presided at the hearings, the cases were almost completely in their hands. The most lasting reform left from the short-lived Civilian Review Board, as it turned out, was the appointment of a group of senior officers, working under a civilian director and beholden to no one, to investigate for the Board alone. When the civilians were struck from the Board by the vote in the referendum, the reforms in the investigative structure remained. Those reforms were desirable from the point of view of objectivity and consistency in handling complaints, yet at the same time they were completely inadequate to the magnitude of the problem. The Sellers complaint was an object lesson.

Under the old system, the first thing that happened to the complaint was that it disappeared. A month after it was filed, a lieutenant from Brooklyn called to ask if I had the names, addresses, and statements of witnesses. I sent him copies of everything I had, and the rest was silence. Months after the complaint had been filed, when the civilian Board had been defeated, I began to hound the new Board to do something about the complaint. Nearly six months after the incident, another man, this time from the Board, asked me again for the names and addresses of the witnesses. I told him about the lieutenant in Brooklyn, inquiring whether he had any record of the investigation. He sighed and said that it was easier to start over. I gave him the information, and a short time later the Board scheduled a hearing.

It was to present a number of problems. One thing I did not doubt was that a nightstick had struck Sellers. All three of my witnesses agreed upon it and the photograph confirmed it. On the other hand, the driver had received an apparently valid traffic summons. The policemen would unquestionably claim that they had attempted to stop the car for the traffic violation. The first officer could claim that he had run after the jeep when it went through the light, and the second officer, down the block, need say only that he threw the stick to help in an emergency when there was no time for questions. Just as he had said to the witnesses, he could claim that he had thrown the stick in lieu of firing his gun. Since I had no way of corroborating Sellers' account of what the policeman standing on the corner had said to him before the light changed, I had no way of convincing the Board that he had stopped the jeep for anything other than a traffic violation.

At the hearing, the officers went even further and denied

that any of them had thrown a stick at the car. This was to be expected, since it was very doubtful that throwing a stick was a legitimate means of stopping a car for a traffic offense. Even without the provocative remarks from the officer, it was bad police work from any point of view.

Sellers and his two witnesses naturally agreed in their testimony at the hearing that the stick had been thrown, but only Sellers could testify to the verbal exchange with the officer at the traffic light. The fourth man and the girl were still nowhere to be found.

Two weeks later I called the office of the Du Bois Club, searching for a bit of evidence in a completely different case, and an unfamiliar voice answered. When I asked who it was, the man identified himself as the missing fourth man in the car. He had just come in from Chicago, he said. I promptly asked him whether he remembered the incident in the jeep. He not only remembered, but volunteered the words of the verbal exchange between Sellers and the policeman:

One cop said, "Hey, kid, do you blow?"
Steve said, "Drop dead. Go to hell."

I hung up and called the Review Board to ask if they would be interested in reopening the hearing for another witness. No luck. We had already had our hearing. The complaint was found unsubstantiated.

This result exemplifies the nearly insuperable problems of a case-by-case approach to police abuses. Here was a case which seemed hopeful from the complainant's point of view. There were witnesses to the abuse, but the most important of the witnesses simply could not be found until after he was needed. Variations of the "disappearing witness" problem appeared in dozens of my cases: witnesses who moved and left no forwarding address, or who simply failed repeatedly to appear in response to a subpoena. In one case, a doctor who examined our client for injuries was committed to a mental institution between the time of the incident and the time of trial.

Serious as this problem is, it arises only in cases that are initially hopeful. In the great majority of cases, there are no known witnesses at all. The problem of witnesses disappearing, or never appearing in the first place, is so endemic that it is not to be expected that more than a fraction of all complaints can be authenticated. The few that can be substantiated are fortunately enough like one another, and enough like the complaints which cannot be substantiated, that they suggest a pattern. But the investigation of the cases one by one can hardly be a very effective deterrent for other abuses.

The Sellers case appears to be one of a mistake by a policeman. The officer in this case mistook Sellers for a "degenerate," as another policeman mistook William DeCristo for a "bum." The policeman who threw the stick apparently acted without knowing anything except that he was trying, however foolishly, to assist another officer. There was an act of violence in response to an act of defiance provoked by the policeman's insult. A stupid abuse by one officer thus often draws in others to assist in re-establishing order. Here again, as with DeCristo the complaint of an ordinary citizen mistaken for a deviant must stand in place of all the deviants who were afraid to complain.

POLITICAL DISSENTERS

Volumes have been written, and another could certainly be added, about discrimination against political dissenters. Here we shall limit ourselves to those forms of harassment used by the police when they encounter peaceful political dissent in the streets. Problems peculiar to riots and demonstrations are saved for a later chapter.

The treatment of political outcasts fits the classic pattern. The policeman often tries to get such pariahs to stop their activities and move along, and he often issues a summons. If the summons does not halt the activity, he makes an arrest. In one case, two young men distributing leaflets for Students for a Democratic Society outside a college in upper Manhattan were simply taken to a police station and questioned for forty-five minutes, but the officers involved in that case were reprimanded, and police methods are usually a little more sophisticated.

The legal support for such police harassment is customarily derived from the Administrative Code of the City of New York, which contains ordinances against peddling and soliciting money, obstructing the sidewalks, and most especially, littering. For many years, the police issued summonses to people handing out political leaflets, even though the city ordinance penalizing littering specifically exempted political handbills [3] (an exemption which was required by the constitutional protection of free speech). In 1967 Alan Levine of the NYCLU finally brought a federal injunctive suit against the practice, based on seventeen incidents during the preceding two years. [4] As this is written, the pressure of that litigation seems to have put a stop to the abuse.

The most interesting of all our multitude of leafleting cases occurred on May 6, 1966. That afternoon there was a demonstration of high school students in front of City Hall to protest a cut in the budget for the City University. Two high school teachers arrived late in the day and began to hand out leaflets opposing the war in Vietnam, with the message that the money that ought to have gone for education was in fact going into the war effort.

As it happened, one of the students demonstrating was the daughter of a police sergeant, and her father and mother were there (her father was off duty) to make sure that there was no trouble. The sergeant and his daughter both felt that they did not want the issue of the war introduced into the demonstration, and the girl asked her father if there were anything he could do to stop it. He asked the schoolteachers to move (they said he ordered them to move), and they refused. He then asked the sergeant on duty at the scene to have a summons issued for littering, and a patrolman proceeded to issue it. When the teachers, incensed, refused to give any identification, they were taken to the police station.*

They were ultimately acquitted of the littering charge, as in fact they had to be as a matter of law. The city ordinance

* The New York City Police Department Rules and Procedures, Ch. 14, §10.00, require that a person be taken to the police station for identification if he refuses to identify himself for purposes of a summons.

against littering states: "This section is not intended to prevent the lawful distribution of any matter other than commercial and business advertising matter." Simply to show that the teachers were distributing something "other than commercial and business advertising matter" was enough to put an end to the prosecution.

The teachers made a complaint of abuse of power to the Review Board. At the time the hearing was held on the complaint, neither the schoolteachers nor I had any knowledge of the personal motives of the sergeant in being present at the scene and ordering them to move on. All we knew was that the complainants had received a patently illegal summons. An extraordinary aspect of the proceedings was that the sergeant not only made no attempt to conceal his motives, but on the contrary brought his wife and daughter to testify that they had all been there and that the daughter had asked her father to do something about the leaflets. He himself said it was partly for political reasons that he had asked the two men to move. He seemed to think that all this evidence strengthened his case, instead of proving his deliberately discriminatory purpose, and I decided that I had to try to find out the reason. I asked him if he had studied the constitutional law and the city ordinances concerning the distribution of handbills, and it turned out that he had graduated from law school and was a member of the New York Bar! I asked him by what law he thought a political handbill could be penalized as litter. He replied that the ordinance made an exception only for political handbills distributed in a "lawful" manner, and these were not being lawfully distributed. Confronted with this tautology, I gave up that line of questioning.

This complaint was found substantiated; it could hardly have been otherwise, because the officer virtually admitted the abuse, though he seemed never to understand that he had done so. The Department decided that the best solution to the problem was a new instruction to the sergeants about the constitutional right to distribute handbills. After NYCLU's federal action to stop the harassment of leafleters was started in June 1967, similar instructions were given to the entire force.

This case was an objective demonstration that education is no panacea for police abuses. Here was a man who was much better trained than anyone could have expected a police sergeant to be, and yet he took the most authoritarian attitude toward the rights of the teachers. Police attitudes are deeply rooted in the requirements of the job and of society. Education alone cannot change them.

The overwhelming urban problem of our time, of course, has nothing to do with derelicts, homosexuals, dissenters, or any other group of outcasts but rather with racial and class discrimination. Aren't Negroes and Puerto Ricans the true outcasts of our cities, and shouldn't a chapter about police treatment of pariahs really be about police treatment of Negroes and Puerto Ricans?

The answer to that question is not simple. Obviously, such deviants as derelicts and homosexuals are outcasts in a different sense and to a different extent than Negroes and Puerto Ricans. Deviants are viewed by the police as essentially or potentially criminal, and many of them do commit minor offenses, such as disorderly conduct, prostitution, and drug offenses, as an ordinary part of their way of life. Some policemen do believe Negroes to be dangerous in exactly the same way as deviants, and Skolnick has said, "the patrolman in Westville and probably in most communities has come to identify the black man with danger." [5] However, it is simply impossible for the policeman working in the ghetto to treat everyone on his beat as he would a deviant outcast. Part of the reason, ironically, is the severe segregation in New York. Wherever Negroes live, they are usually so much in the neighborhood majority that it is difficult to single out any one for harassment. A Negro in the ghetto is just not as visible as a hippie in the Village. Moreover, he is fortunately not quite as defenseless as the deviant. White middle-class people in our society feel more guilt about black people than they do about deviants, and the mistreatment of a Negro will produce much more of an outcry than the mistreatment of a derelict, not only from the black community but throughout the city.

In general, the characteristic of the outcast is that he provokes police action by his mere presence, whereas an ordinary citizen must take some action on his own, however accidental, to clash with the police. In a ghetto community, the simple presence of a Negro does not provoke police action. In most cases, he is an ordinary citizen. It is hardly necessary to add that a Negro outside the ghetto is much more likely to be treated as an outcast.

Accepting the rather obvious fact that the mere presence of a ghetto resident does not provoke the ghetto police to action, we may ask a slightly more subtle question: Does a given provocation to the police in the ghetto produce a more explosive reaction than the same provocation outside it? Everything I have ever observed about street abuses indicates that the answer to that question is yes. Let us be clear that this is not at all the same thing as saying that most police abuses are directed against Negroes or Puerto Ricans. Considering police complaints as a whole, our records show that the majority came from white people and from all sections of town, but most complaints of the use of force came from Negroes or Puerto Ricans (see Analytical Appendix, pages 285–87). Anyone who defies the police is likely to be arrested, but a Negro or a Puerto Rican is more likely to be clubbed in the process.

The chief area of conflict between Negro citizens and the police does not center around violent force, however, so much as around the attitudes and words of the police. It often seems that it is insults and racial slurs, rather than arrest, that make ghetto people most antagonistic to the police. The constant minor irritations make every arrest seem an act of discrimination, even when it is not. I received several complaints of police brutality which, upon investigation, turned out to be perfectly ordinary arrests, or else part of the reaction to truly violent resistance to arrest.

In one case, for example, the police chased two Negro teenagers charged with burglary down a street in the Bronx, firing their revolvers in the air to get them to stop. They finally caught one of the boys in a back yard, and the universal rumor had it that they beat him fearfully. The one eyewitness I could find, however, said that the police simply pushed the boy to the ground and put handcuffs on him. There is a reason why ghetto people see the actions of the police through a distorted lens. It is partly that, living in poverty, they see the police as the authority which oppresses them.[6] But perhaps more important, an arrest often seems to them the last straw in a history of contempt and harassment.

The tools of research available to me, principally investigation through eyewitnesses and court records, were poorly adapted to the problem of racial slurs by the police. Insults are not usually shouted so loudly that others can hear them, and for that reason they are by nature difficult to authenticate. We had a few allegations of the use of racial slurs, but in almost all cases they could not be proved. One such alleged slur, for example, resulted in a charge of disorderly conduct, and for that case we had a witness who disappeared before the trial. Such abuses can be effectively investigated only by neutral observers present at the scene with the permission of the police. This method, while not open to me, was used by the investigators of the President's Commission on Law Enforcement, and the Task Force on the Police did report the use of racial epithets in departments outside New York. A 1966 report on the police in the District of Columbia, still a Southern city in many ways, found that the use of racial insults was widespread.[7]

Unless a racial slur is intended as deliberate provocation, it is difficult to understand why a policeman would use it. In some cases it appears that the phrase is actually intended to provoke a fight, but apart from that restricted class of cases, allegations of the use of racial epithets have often been treated with polite incredulity by investigators from the Review Board. It is so patently dangerous for a policeman to call a black man a "nigger" that it is hard for an investigator to believe that it really happened; investigators, like lawyers, tend to doubt any charge that a man deliberately acted against his own interests. But the policeman's true interests, and his interests as he perceives them, are quite different things. The Department has issued an excellent pamphlet—called "Words Make a Difference"—to the members of the force, warning against stereotypes and racial slurs; but many policemen believe that a contemptuous word, like an angry tone or a threat of force, tends to command respect and compliance. It is part of the reaction described by a policeman to Westley: "I think most policemen try to treat people in a nice way, but usually you have to talk pretty rough. That's the only way to set a man down, to make him show a little respect." [8] A New York City policeman said something similar to one of four lawyers: "It's no use talking to these people nicely. You have to talk to them in the only language they understand." Finally, some policemen are simply so prejudiced that a racial slur is the first thing that comes to their lips in a time of stress. After being told that a Negro subway conductor was a witness against him, one transit patrolman blurted out to the civil rights lawyer Stephen Nagler, "Now that conductor, that's the guy I want to get. There was a platform full of niggers and he wouldn't help me." The use of contemptuous slurs is due partly to the policeman's failure to grasp the humanity of the people with whom he deals, and partly to his desire to assert his authority. He probably sees it as the least serious of all the weapons in his arsenal of authority, whereas in fact it is one of the most destructive.

A central theme of this chapter has been that the police reflect, with surprising sensitivity, the attitudes of the larger society. When that society is fearful and repressive, as it is, for example, toward derelicts, the police are also repressive; when society is ambivalent, as in its attitude toward Negroes, the behavior of the police reflects that feeling as well. In our pluralistic society, an enormous number of groups are tolerated, but if a man does not belong to one of those groups, or if he belongs to a group that is only peripherally tolerated, he is always in danger of attack. Part of the job of the police is to enforce the tolerance and intolerance of our society. Robert Paul Wolff has summarized the attitudes of the society at large, and by inference of the police, in words which might have served as the epigraph for this chapter: [9]

We can thus see the implicit rationale for what is otherwise a most peculiar characteristic of pluralistic democracy, namely the combination of tolerance for the most diverse social groups and extreme intolerance for the idiosyncratic individual. One might expect, for example, that a society which urges its citizens to "attend the church or synagogue of your choice" would be undismayed by an individual who chose to attend no religious services at all. Similarly, it would seem natural—at least on traditional principles of individual liberty—to extend to the bearded and be-sandled "beat" the same generous tolerance which Americans are accustomed to grant to the Amish, or orthodox Jews, or any other groups whose dress and manner deviate from the norm. Instead, we find a strange mixture of the greatest tolerance for what we might call established groups and an equally great intolerance for the deviant individual. The justification for this attitude, which would be straightforwardly contradictory on traditional liberal grounds, is the doctrine of pluralistic democracy. If it is good for each individual to conform to some social group and good as well that a diversity of social groups be welcomed in the community at large, then one can consistently urge group tolerance and individual intolerance.

8

FORCE, ARREST, AND COVER CHARGES

ARBITRARY ARREST AND SUMMARY PUNISHMENT have been recurring themes in past chapters, and we are ready now to draw up an Anatomy of Street-corner Abuses.

The one truly iron and inflexible rule we can adduce from the cases is that any person who defies the police risks the imposition of legal sanctions, commencing with a summons, on up to the use of firearms. The sanction that is imposed depends on at least three factors: the character of the officer, the place where the encounter occurs, and the character of the person with whom the encounter is had. The police may arrest *anyone* who challenges them (as they define the challenge), but they are more likely to further abuse anyone who is poor, or who belongs to an outcast group.

Members of outcast groups, by their mere presence, seem to offer an affront to order such that the police will themselves initiate action against them by ordering them to move along, breaking into a party, or some similar action. To the police, the ordinary citizen begins to assume the status of a pariah only when he actively defies the police, whereas a member of an outcast group need take no such action.

John McNamara, reviewing "critical incidents" involving police and citizens, in his work with New York City police recruits was "struck by the extent to which the handling of relatively minor incidents such as traffic violations or disorderly disputes between husbands and wives seemed to create a more serious situation than existed prior to the police attempt to control the situation." [1] In many of our cases, the police have gone further and caused a situation to degenerate into an argument when it was scarcely a dispute at all to begin with. McNamara attributes the phenomenon to mistaken assumptions on the part of the police about how they ought to behave toward the public. For example, he found that 39 to 40 percent of policemen agree with the proposition that "a patrolman can be pretty sure he will gain compliance from a person who appears to be somewhat frightened of the patrolman," as well as with the proposition that "when patrolmen indicate they will use the force necessary to gain compliance from a citizen, they are helped considerably if the citizen thinks they are getting angry." [2] These police opinions are so potentially dangerous, and in many cases so catastrophically applied, that it is not enough to think of them only as mistaken assumptions. The reason why policemen act so aggressively as to exacerbate street situations is, of course, that they seek to establish their authority by such transactions. The answers to McNamara's questions indicate that a large percentage of policemen will usually try to obtain compliance by an unconditional demand or the use of force. Many people wonder whether police work attracts young men who already have such attitudes, or whether the police role develops those attitudes in them. Most authorities who have studied the problem intensively seem to agree that the second alternative is the correct one. Police recruits are much like other young men of a similar background; it is police mores and the police role that make them adopt police attitudes.[3]

In the paradigmatic street encounter there are three steps:

1. Police perception of a challenge to authority. In the case of a member of an outcast group this step is eliminated, or at least minimized.

2. Police demand for submission. This is most commonly enshrined in the question, "So you're a wise guy, eh?" In my office we sat through many lengthy and excited complaints listening only for the words "wise guy," knowing well that an arrest would have occurred shortly after they were uttered.

3. Response to the demand. The citizen in effect either admits that he is a wise guy, or denies it by complying with the police demand, if it involves an action like moving along, or by apologizing to the policeman if no action is demanded.

People in minority and outcast groups, who are the most likely to be subjected to a police demand for submission, at the same time find it hardest to comply with it. The middle-class man thinks nothing of saying, "Sorry, officer," but to the oppressed and downtrodden those words are galling. It is especially hard for a Negro, for whom such an act seems just one more token of submission. The combination of being an outcast (step one) and refusing to comply in step three is explosive; thereby hangs the tale of many police brutality cases.

The police rationale for this three-step process is that people who present a challenge to them are troublemakers, as the police might put it, or symbolic assailants, as Skolnick calls them. They are, quite literally, potential offenders, and so to arrest one of them is at least the ethical (if not the legal) equivalent of arresting a criminal. The policeman will go on to say that he must maintain his authority against those who challenge it, in order to enforce the laws effectively. In short, his authority over others will be lost if he backs down with one person. It inevitably follows that his authority as a police-man is asserted in situations which are personal disputes, or at least have a personal dimension, like nearly all of the cases recounted in previous chapters. In some of those cases, the provocation comes principally from the citizen, and in others, principally from the police. The point is that they are street arguments, not so very different from those which arise every day between private citizens when one insults another or tries to get him to do something he does not want to do. Al-though it is true that policemen take umbrage very easily, and that they sometimes see a threat where there is none—as in the Bell and Johnson case—it is equally clear that in many instances recounted here—such as George Howard's insulting remark—some sort of retaliation was almost inevitable. The chief difference is that one of the parties is a policeman, and for him no dispute is purely personal. It is no accident that in old-fashioned journalistic parlance the officer was personified as "John Law" or the "long arm of the law." Policemen apparently do see themselves as personifying authority, and a challenge to one of them (or to all of them, as in the case of civilian review) is a challenge to the Law. Everybody knows that when you defy the Law, you go to jail.

The apparently irrational and sometimes provocative behavior of the police in street conflicts has often raised the question whether the police deliberately encourage violence or at least disorderly behavior from a troublemaker, in order to show that he really is an offender and to provide grounds for removing him from the street by arrest. This is one of the unresolved questions about police behavior, and one that is central to an understanding of police abuses. If the police react in a rough manner to provocation from citizens, if they in fact themselves behave in a rude and ham-handed fashion, that is one problem, but it is quite another if the police deliberately provoke to violence people they believe to be troublemakers. Westley, in his research on a Midwestern police department, felt that there was a tendency for the police to provoke anyone who was disrespectful until there was an assault, and then to retaliate with violence.[4] Werthman and Piliavin detected the same thing in their work on police treatment of juveniles,[5] and at least one writer in the professional journal *Police* has criticized the practice, while carefully labeling it "unusual." [6]

The issue is difficult to resolve with the research tools at our disposal in this book. Investigation of a case by interviews with witnesses, the method almost invariably used here, is a very blunt instrument for getting at anything as perishable as the words of a verbal interchange, to say nothing of its tone. Moreover, since we did not accept cases in which there actually had been an assault on an officer, we might possibly have missed cases of provocation. There is a suggestion of egging on a "troublemaker" in the Caulaincourt case, where the policeman repeatedly pushed the defendant. In a later chapter, concerned with the systematic harassment of Galahad and the hippies in his communal apartment, there is a well-authenticated case of provocation during one of the practically constant raids by the police in April and May of 1967. On that occasion a narcotics policeman dared one of the boys in the apartment to take a sock at him. The mind boggles at what might have happened if he had, but fortunately he simply responded, "No, man, that's not my life."

The consensus among the authorities who have studied the problem is that the police do sometimes try to provoke violence in order to make an arrest. It is logical to think that policemen will try such things on with outcasts, whom they fear and dislike and would prefer to see in jail. One young Negro in a ghetto neighborhood in Brooklyn, who had the reputation of being a "cop fighter," complained that the police would not let him alone. Whenever they saw him on the street they slowed down their cars and asked him if he wanted to fight. In New York City in 1967, however, I think that the challenge by a policeman to physical combat, or even to a public disturbance, is the exception. In my office we did not receive more than a handful of complaints of such deliberate provocation, and it cannot be a widespread problem if there are so few complaints. In most cases, even if a policeman wanted to use such crude tactics, they would not be necessary. The New York police are sophisticated enough in drawing charges and making them stick not to need an actual act of physical violence to arrest anyone. If they feel that a man is a troublemaker, they can, unfortunately, charge him with resisting arrest, without the necessity of risking injury to an officer.

The worst problem in street-corner incidents is not that of police quarreling with citizens. Most such quarrels, while never admirable, are at least understandable; they are much like quarrels between private citizens. The worst abuse is not even the police hitting people in such quarrels; pugnacious citizens hit others in private disputes every day. The root problem is the abuse of power, the fact that the police not only hit a man but arrest him. Once they have arrested him, of course, lying becomes an inevitable part of the procedure of making the quarrel look like a crime, and thus the lie is the chief abuse with which we must come to grips. If the police simply hit a man and let him go, there would be an abuse of the authority conferred by the uniform and the stick, but not the compound abuse of hitting a man and then dragging him to court on criminal charges, really a more serious injury than a blow. One's head heals up, after all, but a criminal record never goes away. There is no more embittering experience in the legal system than to be abused by the police and then to be tried and convicted on false evidence.

Police abuse and consequent conviction on false evidence are a combination which feeds the impulse to riot; once respect for the legal process is gone, grievances can be expressed only by force. Despite these obvious repercussions upon community relations, it is rarely that anyone is abused without being criminally charged, not only because of the rationale for such abuses ("he was guilty anyhow") but because the policeman is likely to get into trouble if he lets an abused person go free. There is nothing to cover a later accusation of abuse if an arrest has not been made.

There can be no doubt that police lying is the most pervasive of all abuses. In most of the cases reported in earlier chapters, there was a lie whenever there was a criminal trial. If the charge was disorderly conduct, officers lied to create a breach of the peace where none existed. If the charge was assault or obstructing an officer, they supplied blows by the defendant when none had been struck. In the police canon of ethics, the lie is justified in the same way as the arrest: as a vindication of police authority, by proving that defiance of the police is a crime in fact if not in law. A member of a pariah group, or anyone who defies the police, being guilty at heart and sometimes potentially guilty in fact, deserves to be punished out of hand. Besides, the police dislike such people so much that they consider them unworthy of the protection of the law. By lying, the police enforce these folkways of their own, while preserving the shell of due process of law.

Not surprisingly, police lying is a problem about which little reliable research has been done. William Westley, after breaking ground upon the police use of violence in his first article, went on to open the problem of lying in "Secrecy and the Police." [7] He found that 11 out of 15 men said they would not report a brother officer for taking money from a prisoner, and 10 out of 13 said they would not testify against the officer if he were accused by the prisoner. Comments on police honesty since the publication of Westley's article have often taken the form of avuncular warnings in the professional journals. Richard H. Blum wrote in *Police*: "The conflict of loyalty versus lawfulness is always with the officer, as he is faced with wanting trust, friendship and reliability on the one hand, while wanting to be lawful on the other." [8] Both Blum and Westley deal with honesty about the conduct of a fellow officer; obviously the temptation is even stronger for an officer to cover up when he himself is in trouble, as he usually is when he has abused a citizen.

Once an arrest is made, the police begin to consider what testimony is necessary for a conviction, and what charges are necessary to create pressure on the defendant for a plea of guilty. The Criminal Court is not viewed as a tribunal for the determination of fact, but as a sort of administrative adjunct to the police station for the purpose of obtaining desirable results. Lying is a litigation tool much like, say, investigation. Once the police have arrested a man, particularly under circumstances when charges have been made against an officer, the only real objective is conviction, and the police feel that they have made a mistake if they fail to obtain the conviction, not if they lied to obtain it. The arresting officer who has abused a citizen makes it his business to get out of trouble, as does any other accused party, and his original aim of "preserving police authority" becomes little more than a rationalization. The lie serves the double purpose of preserving his authority and his job.

It seems that there is some sort of folklore or underground

standard circulating in the Department, according to which charges are drawn to cover abuses. Lying to cover a mistake and the use of a criminal charge to buttress the lie are such a natural development that it would hardly seem necessary to do more than give a patrolman a hint. Charges are so invariably preferred, however, and the charges are so much alike from one case to the next, that I am constrained to believe that something a little more definite than a hint is at work. At some level in the Department, something close to this standard has been accepted: when a citizen is injured by a policeman, he must be charged with resisting arrest, together with the underlying crime for which he was arrested. If there was no crime, but rather a personal dispute with the policeman, then the defendant must be charged with disorderly conduct and resisting arrest. Other, more serious charges become something of a matter of taste. Experienced men tend to add other charges, in order to increase the pressure for a plea of guilty to one of the charges. I once heard two transit policemen arguing in the hallway outside the courtroom after one of my clients had refused to plead guilty to disorderly conduct in exchange for a dismissal of the charge of resisting arrest. The more experienced of the two was saying, "You see? He wouldn't take it. I *told* you you should have charged him with felonious assault." These charges—disorderly conduct, resisting arrest, and felonious assault, or all three—together with a story to establish them, constitute the system for covering street abuses. According to a task force of the President's Commission on Law Enforcement, the system exists in many other cities with conditions similar to those of New York, notably in Philadelphia.[9]

It is my guess that the system is perpetuated at the middle level, among the sergeants and possibly the lieutenants. I cannot, of course, be sure, because I rarely hear a reliable account of what is being said at the precinct. However, investigators for a field survey of the President's Commission, covering police departments in major cities outside New York, were able to gain access to the precincts, and their direct observation supports the theory that it is the officers at the middle level who tend to cover for the abuses of the men working under them.[10] This cover may take the form of advice about criminal charges, the system I describe here, or simply of keeping quiet about abuses; in any case, it is characteristic of the extreme solidarity and secrecy of policemen in every city. No doubt the solidarity is as tight as it is because every ranking officer in the typical urban police department has come up through the ranks and shares the mores of the men below him. By the same token, it follows that the introduction of new men at the middle level, specially trained for their jobs rather than drawn from the ranks, would be the most effective way of breaking through the police secrecy. Under present civil service laws, in New York as well as most other communities, it is difficult to alter the system of seniority, but any limitation on the protection of underlings by superiors may be impossible without it.

The Review Board and other institutions in the New York City Police Department do little to discourage the system of cover charges. The Review Board does not hold a hearing until after criminal charges against the complainant have been disposed of, and the charges at a departmental trial are always artfully drawn to avoid any conflict with criminal charges made by the officer involved, even when they have been disposed of. Such tailoring of charges occurred in the Kaplan case (Chapter 6) and the Queens bar case (Chapter 3). These practices encourage officers to believe that if they can cover themselves by a criminal charge, they will escape censure. If the Department were vitally concerned about seeing justice done, it would make sure that criminal charges were dropped against citizens when a departmental investigation showed that they were unwarranted. Instead, the Department sits back to see whether the officer can make his criminal case stick before proceeding against him.

It is worth mentioning here that the ironclad system of cover charges exists in New York City partly because certain other abuses do not. For example, the New York City Police Department does not permit arrests* on "suspicion," a practice al-

* As distinguished from field interrogation, or "stop and frisk," which is discussed in Chapter 12.

lowed by departments in other cities such as Detroit, where
13 percent of the arrests in 1964 were for "detention." [11]
Dragnet arrests for suspicious persons do occasionally occur
after serious crimes in New York, but in general, if a city
policeman has a defendant in custody, he must try to show
probable cause for arresting him, and if he is to account for
a defendant's injuries by resistance to arrest, he must com-
mence his explanation with a lawful arrest. Hence the elaborate
lies about disorderly conduct. It is because the men at the
top of the Department are trying to maintain a façade of probable cause for arrest that the men in the middle and at the
bottom go to such lengths to cover their mistakes. To be an
oppressor is a tricky business in New York, this most liberal
of all possible worlds. In jurisdictions where no attempt is
made to maintain the requirements of probable cause, the
system of cover charges is correspondingly less deeply en-
trenched.

Furthermore, in other jurisdictions a policeman can afford
to be a little lax in covering himself because he can rely on the
district attorney to help him out if he makes a mistake. In
the District of Columbia, for example, the authorities have in
the past preferred charges of filing a false report against people
who made complaints about policemen. [12] In one case from
that jurisdiction the District Attorney started a prosecution
upon minor traffic charges three months after the events were
supposed to have occurred, and solely because the defendant
had complained against the police officer involved in the incident. [13] If there is an instance of equal skulduggery perpetrated
by any of the five New York City district attorneys, I have
not heard of it. The only incident in my experience which ap-
proaches these in depravity was a threat by the prosecutor in
one of my cases, after he had consented to a dismissal of the
charges against two out of three codefendants, to reinstate the
charges against them if they testified in defense of the third.
That is an exceptional incident, however, and it is generally
up to the New York City policeman to provide his own cover
for his mistakes. If he does not make his accusation at the time
of the occurrence, the prosecutor is not likely to look upon

the case with favor. The system is the policeman's only solution.

If officials outside the Police Department in New York do not participate directly in protecting police officers, they do so by their silence. The judges, the prosecutors, even the commissioner himself, cannot appear to condone slipshod police work or police abuses. On the other hand, they know that there is such poor police work, and although they would not participate in it, they do not expect to do very much to improve it. The district attorneys go right on taking waivers of damage claims in return for the dismissal of criminal charges, the remedies for abuses continue to be inadequate, and all in all, with some exceptions, the system works nearly as effectively as if all the other officials participated in it. They become parties to the system in the sense that they know, or should know, that the policeman is covering his mistakes by lying and are content to let him go on doing it. They maintain the rigid standards of due process required in a modern liberal society by letting the patrolman vary the facts to fit the case. They have helped to make the policeman the target for much of the hostility in the city by making him do all the dirty work.

Ironically, the vigilance and sophistication of citizens in pursuing what few poor remedies are open to them have probably helped to make the system as rigid as it is. In rural communities and small towns, where abused citizens are satisfied to forget the whole thing if the police will forget it, criminal charges may not be used by the police as a cover, but in New York, where many abused citizens are very likely to complain to the Department and perhaps even bring a lawsuit, criminal charges are almost invariably preferred. One thoroughly puzzled woman who complained of being manhandled in a welfare center by a policeman told me that the officer had later bought her lunch and said that he would like to drop the charges, but he dared not because she might sue the city. She tried to convince him that she would not sue, but he felt that he could not trust her; regardless of the promises she made while she was under arrest, she might change her mind later. The system was too ironclad for him to let her go.

9

FRAMES

THIS CHAPTER IS, in a way, a postscript to the "system" of cover charges as I have described it up to now. In previous chapters a typical pattern has been for a policeman to become involved in a dispute with a citizen and finally to end by arresting him and charging him with, say, disorderly conduct. In his testimony, the policeman supplies the elements of shouting by the defendant and the presence of a crowd in order to make out a case. Where there was no shouting or crowd, it is obvious that the defendant has been "framed" in the sense that the officer has distorted the facts to obtain a conviction. Nevertheless, we do commonly distinguish between a charge which distorts an incident that actually occurred, in order to cover an abuse, and a frame, in which an incident is alleged that never occurred, or a piece of evidence is manufactured. The line between the two is often extremely fine, and it might be easier to lump the cases together, with the grim pronouncement that almost every police abuse gives rise to a frame, even if only for a minor charge. For purposes of clarity alone, however, the distinction is still useful.

The difference is illustrated in a strange little case arising out of a visit by President Johnson to New York. On June 11, 1966, the President's Club, an organization of Democrats who have contributed more than one thousand dollars to their party, sponsored a dinner for its members at the Waldorf-Astoria Hotel. Without advance notice, the President flew from Washington to speak at the dinner, but despite the impromptu nature of his visit, pickets appeared outside the hotel to protest the war in Vietnam.

In a news story about the dinner, apparently based on police sources, *The New York Times* the following morning reported a curious incident: "At one point a middle-aged woman apparently managed to get into the main ballroom and began shouting at the President. She was immediately arrested by a detective and was taken to the East 51st Street station house." The lady subsequently came to our office, charged under an ancient section of the Penal Law with the misdemeanor of interrupting a lawful meeting. The detective's affidavit alleged:

> Defendant did without authority of law, wilfully and unlawfully disturb an assembly at above location and time, by shouting and using loud and boisterous language, interrupting an address of Lyndon B. Johnson, President of the U.S.

This incident never occurred. The lady did not interrupt the President's speech or the dinner, and *neither did anyone else*. Our investigation and the District Attorney's actions in the case leave not a shadow of a doubt of this. I first interviewed employees of the hotel who had been standing at the entrances to the banquet hall and found that none of them had seen any interruption at all. I then tried to interview the people who had attended the dinner—and I ran up against a stone wall. Naturally the President's Club was not going to give out a list of its members, although one or two whose names had appeared in the newspapers reluctantly spoke to me over the phone. I issued a subpoena for a list of the guests, and on the day the case was called, a lawyer appeared for the club to oppose the exposure of the names. The judge granted his motion to quash the subpoena, and I turned to the lawyer to ask if *he* had attended the dinner. He had, and he confirmed the fact that there had been no interruption. While I began hastily to write out a subpoena for him, he went up and spoke to the

Assistant District Attorney and the policeman. The case was instantly dismissed, and the Assistant stated for the record that "the defendant at no time entered the banquet hall where the speech was to be delivered."

The behavior of the detective throughout can most charitably be described as insolent. While I was waiting for the case to be called, the officer, having learned that I had subpoenaed the guest list, said with a smug smile, "None of those people can be bothered with this case. They're too important." After the case was dismissed, he smiled some more and said, "Sorry about that, chief."

Why were the charges ever brought? The answer, I think, lies in the nature of the arrest and the attitude of the officer. The lady was in the line of pickets opposing the war, and she subsequently went into the hotel, curious to hear the speech. She put her picket sign in a shopping bag and approached the banquet hall, supposing that there might be some sort of lobby or foyer from which she could hear the speech. Oddly dressed as she was, by the standards of the dinner, in a blue shirt, she was immediately accosted by the officer. When she tried to leave, he demanded to look in the shopping bag. She refused, and he took it from her, finding the sign inside. Then she was arrested.

The policeman apparently corroborated much of this story, once he was confronted with someone who had attended the dinner, because the District Attorney's words in dismissing the case tracked the lady's account rather closely: [1]

> The fact[s] here occurred in the foyer outside . . . the defendant here was denied permission to enter, since she stated she had no invitation. There was a brief altercation after which she was placed under arrest and certain signs were found in her possession. However, she at no time displayed the sign and there was no disturbance other than what I have indicated.

The words of the policeman when he arrested her are perhaps the key to his motive. As the lady recalled it, he said to the other officers, "I know she was going in there."

The distinction between a cover charge and a frame is clear in this case. If the lady had been charged with, say disorderly conduct, based upon the "altercation" in the hallway, one might have said that the charges were unjustified, since the altercation was a protest against the policeman looking into the shopping bag. One could hardly have said, however, that the charges were a "frame." The case would have turned upon interpretation of the facts. But to charge the lady with interrupting the President's speech when there was no interruption is a different matter—particularly in view of the fact that disrupting a meeting was at that time a more serious offense than disorderly conduct.* The Review Board did not agree with my opinion about this case. Despite the fact that the abuse was obvious, the lady's complaint was found unsubstantiated without a hearing.

The motive for the frame in this little case appears to be essentially the same as for other arbitrary arrests described in previous chapters. The policeman thought that the lady was guilty *in intent*: she would have disrupted the meeting if he had not prevented her. As we have seen, this is the common rationalization for distorting the facts in a case. The policeman sees his job to be catching criminals, not complying with procedure. He feels that he has done his job when the person who is "guilty anyhow" is convicted, regardless of how the conviction is obtained.

One hesitates to generalize about the problem of planting evidence and other frames, because reliable evidence is supremely difficult to come by. The proof of a frame is usually much more difficult than it was in the case of the lady at the hotel, because it requires a demonstration that a piece of concrete evidence—contraband, for example—was not in the place where an officer said it was. Nevertheless, from our experience with police ethics and the evidence that we have about frames, we can conclude that the motive for manufacturing evidence is usually the conviction of someone whom the police believe guilty in fact or in intent.

---

* Disrupting a meeting, Penal Law §1470, was a misdemeanor and disorderly conduct, P.L. §722, was an offense. As of September 1, 1967, disrupting a meeting became a form of disorderly conduct, P.L. §240.20.

The attempt to establish the planting of evidence as a defense to a charge of possessing contraband (for example, narcotics) is generally hopeless. Defendants constantly claim that contraband has been planted on them, and judges routinely decline to believe it. The problem is that the allegation of a "frame" is the typical last-ditch defense to the charge of possessing contraband. If the police have produced the contraband in court and sworn that they got it from the defendant, and a judge has declared that the evidence was obtained without an unlawful search, there is no defense left except for the suspect to claim flatly that he did not have the contraband. Since the defendant has every motive at such a time to lie about the source of the evidence, the judges cannot believe him unless he can show some really strong motive for the police to lie. In most cases no such motive is discoverable, and there are no corroborating witnesses.

In one restricted class of complaints about narcotics cases, however, there is some evidence, both from circumstances and from witnesses, that suggests a pattern of abuse. These cases occur when the police are lawfully searching an apartment for contraband—under a warrant, for example. Not knowing that the search is in progress, a visitor comes to the door and knocks. The police open the door and arrest the visitor, charging him with possessing contraband. My office received five complaints of this type, differing only in the smallest details, and in each of them, one of the people at the door claimed that he had no contraband on him.

There is no mystery about the possible motives of the police in a case like this. When the narcotics police have searched an apartment, it is usually because they have some cause to believe the tenant is a dealer in contraband. If they actually find narcotics, their suspicions are confirmed, and anyone who comes knocking at the door is immediately under strong suspicion of being a buyer. He is almost as much a party to the crime as if he had been found in the apartment itself. Since he was knocking, he obviously *intended* to get in. The narcotics police see their job to be one of controlling the traffic in contraband, and to this end they are interested in catching narcotics users whether or not they are technically guilty of crime at the time they are caught. The man who knocks at the drug dealer's door is fair game because he is part of the dealer's world.

Most of the complaints about frames that I received, unless they were totally improbable, can be explained in the same way as these cases. For example, one boy who swallowed a bag of heroin when he saw the police coming claimed that the police first pistol-whipped him to try to make him cough it up, and when he would not, they charged him with possessing a different bag of heroin, which they produced. This complaint, if true, is certainly to be explained on the theory that the police thought the defendant was "guilty anyway."

Surely the most outrageous of police abuses is falsification of evidence by officers for corrupt personal motives, or because there is public outcry to find a culprit in a celebrated crime of violence. This is the classic "frame" of the detective story. There is no question that such frames do occur, though I suspect they happen less often than the "law enforcement" frame we have described in the first part of this chapter. We will never know how many frames of this or any other sort occur, however, partly because the evidence is so difficult to come by and partly because the motives of the police are so difficult to fathom. Even in those cases where a defendant confesses to a crime and it is later found that he could not have committed it, it does not follow that he has been deliberately framed. The officers may believe him guilty before they interrogate him, and they almost always do after he confesses. The methods of psychological persuasion used by detectives are powerful enough to extract a false confession without the use of physical force, and one of the most alarming aspects of the interrogation process is that it is possible to take a false confession in good faith. In the famous case of George Whitmore, for example, who confessed in 1964 to the murder of Janice Wylie and Emily Hoffert and was later exonerated, there is no telling whether the detectives who interrogated him believed his confession or not; it seems probable that they did.[2]

One thing we can be certain of is that there are aspects of the system of incentives established by the Department for members of the force that tend to encourage distortion of the facts to maintain or advance the career of the individual officer. Medals and other "departmental recognitions" are given for undergoing conditions of personal danger which may lead to an arrest. These make relatively little difference in advancement to sergeant or lieutenant, which depend chiefly on seniority and the competitive civil service exam.[3] The correlation between the brilliant or dangerous arrest and promotion to detective, however, is very close. In the New York City Police Department, as in substantially all others,[4] the job of a detective is considered a form of specialized police work, rather than a rank attained by seniority. It is not a civil service classification and does not entail an examination, though the pay scale may run as high as that of a sergeant or a lieutenant. The appointment is made by the Commissioner directly, on the advice of the precinct captain, and his recommendation may be based on only one big arrest. The belief on the part of the patrolmen that the facts of an arrest are commonly distorted for such advancement is described by McNamara: [5]

> As an indicator of the extent to which patrolmen felt that mobility through appointment to the detective division was based on effective performance, there exists one of the more dramatic expressions of cynicism, "If you want to get 'out of the bag' and into the 'bureau,' *shoot somebody*." (The "bag" refers to the uniform.) Although it seems unlikely that many officers follow this advice literally, many of those who had chosen this mobility pattern were likely to make a bit more out of situations they encountered than did officers who chose other mobility patterns or chose to remain in the position of patrolman. For example, some officers deliberately antagonized citizens in the hope that the citizens would assault them and that the officer would then have some grounds for making a felony arrest or for using the "necessary force in order to effect the arrest."

One case in 1966 cast an extraordinary light upon the abuses to which this attitude may give rise.[6]

On a Sunday morning in November 1965, a middle-aged

Negro named Robert Nichols was arrested in a fight with a
white man in Harlem. The charges against him were extremely serious. The white man, owner of two local bars,
claimed that Nichols had attempted to hold him up at gunpoint. When he grappled with Nichols, the pistol went off
and the bar owner was wounded in the shoulder. Two policemen appeared in a squad car while the struggle was in progress, and the police and the bar owner agreed that Nichols took
a shot at the officers. One of them fired two warning shots,
then they moved in and subdued Nichols. He was charged
with robbery, assault, and possession of a dangerous weapon,
as well as felonious assault on the policemen. The two patrolmen applied for departmental recognition for having subdued
Nichols under conditions of danger.

Nichols claimed that once they got to the precinct, one of
the officers had struck him in the face with a blackjack; the
police claimed that he had fallen down. In either case, there
was no doubt, as his Legal Aid lawyer later said, that "he
walked in and was carried out" of a Harlem station house,
and was taken to Harlem Hospital. His trip to the hospital
proved to be a blessing in disguise, because shortly after he
got there the electric power failed all over the Northeast. He
was able to escape from the hospital's prison ward, not to be
apprehended again until over a month later, when a charge
of escape was added to the already extensive list pending
against him. The Grand Jury of New York County indicted
him on nine counts, and, especially in the light of his previous
criminal record, his case looked hopeless.

Nichols now began a long sojourn in jail awaiting trial,
while he steadfastly maintained his innocence of the original
charges. He claimed that he was coming along the street at
a time when the bar owner was getting out of his car, and had
accidently run into the door as it swung open. An argument
followed, and Nichols started to walk away, when the man
struck him and drew a gun. Nichols punched at the gun, which
went off, and the two began to grapple. Nichols got hold of
the gun and threw it down a cellar stairway. The two patrolmen did indeed arrive and separated the two. As more police-

men came, there was a private conversation between the white man and the officers, and finally Nichols was arrested. The officers searched the cellar stairways and came up with the pistol.

Nichols said that on the steps of the precinct one of the officers had told the other to "go to the roof and fire two shots." Nichols had not understood the meaning of the order until he realized that he was charged with firing the gun at the patrolmen, and that they claimed they had fired two warning shots before arresting him.

At first no one believed any part of this fantastic story, but doubts began to grow after the Legal Aid investigator and the District Attorney's office interviewed the witnesses to the fight. Not one of the fourteen witnesses had seen the beginning of the fracas; their attention had first been attracted by a shot fired while the bar owner and Nichols grappled, but they all agreed that they had heard no shots fired after the police arrived. Some of them had seen the officers searching the cellar entrances.

After a number of interviews by the District Attorney's office, one of the two patrolmen suddenly admitted that he had lied about the warning shots at the scene. He had in fact discharged his revolver into the Harlem River* and had claimed that it was fired at the scene. He finally admitted that Nichols had not fired the pistol at the policeman at all.

Consternation. Half of the case against Nichols was blown up and the other half thrown into doubt. Nichols' credibility had been poor, but it was enhanced by the truth of the latter part of his story. The bar owner's credibility had been good, but it was tarnished by the fact that he had corroborated the story of the assault on the officers. The ownership of the gun could not be determined. The only count of the indictment that could reasonably be preserved against Nichols was the charge of escape, because, innocent or not, he had apparently at least been lawfully arrested. Seized as he was

* By the NYCPD Rules and Procedures, Ch. 2, § 38.9, when a revolver is discharged the fact must be reported and the weapon checked by the ballistics squad.

during a fight in which a pistol was used, the police perhaps had a right to arrest him and settle the issue of ownership later. Nichols finally pleaded guilty to the escape count, in return for having the rest of the indictment dropped, including the robbery and assault charges. He received a suspended sentence on June 22, 1966, slightly over seven months after he was incarcerated. Considering his record, it was no doubt wise for Nichols to avoid a trial on the robbery charge, but his plea of guilty to escape effectively destroyed his chances of recovering damages in a civil action.

A month later, the two patrolmen were tried by the Department before a deputy commissioner for filing false statements with their superiors and with the courts and fraudulently applying for departmental recognition of their alleged act of heroism in arresting Nichols. The conduct of the trial was superficially smooth, but in fact it minimized the extreme seriousness of the offense. The prosecuting police officer failed to follow some avenues of inquiry that would have shown how the officers had damaged Nichols. There was an implicit assumption, for example, that Nichols was guilty of the attack on the white bar owner. The pistol was several times referred to as "Nichols' gun" and no attempt was made to show that no evidence of ownership had been established. More important, the bar owner testified to his version of the assault, and the prosecution did not try to impeach him with his affidavit corroborating the false stories of the patrolmen. The Deputy Commissioner, on the other hand, contemptuously refused to listen to Nichols and ordered him to leave the stand. The implication of the trial, as the defense lawyer for the policemen pointed out, was that the officers had hurt no one but themselves. They had not hurt but helped Nichols, as the Deputy Commissioner agreed in his opinion, for if they had not ruined the criminal case against him, he would have been fairly convicted of the assault on the bar owner. Since that charge against Nichols had been dismissed before the departmental trial, this was, to say the least, an extremely highhanded assumption.

The patrolmen testified and admitted that they had made the false statements to obtain departmental medals. One of

them added that he did not hope for a promotion as well, but
that of course was a little incredible. The most fascinating
witness was a Catholic priest to whom one of the patrolmen
had first confessed his crime. With the consent of the officer,
the priest dramatically recounted how the officer had confessed after he learned in his class at the College of Police
Science that Nichols could get a stiffer sentence if the lie
were permitted to stand. The priest said he had directed the
penitent to tell the truth.

At the close of the trial, the Deputy Commissioner described the acts of the patrolmen as "insane," but in fact they
seem quite rational. The patrolman who first confessed could
have believed that the extra charge would have made no
difference in Nichols' sentence. His previous record was suf-
ficiently damaging for the officer to have thought that the
sentence for the assault on the bar owner alone would be so
severe that another assault would make no difference. The
officers chose their victim very well. His protests about their
story would not have been believed, and they supposed that
they could have advanced their own careers while injuring
him very little (if he had been guilty of the attack on the
bar owner). The scheme would probably have worked, if one
of the officers had not been a devout Roman Catholic. It is
perhaps because they admitted their guilt that the Commissioner limited their sentence to a penalty of thirty days' pay
(the most serious penalty short of dismissal).

Here was a case where the closed character of the departmental trial showed its weaknesses. The prosecution was conducted entirely by a member of the Department. I was Mr.
Nichols' counsel, but I had no standing at the trial to cross-
examine any of the witnesses, either for the Department or
for the defense. I felt that I could have brought out elements
that the prosecutor did not, but I was prevented by the regu-
lation that makes the Department's legal officer the sole agent
for the prosecution. It would be a small but valuable reform
in the departmental trial procedures to permit the complainant or his attorney, as well as the Department, to put questions to the witnesses.

This case is unique. There is no telling how many times

officers have added acts of heroism to the charges in the arrest of a person with a criminal record, in order to obtain advancement, but there can be no doubt that such an act is difficult if not impossible to discover unless one of the officers is willing to confess. I think the punishment in this case shows that the Department knows such cases occur and does not wish to penalize too severely the rare officer who is willing to admit his guilt.

It is difficult to solve the problem of administration posed by a case like this. Obviously the Department properly encourages initiative by advancing those men who take risks, but it must not encourage perjury or wanton acts of violence to give the appearance of initiative. At the present time, officers in the ranks believe, whether rightly or wrongly, that a large number of arrests, or a dangerous arrest, will lead to advancement. The Commissioner should take more direct control of the advancement of patrolmen, to make sure they know that arrests which unnecessarily injure police-community relations will not help them to get ahead. In the long run, it is likely that a real solution can come only from an overall change in the attitude of the men in the Department. So long as the system of cutting corners in procedure is permitted to exist in other activities, like arrest and testimony in court, some men are going to be cynical about the reports they make to the Department itself. The problem of lying to obtain advancement cannot be solved unless officers are expected to be truthful generally in their testimony.

Policemen occasionally make arrests or exaggerate the importance of an arrest, not only to obtain promotion, but to avoid demotion. One of the hallowed legends about the police concerns the "arrest quota" alleged to exist for some crimes. A gambler once told me that a policeman assigned to the gambling detail had to make fifteen arrests a month to stay in plainclothes. If it were true that there is such an ironclad quota, it would obviously give rise to false arrests and trumped-up charges, but interviews with policemen have convinced me that it is only partially true. Plainclothesmen assigned to enforce narcotics and public morals laws (gambling and prostitution) have an informal quota in the sense that they are expected to make about as many arrests as other men working under the same conditions. If over a period of time they do not approximate the average, their work is questioned. The reason seems to be that the enforcement of the public morals laws offers a tremendous temptation to take graft, and the maintenance of the arrest average tends to eliminate the man who takes a payoff instead of making an arrest.

Undoubtedly, this system does give rise to abuses. Under the gambling laws, betting on the numbers (a lottery based on horse-racing results) is not illegal, but it *is* illegal to sell bets on numbers, and the possession of ten or more bets is presumptive evidence that bets have been sold. Thus a known gambler may be charged with selling policy (numbers) at a time when he is not actually engaged in selling but has a small number of policy bets in his possession. A gambler's lawyer explained to me that in one case when the police found two men with lists of bets, one containing seven and the other five, they charged one man with having twelve bets and let the other go. When the other man appeared to give testimony, the case was dismissed in court.

The arrest quota thus creates real problems, but as long as it is restricted to people who are in a criminal class (gamblers, narcotics users, or prostitutes) the Department no doubt feels that it is preferable to taking graft. Society's attitude toward the criminal law is as much responsible for this situation as the police. We have by statute created a number of "business" or "cooperative" crimes which in turn create an illicit traffic and a criminal class. The traffic affords an enormous temptation for graft, and the criminal class is viewed by respectable people with aversion. The result is that unlawful actions can be taken by law enforce· ment officers against members of the class, and hardly anyone else in the society really disapproves. If those actions are encouraged for the purpose of stopping the taking of bribes as well as stopping the illicit traffic, the quota system must seem a positive gain for the public. In short, by establishing a quota for public morals arrests, the police do what the public asks them to do: try to control an illicit traffic without themselves getting too deeply enmeshed in it. The fact that due process is sometimes a casualty of the system does not appear greatly to concern either the police or the public.

As this is written, the Department's Narcotics Bureau is being shaken up by a scandal of an interesting and characteristic nature. According to newspaper reports,[7] high-ranking officers have been transferred, apparently because a fund intended for the payment of outside informers has been used by some officers for private purposes. Complaints, made over many years, that officers had framed defendants either for "law enforcement" reasons (because they thought the suspect guilty) or to meet a quota, and that officers had distorted the circumstances of arrest and search, have never been able to effect this shakeup, even though many assistant district attorneys and high-ranking policemen knew that those allegations were often true. So long as officers were "doing their job" by making arrests, they were protected. The consideration that someone who was actually innocent might go to jail as the result of a false statement, or that an officer might advance to the rank of detective by exaggerating the importance of his arrest, never led to reform. It was not until the narcotics policeman was thought to have put his hand into the public purse that the Department cracked down on him.

10

MASS POLICE
ACTION

THE REASONS FOR CIVIL DISTURBANCES, both the underlying
causes and the immediate catalyst, are surely among the most
important questions now confronting the social sciences. I
cannot effectively explore those reasons here, however, ex-
cepted insofar as the police are responsible. I have already suggested that the disappointment with the legal process
created by the individual police abuse, with its usual attendant criminal conviction, feeds the frustrations and the cynicism about peaceful remedies which are the stuff of riots.
A study of the causes in depth would require another book,
perhaps longer than this; in this brief chapter I can only
focus on mass police action.

There are always two aspects to any civil disturbance.
One is the action of the crowd, with which we have become
so familiar in the past five years, and the other is the action
of the police. The two are surprisingly alike. Just as a man
in a rioting mob does not behave as he would by himself
on an ordinary working day, a policeman does not behave
the way he would on patrol alone or with one other man.
When we investigate abuses by policemen in a large disturbance, we are not examining the same kind of abuses

that we have described in earlier chapters, although the origins of the abuses may be similar. The psychology of policemen acting in the mass is bound to be different from that of the officer on the beat. The descriptions and photographs of mass police action in Newark in 1967, for example, are impossible to explain adequately in the way I have described individual police action.[1] Indiscriminate beatings and killings with little or no provocation are as difficult to understand by the standards of individual police conduct as the killing of a policeman by a mob in Plainfield, New Jersey, in the summer of 1967 is incomprehensible by the standards of conduct of the individual citizen.

The reasons are probably similar in both cases. The individual draws strength for violence from his fellows. If a spirit of destruction springs up, the individual feels that he has support for his actions from the others in the mob. The sense of a threat to the whole group from another anonymous crowd gives extra courage to take violent action against the crowd. Most obviously, the presence of others, whether policemen or citizens, gives a cloak of anonymity to the actions of the individual. Whatever he does is unlikely to be detected.

These characteristics of mass action do not entirely explain the behavior of the police, any more than they explain the actions of the crowd. The hatred and frustration which are exposed on both sides by a civil disturbance are merely channeled by the mob. It is here that the attitudes of the individual policeman come into play. The policeman no doubt sees a drastic threat to authority from a civil disturbance, and it is perhaps this which originally provokes him to angry reaction. The anonymous and continuing nature of the threat brings out hostility against Negroes, Puerto Ricans, hippies, leftists, or whoever else is or appears to be involved in the mass action. The mob psychology reinforces the impulse to take violent action against the threat, until the impulse is distorted out of all proportion to the original cause. If there is any real destruction of property by the crowd of citizens, the situation often degenerates further because the police find that the middle-class public expects them to put down the riot with violence, will applaud them if they do, and will criticize them if they do not. They then have a kind of external support for their actions that the mob of citizens never enjoys short of a revolution.

The problems of the case-by-case approach to police abuses are magnified in a civil disturbance. Witnesses are themselves difficult to identify, and when they appear they usually cannot pick out one policeman from the many wearing similar coats and hats. When they can identify an officer, they frequently cannot tell how an incident started and they do not know whether his actions were justified. The fact-finding tools of a board of review are particularly inadequate for complaints of abuse in mass police action.

After many frustrating interviews with witnesses to mass police action, I had occasion to experience their problems at first hand in the enormous Spring Mobilization for Peace of April 15, 1967, the same rally at which Professor George Fischer was arrested (see Chapter 6). The prescribed course of the march from Central Park to the United Nations Plaza was a little over a mile. Many thousands marched peacefully along that route, but the tougher militants literally ran down Broadway and across Forty-second Street, stopping traffic and chanting, "Hell, No, We Won't Go." This bid fair to cause conflict with the police, but it was at first handled very skillfully, with the police closing off streets temporarily as the crowd passed. When the crowd reached the foot of Forty-second Street at the East River, however, they began to fill the entire street, because they could not get around the corner onto the avenue facing the river. The police began to push them, and some demonstrators sat down. They were picked up and pushed or thrown out of the crowd, as I looked on. One young man was pulled out by several officers and hustled unresisting from hand to hand along a fence at the edge of the avenue. So far all of it seemed rough but not unreasonable. But as I watched, a hand reached over the fence, I saw the flash of a daystick (a rubber truncheon with a thin steel rod in the center), and the boy tumbled bleeding to the ground. I had not the faintest idea which of the officers had done it; all I could see was a group of men in blue. The cloak of anonymity was working well.

During the period of this project, there were no major riots in New York City, though there were a number of smaller incidents resulting in mass police action. Perhaps they illuminate the problems better than the description of a major disturbance, because the facts can be learned from the witnesses with some hope of accuracy. The comparatively small number of people involved may mean that these incidents are quickly forgotten, but it helps us to better determine what actually happened.

CONEY ISLAND

The neighborhood bordering the Coney Island amusement park along the southeastern shore of Brooklyn is a microcosm of the city. In a midsummer report on the community, *The New York Times* quoted an employment counselor who said that it "is the most integrated area in the city." [2] There is some truth to this, in the sense that there is little conflict between the races, but the several thousand Negroes living there do inhabit a ghetto. It runs down Mermaid Avenue, a block away from the sea, like the spine of a fish, branching out into the side streets in either direction. This tiny ghetto, encysted in a community of Irish, Italian, and Spanish people, has experienced intense conflict with the police. The problems are concentrated because the ghetto is so small, and "new"— most of the Negroes are recent arrivals. The police are unfamiliar with them, and even afraid of them. The police problems of Coney Island seem like those of a small Midwestern city, rather than New York. It is chiefly from this ghetto that I had complaints of police attempts to get a "rise" out of youths by openly taunting them on the streets, or of their harassing Negro community leaders by taunting or arresting them. The conflict between the police and the black people there is so bitter that some Negro leaders claim that the city is trying to harass them into moving out of the neighborhood. Whether this is true or not, it is a measure of the estrangement that the black people feel.

On July 12, 1966, the YMHA on the Coney Island water-front sponsored an interracial dance as a symbol of the good feeling between Negroes and whites. It was only a qualified success. A shouting argument came to a head outside the dance, and the police arrived to disperse the crowd. White observers at the dance remarked upon how well the police appeared to keep their heads under some ferocious cursing by Negro youths. The Negroes, on the other hand, said that the police were sending all the blacks in one direction and the whites in another. One man said that he had been poked in the back with a nightstick.

Negroes streaming home from the dance began to converge upon the northern end of the narrow mile of ghetto on Mermaid Avenue. There an argument started between two Negro girls, with several dozen passers-by, mostly black as well, stopping to watch. It was a simple private dispute, having nothing to do with race.

The police, probably tense because of the threat of violence at the dance, arrived forthwith in squad cars and a patrol wagon. Several women began shouting at them to go away and not interfere; the police finally lost their tempers and began summarily arresting those standing around, putting them in the patrol wagon. The crowd grew larger, firecrackers and bottles began to come down from the buildings facing the street, and officers fired their pistols into the air. Before the night was over, some sixteen people, ranging in age from fifteen to twenty-six, had been arrested and charged in each case with disorderly conduct, resisting arrest, and feloniously assaulting a police officer.

Those sixteen cases were to be a painful lesson in the intractable difficulties presented by criminal charges arising out of a riot. To begin with, the "bid" by the police was very high. Sixteen separate charges of felonious assault were an obvious demand for a plea of guilty to a lesser offense. To make matters worse, the cases were in two entirely separate courts. The teen-agers under sixteen were all charged in the juvenile court; the adults and older adolescents were arraigned together in Criminal Court in Brooklyn. The juveniles were released in the custody of their parents, but the bail in

Criminal Court was high, ranging from $500 for two mothers with large families on welfare, to $2,500, and in one case to $10,000. High bail is common for mass arrests in civil disturbances because judges seem to think that it will keep the participants out of trouble until the community cools off. This tactic effectively denies the defendants the benefit of their presumption of innocence, but there is not much anyone can do to prevent it until the lawyers take action to reduce the bail. The judges tipped their hand in the case of the man held in $10,000 bail. Several weeks later, when everyone presumed that conditions were quiet, he was simply paroled without bail. After that, it was difficult to believe that high bail had ever been necessary for him.

The day after the arrests, federal Vista* volunteers working in the neighborhood got in touch with me, and Clift Johnson and I went out to a crowded, hot mass meeting at the Family Center on Mermaid Avenue. By that time, the community had succeeded in collecting bail for some of the defendants, and they were there, the older ones passionately denouncing the police, while the younger people just sat on their folding chairs, looking thoughtful and scared. I agreed to represent three of the adult defendants, a man and his two married sisters, together with a nineteen-year-old girl who had been arrested at the same time. I thought that would be about as much as I could handle.

Our first job was to bail out the one defendant we still had in jail. His bail at first was $3,000, and in view of the fact that his mother was on welfare, it was absurdly excessive. One of the Criminal Court judges was kind enough to put it down to $2,500, but we had to obtain a writ of habeas corpus to have it reduced even to a figure as high as $1,000. The community finally succeeded in raising the collateral for this bond, and he was released after twenty-three days in jail.

After that, there began a wearisome round of bargaining with the District Attorney. At first we were all, defendants and attorneys alike, spoiling for a trial. Once the defendants were

* Volunteers in Service to America, a federal antipoverty project similar to a domestic Peace Corps.

indicted by the Grand Jury for felonious assault, however, it became obvious that a trial was almost impossible. The case would have taken literally months to try before a jury. On the other hand, it was equally obvious that it would have been nearly impossible for a private attorney, as distinguished from an institutional fellow like me, to represent the defendants in a case like this. The cases of the three women alone required more than twenty court appearances for me or one of our volunteer attorneys; they were constantly being adjourned because no one could make a decision about how to dispose of them. It was only because I was employed by the Police Practices Project that we could afford to give the time required to defend the case as long as the District Attorney's office wanted to prosecute it. When it finally became clear that we would indeed stay with it to the end, the felony charges were reduced to the minimal offense of disturbing the peace. We all thought "disturbance of the peace" was a roughly adequate description of what had occurred, and the ladies left the court with a warning from the judge after a year and a half of litigation. Many lawyers think it a triumph for a felony to be reduced suddenly to a mere offense, but the truth is that it requires only two simple ingredients: guiltless clients and infinite patience. If I had had to subsist upon the fees that my unfortunate clients could afford, I would still have had the first requirement, but not the second.

From the confused scenes of shouting and arrest on July 12, only two incidents stood out in the minds of the witnesses clearly enough to be authenticated.

The first of these arose when policemen were walking down the streets trying to herd people into their houses. They chased one group of four teen-agers, including our nineteen-year-old defendant, into the doorway of a house just off the corner. The young people were in fact attempting to comply with the orders of the police; one of them lived in the building and they were trying to get off the street and into his apartment. They were partway up the stairs when the police ran in and pulled them back out into the street and over to the paddy wagon. The girl was struck on the side of the head as she was put into the wagon. All were charged at the same time as the other twelve defendants, with disorderly conduct, resisting arrest, and felonious assault on a policeman.

Three witnesses, women who lived in the building, agreed on this account of the facts for all four of the teen-agers in the doorway, and yet the results in the four cases are completely at odds. The youngest of the four was declared a delinquent in juvenile court, a second, being over sixteen, was adjudged a youthful offender, and for two defendants the charges were dismissed. Such wildly inconsistent results can only be explained by the vagaries of judicial decision and the bargaining process in criminal cases.

This incident was only the beginning. As the scene got rougher, the police exhibited a kind of frenzy. A young woman who lived in the house on the corner was hurrying home along Mermaid Avenue when she met her mother coming from the disturbance. The mother said that her son had been arrested. The girl came up to her doorway, and finding it blocked by officers, demanded to know why her brother was in the paddy wagon. The officers seized her and started to put her in the wagon, while one of them held a rubber club under her chin. One of the women already in the wagon reached out to help her in, and finally fell or jumped out of the wagon. As she fell to the ground, the police began to hit her, ignoring the other woman, who fled around the corner. Bottles began to fly from the houses, and one or more of the officers fired their revolvers into the air. A large number of witnesses watched this, including one of the Vista volunteers, and the president of the local NAACP finally helped the lady to her feet and got her seated near the curb. Like the others, she was charged with disorderly conduct, resisting arrest, and felonious assault, but she was finally found guilty, as we have seen, only of the offense of disorderly conduct.

One policeman had been knocked out in the fray, and the problem from the beginning of the litigation was to find out how this had happened. The two married sisters who were my clients were at first accused of knocking him down and kicking him, but in the end it became clear that he had fallen and hit his head. His assailant, if there was one, was simply un-known.

This was a classic ghetto conflict with the police. The two incidents that I have been able to "authenticate," according to standards that are at best awkward, can give only the faintest idea of the anger, as well as the confusion, that was obvious after the disturbance and must have prevailed while it was going on. I talked to more than a dozen witnesses over many months, in interviews yielding false leads, mistaken identifica-tions, personal animosities, a pervasive fear of trouble for any-one who testified—and a few hard facts. The furious desire to resist oppression always shone through the confusion, never-theless, particularly in the three young people from a single family that I represented. The older sister demanded on every court day what I was going to do about the way the police had treated her younger sister. The younger girl just came silently to court, busying herself taking care of the children she had brought with her. The first few times she wept at the bar in indignation and apprehension at the charges, but her spirits revived a little as the case wore on. At the end, she went away relieved, but the older and more militant girl was exasperated at the results. She said, "So they're just going to say there was a disturbance of the peace and no one's going to do anything about this place and these cops out here." Another of the de-fendants said, "You learn a lot when they hit you in the head a few times. At first you want to hit back, but you learn you can't fight City Hall with your hands." As the cases grew older, and defense witnesses from the neighborhood became more reluctant to testify, he said sadly, "My people. They just fall away like feathers out of a pillow."

We made complaints to the Department's Review Board shortly after the disturbance, but the results were disappoint-ing. A hearing was held only after the criminal charges were disposed of, a year and a half after the fracas had occurred. The usual problem in reviewing the events of a civil disturb-ance—identification of individual officers—was exaggerated by the delay. One of the witnesses was so angered at the absurdity of being asked to identify the face of an officer after eighteen months that she stood up in the middle of her cross-examination and stalked out of the hearing room. I had a difficult time convincing her to come back. One of the chief weaknesses in the Review Board procedures, its subservience to the criminal courts, was dramatically revealed in a case where the criminal proceedings took so long to dispose of. The weakness is not always so obvious, but it is always there. The Review Board should never permit its hearing procedures to be influenced by the courts.

Mass police actions like the one in Coney Island are familiar to us from other ghettos and other cities. So great is the inflammatory effect of mass police action that it is said sometimes to keep a riot going after it would otherwise have worn itself out.[3] Totally different in origin, but similar as far as mass action is concerned, were two other disturbances from which complaints came to my office. They were actions against outcast groups, radicals and hippies, rather than against a spontaneous outburst by black people. In essence, they were highly charged versions of the typical cases we have discussed in previous chapters—reactions by policemen, this time in a body instead of as individuals, to defiance or some other provocation. Though these cases are unusual, they help to cast a special light on police action in ghetto disturbances as well.

THE DU BOIS CLUB RIOT

On March 4, 1966, United States Attorney General Katzenbach announced his intention of investigating the Du Bois Club to determine whether it was subversive. No such announcement had been made about any other peace or civil rights group, and the young people in the club were angry and alarmed. They called a press conference for the next day to reply to the accusation implied in the Attorney General's announcement. It was to result in a disturbance and an ensuing investigation that kept us occupied for months, and interfered with our work in cases I have discussed in previous chapters.

The conference was held at Vanderbilt and St. Mark's Avenues in downtown Brooklyn, at a now defunct branch office of the club. As the press converged on the Brooklyn office that day, a Saturday, dragging in a tangle of cables and television cameras, neighborhood people began to gather outside. Most of them were middle-aged, and they had never paid any attention to the club until the Attorney General's announcement. A few bystanders shouted and threw eggs. It developed that the Du Bois office was located next to a men's social club, and its members repeatedly expressed for the television and radio microphones their surprise and anger at finding out that their neighbors might be Communists.

After explaining their program and denouncing the Attorney General to the press, the members of the Du Bois Club began to leave the branch office, and a brawl started. Its origins are complex, yet unusually easy to trace because the television cameramen lingering after the press conference recorded it in detail.

The fracas began when neighborhood youths chased a group of five people leaving the club to their car and beat one of them ferociously with steel garbage cans. From inside the car, one of the club members flashed an air pistol, apparently for the purpose of frightening off the assailants. The police, thinking that it was a real pistol, opened the doors of the car and arrested all five. No attempt was made at that point to arrest their assailants. As the five were being handcuffed against the car, fighting among the police, club members, and local toughs became general in the entire block.

The behavior of the police and of the youths in the neighborhood who set upon the club members was curiously similar. When the driver was arrested, he was pulled violently out of the car, and the television films show a citizen standing among the policemen, hitting him as he is on the ground. Presumably the police felt as threatened and angered as the neighborhood people by the presence of the air pistol, and they reacted by arrest and violence. Many of them shared the prejudice toward the club's political views; in fact, one witness later said that she actually heard officers singing "America" on the steps of the precinct when the club members arrested were brought there.

This is not to say that the police took no action that day against anyone from the neighborhood. The films show a general melee, with private citizens grappling and the police pushing them all around in a disorganized way. The anger and tumult of mass police action was revealed in a film sequence shot by a CBS cameraman. The film shows a young member of the club being held by a neighborhood man. As the man lets him go, a policeman, face contorted in a yell, grabs the young man by his shirt, puts him up against a car, and slugs him.

Shocking scenes of the club members being pelted with garbage cans appeared that night on the six o'clock news, and many viewers demanded an explanation of the arrests. This case would ordinarily have been handled by the Review Board, but because of the publicity an investigation was started directly out of the Commissioner's office, by his Confidential Investigating Unit (PCCIU). This group of senior officers and detectives, now absorbed into the Bureau of Internal Affairs, customarily handled charges of corruption, or charges which originated within the Department, as distinguished from civilian complaints. Occasionally they were assigned to a case like this, where there had been a public outcry.

The PCCIU investigators looked at the films, made stills from them, and interviewed everyone whose faces they could identify, more than a hundred witnesses in all. Most witnesses were unable to remember the faces of the policemen who had hit them. Even the films did not entirely solve the problem because some incidents did not appear on the films, and in those which did, the actors themselves sometimes could not remember the events. The young man who was struck in the sequence of shots from the CBS film did not remember the episode at all! Curiously, he remembered being struck at another place by another policeman. The events which occur during mass police action are often so rapid that they simply defy the wide net of the standards of legal proof. Not surprisingly, after the investigation the Department informed me by letter that the Commissioner had reached the conclusion that "none of the allegations could be substantiated. This is due, in part, to the inability of those assaulted to identify any police officers as their assailants."

The Du Bois Club riot very nearly convinced me that mass police action is unreviewable, as far as abuses committed by individual officers involved are concerned. It does suggest something about the underlying causes for the mass action as a whole, however. The same sort of conduct which tends to provoke a sanction from the individual policeman—namely, a threatening act by an outcast, in this case a putative Communist—provoked action from all the policemen. They reinforced one another's reactions, and the crowd contributed as well.

TOMPKINS SQUARE

The lessons of March 1966 about mass police action were writ large, if not actually caricatured, a year later, on Memorial Day, 1967.

Tompkins Square is one of the centers of that part of the Lower East Side known as the East Village. As the neighborhood became a haven for hippies in 1966, the park increasingly became a setting for hippie outings. There they rang bells, sang Hindu chants, and occasionally smoked marijuana. The police opinion of these apparently bizarre loungers was perhaps summed up by an officer who, watching such a group in another park, muttered to one of our lawyers, "I wish one of those characters would make a false move, so I could plug him."

In the spring of 1967, there were a number of minor disputes with police in the park; on fine days it was crowded, and the police sometimes tried to get the hippies to move along. On Memorial Day, however, a special legal dilemma was brewing. The City Parks Department had issued a permit for an art show and music in Tompkins Square on that day; the event was intended to accommodate six thousand people. Tompkins Square is only a block wide and two blocks long; six thousand people would have made it uncomfortable indeed. Fortunately, only a few hundred gathered. They were peaceable enough, although they violated then-current Parks Department regulations by sitting on the grass.

Around 4:30 P.M., a group of about twenty hippies were sitting on the grass, playing a bongo drum and guitars and chanting the "Hare Krishna." It is more of a drone than a chant, and the witnesses were probably correct when they said that it was not loud. A policeman came up and told the singers to stop. They did stop for a while, but shortly they began to play again. The policeman returned with a few others, including a sergeant, who ordered the group to move on or be arrested. They refused, and linked arms to prevent the arrest. The police attempted to pull those at the end of the line loose, amid the protests of those sitting down. While this was going on, the crowd in the park grew larger, and patrol wagons with perhaps seventy more policemen arrived, making about one hundred in all. They began to push the standing crowd out of the park, leaving the few hippies in isolation on the ground with their arms locked.

The final stage of the mass action was triggered by the events of the next few moments. Frank Wise, one of the group on the ground, stood up and addressed the crowd, telling them, as he himself remembered it, "What is happening here? This is America. This is the land of life, liberty, and the pursuit of happiness." A photograph in the *New York Post* of May 31 shows him standing with his arms upraised. A policeman ran toward him, his club in the air, and two witnesses saw him trip and fall toward Mr. Wise, as Wise himself fell back. The *Post* account substantially agreed about this curious incident. Other policemen rushed in and began to club Mr. Wise and the others near him, with little or no resistance. Forty people were ultimately arrested, including some who protested the treatment of those on the ground. A grisly photograph, printed the following week on the front page of the local underground paper, the *East Village Other*, showed Wise being dragged away by the handcuffs on his wrists, his arms twisted up over his head, blood streaming into his eyes and onto his shirt. Mass police action had turned an ordinary arrest in response to a threat to authority into a ferocious act of brutality.

When the forty arrived in night court, the charges had been attuned to their injuries with unusual delicacy. All were

charged with disorderly conduct and nearly all with resisting
arrest. In addition, Anthony DiStasi and Frank Wise, who were
injured, were charged with felonious assault.

All the charges were dismissed at the preliminary hearing
a month later, in a decision of Judge Herman Weinkrantz.
The opinion was an extraordinary application of the doctrine
that it was lawful, if inadvisable, to resist an unlawful arrest.
Judge Weinkrantz said:

> The cases are before the Court for preliminary hearings
> on all the misdemeanors and the one felony; the Dis-
> orderly Conduct charges, being offenses* are not before
> the Court at all and are not being tried at this time. It
> has been conceded, however, that in determining the
> pertinent issues in the misdemeanor and felony charges,
> if the arrests were not made in accordance with law, then
> the resistance to the officers, if not unreasonable, and
> some of the other charges, would thereupon not be viola-
> tions of law. To ascertain all the facts the people have
> presented their side of the Disorderly Conduct charges
> so that the Court could determine whether those arrests
> complied with the provisions of Section 177, subdivision
> 1 of the Code of Criminal Procedure, to wit: "for a crime
> committed or attempted in his presence or where a
> police officer has reasonable grounds for believing that
> a crime is being committed in his presence."

Since the judge found no case for a disturbance of the peace,
he dismissed all the charges. This decision shows how salutary
the rule was. On March 6, 1968, nevertheless, in a wave of
repressive "anticrime" laws, the legislature took the extraordinary step of abolishing that right and making every resistance to an officer a crime. The ostensible rationale for the
decision was that resistance is dangerous to both the citizen
and the officer, and there is some truth in this, of course;
resistance, if there was any, was certainly dangerous to Frank
Wise. The trouble is that the conclusion does not follow. It
would certainly not have been justice to permit Wise and the

* In New York a preliminary hearing was available only for crimes,
not for offenses. The judge had to determine whether there was an offense,
however, to know whether there was a crime.

others to be convicted of or even tried for a crime as a result of their actions. It is equally absurd to pretend that the hippies would have behaved any differently if it had already been a crime to resist an unlawful arrest on Memorial Day, 1967. The refusal to comply with an arbitrary order is not rational but a natural reflex action. As the highest court of New York once said: "For most people an illegal arrest is an outrageous affront, and intrusion—the more offensive because under color of law—to be resisted as energetically as a violent assault." [4] More important than these considerations is the familiar fact that charges of resisting arrest and assault are so often used as a cover for a false arrest or an act of violence. Frequently, when a defendant is accused of one of these crimes, there are no witnesses except the defendant and the policeman. If a defendant subsequently appears at his arraignment with injuries, there is really no way to defend him against a charge of assault except by trying to show that the original arrest was invalid. The change in the law permits a policeman to make every arrest valid simply by adding a charge of assault. The problem appears most poignantly in the case of Frank Wise, who was charged with taking a police officer's stick away and striking him with it. Of course, there were plenty of witnesses to say that he had not done it, but if there had been none, he might easily have been convicted of the charge. Under the law as it is now, he would have received nothing for his bloody injuries but a criminal conviction.

The complaint made to the Review Board in this case seems to have been disposed of in a characteristically hippie way. The Board's staff and the defendant's attorney, Ernst Rosenberger, tried to get some one, any one, of the injured parties to come in for a hearing. But they drifted away to California and points unknown. The complaint failed by default.

I think these cases give us enough material to formulate a rough sort of theory about mass police action. Conditions are ripe when the police are faced in the streets with an outcast group toward which they feel alien and consequently fearful. The action is then triggered by an act of defiance or assumed threat to authority of the same sort that will set off a violent response by an individual policeman. In each of our cases—poor Negroes in Coney Island, leftists at the Du Bois Club, and hippies in Tompkins Square—the police were faced with a group toward which they could adopt a common hostile attitude. Then in each case there were threatening acts which set off the action—arguments in Coney Island, an air pistol at the Du Bois Club, and a defiant speech in Tompkins Square.

What is to be done about the abuse of mass police action? It is one of the most important and potentially incendiary problems of police work, and as we have seen, review of civilian complaints is even less effective as a deterrent for mass police action than it is for the individual police abuse. The solution, I think, is not quite so difficult as it might seem at first. It requires the presence on the scene of responsible civilian officials and superior officers of the police. This is impossible in many relatively minor confrontations such as the ones described in this chapter; they frequently occur without warning. But most planned demonstrations, such as peace marches, which give rise to mass action are announced in advance. A major civil disturbance like a riot takes hours, if not days, before turning into a rampage, and it is no problem for reliable witnesses to get to the scene. By their presence, the cloak of anonymity is removed from the police, and the mob psychology of the mass is minimized. Unlike most police abuses, mob violence by the police is relatively predictable, and therefore it can be controlled. It is the job of civilian and police observers to get there and help control it.

The work of the official observers should be supplemented by film teams, both officially sponsored and independent. In addition, civil rights and civil liberties groups ought to send their own observers, clearly marked by hats or armbands, and their own film teams as well. If the official observers are prejudiced, the films and the unofficial observers will act as a control. Some may be arrested at first, but in the long run that practice can be stopped. All of this paraphernalia might seem like an attempt to catch the police out committing crimes, but in fact, my hope is that the observers will have nothing to

observe, the film teams nothing to shoot. They are only a deterrent, and they will become a more effective deterrent when
their presence is better known to the police.

All these techniques of control have been used in New
York, with varying degrees of success. The device of sending
civilian and high-ranking police observers to potentially dis-
ruptive events has been used for two years, and it has
worked passably well, although it often breaks down. In the
East New York section of Brooklyn during the summer of
1966, the Commissioner went to the scene of disturbances
there to make sure that the police used restraint.[5] They did,
and the situation never escalated into a full-scale riot. In East
Harlem in the summer of 1967, the Commissioner's chief
deputies as well as the Mayor and his aides went to the scene
of an incipient riot to calm both the crowd and the police. The
attempt was not entirely successful, but once again the riot
died down. At the peace demonstrations during the week of
December 4, 1967, the Mayor's aides went along to try to
keep the peace, again with mixed results. This is in fact a
form of civilian control of the police, and for its limited purposes it is more effective than civilian or any other kind of
review. The Patrolmen's Benevolent Association showed that
it understood this very well by objecting strenuously to the
presence of the Mayor's aides at the December peace demonstrations. It was consistent with the record of the PBA in
opposing a civilian review board or any other civilian
surveillance.

The use of film as a tool of civilian control, though much
discussed, is in its infancy. At this writing, one small film
group in New York, the Newsreel, is undertaking a project
of filming police work at peace demonstrations. The idea
ought to be applied widely, because such films would act both
as a deterrent and as a record of extraordinary events. As we
learned in the Du Bois Club riot, films cannot solve all the
problems of mass action, but they will be more of a help as
their existence comes to be generally known.

The techniques I have described here cannot, of course,
prevent the outbreak of civil disturbances, but they can help

to prevent the exacerbation of those disturbances by mass police action. The techniques are so simple and so obvious that they come down to an expression of good faith on the part of the civil authorities. If a pitched battle between police and citizens—such as often occurs in a riot—can be easily avoided, then it is the duty of the authorities to take measures to avoid it; the failure to send observers to watch and attempt to control the police becomes an inexcusable act of official revenge against the impulse to rebel. If the authorities will not take those measures, there is no choice but to believe that they invite the carnage that ensues. It is to the credit of the Police Commissioner and other New York City officials that they have at least made a start in the direction of minimizing such conflicts, and it is to the eternal discredit of the administrators in most other cities that they have refused even to try to prevent them. It is less to the credit of the New York officials that they have frequently denied the existence of police misconduct in demonstrations and disturbances where everyone knew that it had occurred, but in the long run, their admission or denial does not make as much difference as their presence. As we have seen, mass police action is nearly impossible to review; the important thing is to get there ahead of time and prevent it.

At this writing (May 1968), recent weeks have shown an apparent increase in mass police action, and the New York City police have come under heavy fire, especially on account of their actions at Columbia University. Everything that has occurred in the Columbia demonstrations and other similar ones tends to confirm the theory that police abuses originate in defiance. If anything, it seems that recent events demonstrate that the control of police and civilian authorities over mass police action at demonstrations in New York is beginning to weaken, as individual officers become accustomed to it.

SEARCH AND
SEIZURE

Despite intense litigation in the courts during the past few years over the privilege of official instrusion, the single sentence of the Fourth Amendment still summarizes the law of search and seizure very well:

> The right of the people to be secure in their persons, houses, papers, and effects, against unreasonable searches and seizures, shall not be violated, and no warrants shall issue, but upon probable cause, supported by oath or affirmation, and particularly describing the place to be searched, and the person or things to be seized.

While we commonly think of an official search as the ransacking of a house, with the cottager trembling on the doorstep at the tramp of the constabulary's boots, many searches in fact do not involve entry into a house at all. Searches of the person are quite common, and with certain exceptions they too are covered by the Fourth Amendment.

The words of the amendment emphasize warrants, and many people who have called me to complain of unlawful searches believe that a house search cannot be made without a warrant. This is probably a healthy prejudice on their part, but the law is that a search, either of a house or a person, can be made without a warrant, and it is routinely done in connection with an arrest. If the police come to a citizen's house, or stop him on the street, to arrest him lawfully, they can search his person and the place where he is arrested.

The phrase around which nearly all the law of search and seizure revolves is "probable cause." It is defined rather generally, as evidence which would "lead a man of prudence and caution to believe that an offense has been committed, and that the accused committed it." The words are used in the Fourth Amendment only in connection with warrants, but the Supreme Court has held that exactly the same probable cause must be shown to justify a search without a warrant, lest the police be tempted to neglect the use of warrants. In other words, when a defendant seeks to exclude from a trial evidence seized without a warrant, the police must show that they made the search upon facts which would have justified issuing an arrest or search warrant if there had been time to get one.

For our purposes, "probable cause" usually refers to the information an officer must have to make a lawful arrest, because almost all the searches discussed in this chapter were made without a warrant and as part of an arrest. Under New York law, a policeman has a right to make an arrest and an incidental search for a crime committed in his presence, however petty it may be. His power to arrest for a more serious crime (a felony), however, extends beyond those crimes which he has actually witnessed. He may make a felony arrest (and an incidental search) without a warrant, for example, upon the complaint of a reliable third party. While both street searches and house searches theoretically require the same probable cause,* then, this law of arrest actually operates so differently in a public place from the way it does in a private home that street searches bear almost no resemblance to house searches. It is obvious that relatively few acts committed in the home can be said to be committed in an officer's pres-

---

* With the exception of the stop and frisk law, New York Code of Criminal Procedure, §180-a, which will be discussed later in this chapter.

ence, unless he has already obtained access unlawfully,
though there are cases where policemen have seen crimes
being committed through a window or heard them through
a door. Most arrests and searches for crimes committed in
the officer's presence are perforce made in public places.
The search of a private residence without a warrant is usually made in the relatively rare case where a person accused
of a felony is lawfully arrested at home. This happens when
the complaining witness in a robbery, let us say, has recognized the assailant and goes with the officer to the address to
pick him up. But if a person claims that he saw the defendant
committing a misdemeanor—using narcotics, for example—
a police officer cannot go and arrest him (or search him) without a warrant.

It is apparent from this brief sketch of the law of arrest
that a lawful search without a warrant is usually made in a
public place and incident to a crime the officer claims to have
witnessed. A variation of this is called abandonment, when
the culprit throws something to the ground, or occasionally
out of a window, and the policeman picks it up and identifies
it as contraband. This, of course, is not a search at all, though
it is similar in the sense that the crime of possessing the contraband is committed in the officer's presence. Abandonment
is so commonly claimed by police officers as the basis for an
arrest on the street that it has a name, "dropsy," in the argot
of the criminal courts.

Much of the law defining probable cause has come into
being since the decision of the Supreme Court in *Mapp v.
Ohio* in 1961.[1] Until then, the Supreme Court had held that
while the Fourth Amendment forbade unlawful searches, the
states were free to use unlawfully seized evidence at a criminal trial. The evidence obtained in the search, after all,
whether it was a murder weapon or contraband narcotics,
was no less incriminating, and the accused was no less guilty,
because he or his house had been searched unlawfully. He
was theoretically able to sue for damages for the search,
though it is doubtful that a jury would give him any damages
if contraband had been found. Under this rule, the law de-

fining probable cause did not develop in the state courts because evidence was admissible at a trial whether or not there was probable cause to obtain it. In the *Mapp* case the Supreme Court finally recognized that the old rule had made the Fourth Amendment ineffective, and the result has been that a defendant now cannot be convicted upon evidence obtained without probable cause to make an arrest or a search. In New York, a defendant makes a simple motion before trial to suppress evidence seized from him, and if he can show that there was no probable cause for the arrest or the search, then the evidence is excluded. For most crimes involving contraband, a successful "motion to suppress" ends the prosecution, because there can be no conviction without the concrete evidence.

The exclusionary rule of the *Mapp* case conflicts directly with the standards of police practice discussed in previous chapters. If contraband has been taken from a man, then he is guilty of having possessed it, and it is extremely difficult for the policeman to see why he should not be convicted. The fact that the exclusionary rule was established as a means of enforcing the Fourth Amendment matters very little, because the policeman sees his job as one of catching criminals, not of enforcing the Constitution. Once he has caught someone who really is a criminal, he does not feel that it is wrong for him to vary the facts in order to comply with the legal rules.

The search of an apartment on the Lower East Side in the spring of 1967 admirably illustrates the legal problems, as well as the police reaction to them. A man whom we shall call by the fictitious name of Francis White occupied an apartment on East Tenth Street. It was a three-room railroad flat on the first floor, with a living room facing on the street, an open arch into a large kitchen, and a bedroom behind the kitchen. The front door opened into the kitchen from an entrance hallway. On the evening of April 3, 1967, Mr. White was committing a misdemeanor by smoking marijuana with three friends, in the bedroom with the door closed. His wife was sitting in the kitchen with Linda Johnson, a friend of the family. When Miss Johnson got up to leave, she opened the front door and was confronted by the police, who shouldered by her into the apartment. They made no attempt to arrest her, and she simply walked away, to return later after they had left. They opened the door to the bedroom and made for Mr. White, passing by one of the four men, here called Jake Sharp, who quietly stepped into the kitchen. After the police had arrested the three remaining in the room for the possession of marijuana, they searched Mr. Sharp out in the hall. Finding no contraband on him, they released him.

I was familiar with the pattern as Mrs. White described it when she called my office to tell me that her husband was in jail. The one factor that set this apart from similar cases was the witnesses, Jake Sharp and Linda Johnson. When the police find contraband in an apartment, it is customary for them to eliminate all the disinterested witnesses by arresting everyone in the place and charging each person with loitering for the purpose of using narcotics, if not with actually possessing the stuff. In this instance, we had at last found one case where the witnesses had been left at liberty. The reason, perhaps, was that the arrests were made by patrolmen unaccustomed to searching houses rather than by experienced narcotics police. At Mr. White's apartment the same night, I met his attorney, John Mage, and interviewed the two witnesses as well as the defendants. Mr. Sharp was a welfare investigator by profession, although his avocation was the hippie life. Neither he nor Miss Johnson had any previous criminal record. They seemed to be excellent witnesses, and were properly incensed by the police tactics in the case. They demanded to know how the officers could hope to justify the search under the exclusionary rule, as I had explained it to them.

Since White was charged with a misdemeanor, the police could justify their search without a warrant only by saying that he had committed the crime in their presence. This could have happened in two ways. Either the police, standing in the street, saw one or more of the defendants smoking a marijuana cigarette through the living-room window, or the police, standing in the hallway, saw one or more of the defendants holding the contraband when Miss Johnson opened the door. The second story struck me as the most likely choice, since it was closer to the truth. When I outlined these alternatives, Miss Johnson burst out, "But they can't say that. I was here and Frank and the others were in the bedroom."

The police took the second choice. At the preliminary hearing, conducted by Mr. Mage, they said they were in the building "on another matter." When a girl opened White's door, they saw him holding the contraband and walked in and arrested him.

The defense witnesses were sitting in court. I had instructed Jake Sharp to wear a jacket and tie, and he had painstakingly complied out of his hippie wardrobe. He was wearing a tweed sport coat with a wide psychedelic cravat depicting a sunburst apparently of steel and blood. He did not get a chance to testify, however. From the outset, the hearing judge appeared to be unhappy about the entry into the apartment, and the laboratory report on the marijuana gave him a chance to dispose of the case gracefully. The police testimony had connected each of the defendants with a separate cigarette, but the exhibit from the police laboratory contained only a single package with a small amount of marijuana in it. Since this could not be assigned to any of the defendants in particular, Mr. Mage made a motion to dismiss as to all, and it was granted. The case was decided solely on a technicality, but the entry into the apartment may have influenced the strictness the judge used in evaluating the laboratory report.

After the hearing, I had a few questions for the defendants. I was curious to know their opinion of the reason the police had come in. They thought it was simple. White was known as a hippie in the neighborhood, and his apartment was likely to be identified as a place where narcotics users hung out. Everyone thought that the police had been waiting for the chance to arrest White, and this appeared to be correct since other people in the apartment had been so casually released. Whatever the reason, White's is the classic case where the police had a suspicion which, finding it to be well founded through trial and error, they attempted to cast in the mold of probable cause. This they could do only by saying that the crime, a misdemeanor, was committed in their presence, and for that reason White was efficiently transported from the bedroom to the kitchen door.

If the police had caught White with a large amount of marijuana (more than a quarter of an ounce), the possession of it would have been a felony, and the case might have been quite different. An arrest without a warrant could have been made even if the officers did not witness the crime being committed. The police can make such an arrest upon the word of a reliable informant who has seen the narcotic or bought some of it. When the police do find enough contraband to constitute a felony, they can fall back on the informer to justify the search, but if the contraband is only enough for a misdemeanor, as in this case, they are faced with permitting the case to be dismissed, or contriving to have seen the crime committed.

STREET SEARCHES

While a search like that of White's apartment is not a rare event, and was especially common in the East Village in spring 1967, the overwhelming majority of searches without a warrant are not house searches but searches of the person "incident" to an arrest in the street. These operate so differently from house searches that it is profitable to consider them in a class by themselves.

Searches of the person, in public places, have always been one of the principal ways of enforcing laws penalizing the possession of contraband. When the law makes mere possession, whether of narcotics or anything else, a crime, search of the person is an almost inevitable concomitant. Occasionally, one does see someone holding contraband in his hand or surreptitiously throwing it away. I myself once saw two schoolboys in front of the Criminal Court, passing back and forth what looked and smelled like a marijuana cigarette. But it is apparent that these events are rare, and the most

effective way to police possessory crimes is to dig into people's pockets.

After the *Mapp* decision in 1961, the direct conflict presented between police practices and the exclusionary rule
created a crisis in the administration of possessory crimes
that is not over yet. The first sign of the crisis was an extraordinary rise in the number of "dropsy" cases—in which the
arresting officer's affidavit showed that the defendant was not
searched but had abandoned the contraband, usually by
dropping it when he saw the officer coming. In the years after
1961, allegations of abandonment became the subject of extreme suspicion, first to defense lawyers and ultimately to
judges and prosecutors as well. Mobilization for Youth finally asked a Yale Law School student, Sarah Barlow, to
analyze the arresting affidavits filed at Manhattan Criminal
Court in narcotics possession cases for two six-month periods
straddling the date of the *Mapp* decision. Mrs. Barlow's is
one of the first attempts to study quantitatively the effects
of a constitutional decision on police behavior (including
police testimony).[2] Her records show that the percentage of
narcotics misdemeanors in which abandonment was alleged
by all policemen rose from about 14 percent in 1961 to 31
percent in 1962, and for specialized narcotics police it rose
from 14 to 47 percent. It is difficult to avoid the conclusion
that some proportion of the allegations in the 1962 cases were
totally false. There is some possibility, of course, that the
Mapp decision actually affected the conduct of the defendants rather than of the police, but if this had been true, it
would not have increased the number of abandonments.
Before the *Mapp* decision, it was to the advantage of a culprit to get rid of his contraband if he could do so without
being caught, because evidence found in any search could be
used against him. After the decision, it was much less to his
advantage to abandon the contraband, because (theoretically)
he could not be searched unless there was probable cause
to believe he had it. If defendants were familiar with the
Mapp decision (which in most cases is unlikely), then the
number of "dropsies" should have declined, whereas in fact it

increased. There is no practical alternative to the conclusion that the proportion of abandonment cases rose because the police could no longer admit that they had made searches for narcotics without probable cause, but they were not inclined to forgo the practice entirely.

A second fascinating discovery by Mrs. Barlow was that the total number of narcotics misdemeanor cases dropped off drastically in the same period, about 30 percent for the police generally, and 47 percent for the narcotics police.[3] This suggests that a great many policemen, especially the experts, were unwilling to enforce the laws in violation of the *Mapp* decision. Thus the decision was effective in reducing the number of unlawful searches, but if a policeman really wanted to arrest a defendant—for possessing, say, narcotics—he could find a way to do it. The figures do not indicate that all or even most policemen were lying, but only that a conflict between the police ethic ("he is guilty anyhow") and a rule of law increases the tendency to lie.

While that study was in progress, I was attempting to find witnesses in cases where an unlawful search was alleged, in an effort to establish the pattern of practices current in 1967, six years after the *Mapp* decision.

At first we had relatively few complaints about searches, but in the winter of 1966–67 we were suddenly flooded with them. The reason for the increase is not entirely clear, but it is probably related to the fact that the personnel in the Department's Narcotics Bureau increased 50 percent during the latter part of 1966.[4] Perhaps more important, some of the men in the Bureau began to turn their attention away from the ghettos to new neighborhoods, like the East Village, where the people searched were more likely than ghetto people to complain about the practices of the police. Of late years, as the use of narcotics, or at least marijuana, has become an increasingly casual practice with middle-class people and expatriates from middle-class life like the hippies, the incidence of searches—both lawful and unlawful—which are likely to be reported has inevitably risen. The increase in the personnel of the Narcotics Bureau, combined with its shift in tactics, seems to have produced a "drive" against drugs resulting in hundreds of searches. John Mage, an attorney interested in protecting the hippie life, appeared in night court for many weeks running in the spring of 1967, defending literally dozens of people at a time. Street searches in which some contraband has been taken from a defendant are relatively difficult to study except in the quantitative manner that Mrs. Barlow used, because many such defendants do not want to complain and the witnesses are often unidentifiable passers-by. Two authenticated cases, however, occurred in practically the same spot seven months apart, and they help to illustrate one of the ways the police circumvent probable cause.

Along MacDougal Street, the main thoroughfare of Greenwich Village, there are a number of small shops which sell an assortment of trinkets, all innocent in themselves, but a few of them also useful in connection with the smoking of marijuana (cigarette papers and water pipes, for example). Although it is not a crime to possess such implements, the police occasionally search people who buy them to see if they also possess narcotics.

These shops did not figure at all in the police account of the facts in our cases. In each case, the police swore that they actually saw the crime being committed, by catching the defendant with the marijuana cigarette openly visible in his hand, even though the officers were in uniform at the time of the alleged act. One of the defendants was a twenty-one-year-old Negro college student from Queens, in the Village for the evening with some friends. The officer reported that he saw him in a hallway, passing a cigarette back and forth with another boy. The second defendant was a white student from out of town, and the officer claimed to have seen him carrying the marijuana cigarette in his hand right on the sidewalk.

The testimony of the defense witnesses was equally similar, although neither of the defendants knew the other. In each case, the young man, accompanied by friends, came out of a store with a paper bag, and in both cases the policeman stopped him and searched him in a hallway. In one case the defendant was stopped on the hall stairs, and in the other the police detained him on the street, as he was talking to his friends outside a pizza parlor, and took him into the hallway to be searched.

A small amount of marijuana was found in the possession of each defendant, and in each case a motion was made to suppress the evidence. The motion for the Negro student was won through a classic device of cross-examination, attempted a thousand times but rarely successful. The officer gave the address of the building where he had seen the defendant sharing the cigarette with another; he said he had been standing on the sidewalk and had seen the defendant at the end of the hallway through a glass door. A photograph of the entranceway, however, showed that there was a high stoop of six steps, and that it was quite impossible to stand in the street and look down the hall. The testimony of the defendant and his witnesses, on the other hand, was credible and consistent, and was accepted by the judge.

The case of the out-of-town student was won by a strange method indeed. The defense attorney, an experienced criminal lawyer, put a tape recorder in the pocket of the student's witness, who then had a long conversation with the policeman in the hallway outside the courtroom. The officer gradually admitted some of the facts about the search, and the taped evidence resulted in the dismissal of the charges. More important for our purposes here, it revealed some of the officer's motives. He said that going into a Village shop to buy paraphernalia "sets a pattern," and that his suspicions were further aroused when he saw the student try to conceal the paper bag (which contained cigarette papers) in his pocket.

It is easy to see how the police method works in these cases. The police were operating upon the assumption, first, that shopping in certain of the stores along MacDougal Street was in itself a suspicious activity. Any other odd occurrence, presumably the fact that the student from Queens was black and that the other concealed his purchase, was enough to cause them to make a search. These facts perhaps did not rise to the level of probable cause, but they at least gave the police a framework for investigation.

The searches were not the most serious abuses in these two cases, because the actions of the officers were not totally unreasonable. The shocking element is that the police thought it necessary to lie about the way the searches occurred, in order to avoid the suppression of the evidence.

I suspect that, apart from the falsehood in these cases, many readers do not feel much sympathy for the defendants, and that is the sad thing about all search cases litigated in the criminal courts. The Fourth Amendment has never enjoyed much popularity, because it frequently appears as the champion of the guilty. The late Justice Robert Jackson had occasion to remark upon this phenomenon in a famous dissent:[5]

> Only occasional and more flagrant abuses come to the attention of the courts, and then only those where the search and seizure yields incriminating evidence and the defendant is at least sufficiently compromised to be indicted. If the officers raid a home, an office, or stop and search an automobile but find nothing incriminating, this invasion of the personal liberty of the innocent too often finds no practical redress. There may be, and I am convinced that there are, many unlawful searches of homes and automobiles of innocent people which turn up nothing incriminating, in which no arrest is made, about which courts do nothing, and about which we never hear.
>
> Courts can protect the innocent against such invasions only indirectly and through the medium of excluding evidence obtained against those who frequently are guilty.

Many law enforcement officers believe that Justice Jackson's opinion is of doubtful validity. While they would concede that their reasons for a search may not constitute "probable cause" in the opinion of a judge, they maintain that their experience enables them to detect suspicious behavior that is too subtle to express in a rule of law, and sometimes they do show such expertise.[6] For example, the admissions of the policeman in the out-of-town student's case tend to show that while he shifted the facts of his testimony to fit the formal requirements of probable cause, he did genuinely believe that the defendant had attempted to conceal something.

It is not quite accurate to say that the Fourth Amendment is intended *only* to protect the innocent through excluding evidence against the guilty; it is intended also to protect the "guilty," particularly in the realm of political offenses, from unnecessary harassment. But it is true that the exclusionary rule would be more difficult to justify if in fact illegal searches were always directed against the guilty. If the police really can distinguish the actions of the guilty from those of the innocent, say through the observation of some subtle furtive motion, then there is something wrong with the rule of law. If every search without a warrant were based on some "suspicious behavior" that was an actual index of guilt, then it might be wise to change the definition of "probable cause," at least for searches of a person in the street.

The legislature and the courts of New York concluded in 1964 that the law enforcement officers who were growing restive under the strictures of probable cause were justified; the definition of probable cause was too narrow for street searches. The so-called stop and frisk law[7] permitted the police to detain a person for questioning upon "reasonable" suspicion of certain serious crimes. By its terms, the law did not permit a search except when the officer "reasonably" suspected that he was in danger, but the New York Court of Appeals interpreted it to permit a search virtually whenever an underlying crime was suspected. The term "reasonable suspicion" was admittedly vague, but the court frankly felt that it was intended to afford some scope to that unarticulated expertise of the police.[8] The statute was a further reaction to the crisis created by the exclusionary rule of the *Mapp* decision, somewhat more honest and rational at least than the sudden rash of "dropsy" cases, but similar in the sense that it was an attempt to change the requirement of probable cause for street searches.

This study is concerned with the stop and frisk law only as it was being applied in New York City during 1966 and 1967, but in fact, of course, the practice presents one of the frontier controversies in the administration of the criminal law throughout the country. At least five other states have recently granted the privilege to the police by judicial decision or statute, but it is apparent that its actual practice is much more widespread than this. Many police departments (a field survey of the President's Commission on Law Enforcement listed twenty-seven[9]) have carried on the practice, also called field interrogation, but it never became a legal problem until after 1961 when the *Mapp* case brought the issue of probable cause to the states. As this is written, the United States Supreme Court has just decided that evidence seized in accordance with such laws is admissible at a criminal trial, and in 1966 and 1967, the New York police understandably considered the practice to be authorized by law because the New York courts had ruled that it was.

Despite the furor over the right to stop and frisk as a matter of law, the statute was rarely invoked in New York City during the period of this study, because it was under attack on Fourth Amendment grounds practically from the day a policeman first attempted to use it to justify an arrest for the possession of contraband. Until the appeals were completed, no one could tell whether a conviction upon evidence obtained under the statute would withstand a challenge or not. This is not to say that there were no field interrogations and frisks, but if a search in the street without a warrant turned up incriminating evidence, it was standard practice to try to show ordinary probable cause for the arrest and thus avoid the constitutional problems of the stop and frisk law. For a search which yielded no evidence but showed signs of yielding an irate civilian, on the other hand, the law was quite useful. It operated very successfully as a defense against civilian complaints, because the Commissioner could hardly discipline a man for following a law which was on the books at the time the search was made, whether or not the law might later be found unconstitutional. One of the results of this state of affairs seems to have been that relatively few stops were reported—only 1,142 in a period of two and a half years [10]—for purposes of New York City Police Department records.

I was doubtful at first that any street search could be considered an abuse if the statute was used by the officer as a
justification. It is hard to know just what "suspicions" leading
to a stop and frisk are so absurd as to be unreasonable, and
one is tempted to lay down a general rule that a police abuse
cannot officially occur under such a vague statute. The abuse,
one would be inclined to say, is legislative. In some cases,
nevertheless, it is so obvious that the stop and frisk law has
been used as a cover for an egregious mistake in a search
that we are compelled to consider those cases here.

On November 30, 1966, two young white men employed at
the federal Social Security office in Harlem were driving downtown after work, in a car with license plates originating outside the city. As they were waiting in line to get onto the East
Side Drive, one of the enormous highways encircling Manhattan, the doors of the car in front of them opened. Two men
in plainclothes got out and ran back to them, one on either
side of the car. The one on the driver's side had a revolver
drawn, and demanded that the driver get out, asking, "What
are you carrying? How many times have you been busted?"
As the terrified driver began to roll up the window, the man
pointed the pistol at him. When the young men got out, the
plainclothesmen handcuffed them and frisked them. They
then tried to take the two into their own car, but the driver,
afraid that the men were thieves, began to yell for help and
pull away. The passenger, who had seen full identification and
realized that the men were policemen, managed to calm his
friend. The two were driven away by one of the officers, while
the other officer followed in the young men's car. After parking
outside a station house, the officers searched the car, and conferred over what they ought to do. At last they filled out a
mysterious green form for each of the boys and permitted them
to drive away.

The explanation for the search offered at a hearing on the
complain of the two boys was complex. The green slip
turned out to be a stop and frisk report, called a UF250 in the
departmental list of forms. The UF250 records the date, place,
and circumstances of a stopping by force or a stop accom-

panied by a frisk, together with "factors which caused officer to suspect person stopped." Both officers said that they had first seen the two young men some blocks north of the scene of the search. They were sitting in their car at a corner which happened to be a block away from a house occupied by a narcotics dealer. The policemen thought it odd to see two white men from outside the city stopped in Harlem. When a narcotics dealer walked by, close to the car, their suspicions were further aroused, and they started after the men, who began to drive away. They ran two red lights before they were stopped. The two complainants did not remember stopping at any corner, or running a red light.

Sherwin Goldman, one of our volunteer attorneys, made strenuous efforts through cross-examination to show that the officers' explanation did not hold together. One curious fact was that no summons had been issued for passing the red light. Even more oddly, each of the officers named a different crime as the one suspected; one suspected the possession of narcotics, and the other thought the car was stolen.

More important, from a legal point of view, was Mr. Goldman's contention that many of the actions admitted by the officers were not authorized by the stop and frisk law. One of the officers conceded that he drew his gun after the car was stopped. He said that he was afraid the driver might try to run him over, though he certainly would not have been justified in using the weapon under either version of the facts. Mr. Goldman also argued that handcuffing the complainants, taking them to the station, and searching the car were not authorized under the statute, but in fact those were unsettled issues of law, and the Review Board could not call them abuses.

At the time of the hearing we were amazed at the attitude of the hearing officer, a long-time employee of the Department, who seemed to feel that there was little substance to the complaint, whether it was true or not. The inconvenience, to the complainants, he said, had been slight; after all, there had been no arrest and no injuries, and no property had been taken. This opinion, a most significant bias, he shared with other members of the Department and probably with the two policemen involved in this case. According to the account of the two young men, one of the plainclothesmen had at first threatened to arrest them and had added, rather bleakly, that it was a shame that they would have to lose their civil service jobs. The policemen apparently relented after searching the car, however, and settled for the stop and frisk form. They must have felt betrayed by the complaint to the Police Department. From their point of view, they had done the complainants a favor by limiting themselves to a UF250 when they could so easily have charged them with, say, reckless driving and resisting arrest.

The complaint was found unsubstantiated. In essence, we concluded, it was practically impossible to show that the policemen had abused their power. As long as the policemen were permitted to rely on a subjective "suspicion" rather than on objective facts, how could one hope to show that their explanation was untrue? As long as the limits of their powers of detention and search under the law remained undefined, how could one hope to show that they had exceeded them?

Lest the reader think this case is unique, I may add that practically the same incident occurred a few months later on the Lower East Side, this time involving two teen-agers, a Negro and a Puerto Rican. Once again, these two were stopped at gunpoint by plainclothesmen, pulled out of the car, searched, and taken to the station. The detention was much longer than in the first case, extending to three hours. In the Review Board investigation, the UF250 was again offered as a defense. The explanation given for the stop was that the car was speeding (again, no traffic ticket had been issued), and the explanation for the detention was that the officers thought the automobile registration was defective. The complaint to the Review Board was found unsubstantiated without a hearing.

The Lower East Side produced another extraordinary case in which the UF250 form appeared as the defense. Early in the afternoon of May 18, 1967, I received a call from a young painter living in one of the old tenements. He reported that he had been stopped outside his house by several plainclothesmen in a Volkswagen, who had searched him and then taken his house key and searched his apartment, while he was held in handcuffs in a nearby drugstore. He had then been escorted back to the car and released. As soon as he got back into his apartment he had called the Civil Liberties Union. Eve Cary and I promptly went down to his apartment, but he had set most of his belongings in order by the time we got there.

There was no question that the men had stopped and searched the painter and taken his door key. The superintendent of the building, a middle-aged woman, had seen the officers searching him in the first-floor hallway, and she had heard them ask for the key. The owner of the drugstore had seen him there in handcuffs.

At first this seemed to me a potentially tight case for an unlawful search. The defense given to the Review Board, however, was ingenious, if a little implausible. The plainclothesmen claimed that they had seen the painter come out of a building at the same time as some narcotics dealers whom they were waiting to arrest. They stopped him because he appeared to be part of the group. They said they took the key, not to search his apartment, but to see whether it fit the door of the apartment where the dealers lived; in fact, they denied that they had searched his apartment. I asked by what right they had taken the key for any purpose whatever, and they claimed that the painter had volunteered to give it to them.

This case was handled through conciliation, a special proceeding of the Review Board. It is used when the staff at the Board does not think that a substantial abuse can be established, but that some measure should be taken either to help the public understand the police practice or to improve the practice itself. I usually felt that the cases in my office presented abuses much too flagrant to admit of conciliation, but in this case I made an exception. With the stop and frisk law on the books, it was all but impossible to prove that the police had abused their privilege to search people on the street. Short of the defeat of the law in the courts, which I still hoped for, there was no solution except to require more careful practices under the statute, and the painter and I appeared at the Board's offices to learn what they might be.

At a conciliation proceeding there is no direct confrontation between the complainant and the officers, as there is at a formal hearing. A civilian officer of the Review Board explains to the complainant the reasons given by the police for their actions, and attempts at another session to explain to the officers where they can improve their procedures. In this case, the conciliator said he would recommend that searches be conducted in more privacy, to avoid embarrassing citizens before their neighbors. Handcuffs should not be used, he said, and the detention should be shorter than the half-hour period for which the painter had been held. I pointed out that the insignificance of these suggested improvements in the conduct of such a patently unlawful search revealed how dangerously vague the stop and frisk law really was. I also said it was obvious that the officers were not telling the whole truth: their assertion that the painter's key had been surrendered voluntarily was not only unlikely on its face; it was contradicted by the superintendent who had heard them demand the key. The police, furthermore, admitted that the superintendent had come to the door, and she would surely have been able to verify that the painter lived in her house. But the stop and frisk law was on the books, and despite my objections I could not prove either that the officers' suspicions were unreasonable or that their story was untrue.

The problem in all of these cases was the same: we could not tell what standards were being used in applying the law, and therefore could not assert that any given ground for suspicion was unreasonable. We began to search for standards under the statute.

Shortly before the stop and frisk law went into effect in 1964, the New York State Combined Council of Law Enforcement Officers had issued a policy statement, intended to define "reasonable suspicion" and to act as a guide in the use of the statute by law enforcement officers. The policy statement had this to say: [11]

No precise definition of "reasonably suspects" can be provided, other than that it is such a combination of factors as would merit the sound and objective suspicions of a properly alert law enforcement officer, performing his sworn duties. Among the factors to be considered in determining whether or not there is "reasonable suspicion" are

i. The demeanor of the suspect.
ii. The gait and manner of the suspect.
iii. Any knowledge the officer may have of the suspect's background or character.
iv. Whether the suspect is carrying anything, and what he is carrying.
v. The manner in which the suspect is dressed, including bulges in clothing—when considered in light of all the other factors.
vi. The time of day or night the suspect is observed.
vii. Any overheard conversation of the suspect.
viii. The particular streets and areas involved.
ix. Any information received from third persons whether they are known or unknown.
x. Whether the suspect is consorting with others whose conduct is "reasonably suspect."
xi. The suspect's proximity to known criminal conduct. (This listing is not meant to be all-inclusive).

In the cases of the two Social Security workers and of the painter, it appears that the last two factors were used by the police officers as the grounds for their suspicion. (In the first case, the police had said that they saw the car stopped near a known narcotics dealer, and in the second, the painter had seemed suspiciously close to a group of narcotics dealers.) The causal connection between any possible criminal activity and the factor which supposedly gives rise to suspicion is so tenuous that it begs for a mistake like the ones made in these cases. To have stopped a car near a criminal, for example, is ludicrous at best as a reasonable ground of suspicion.

Quite apart from their vagueness, these standards are extremely subjective. The claim that a person was standing next to another unnamed person is not really susceptible of proof by the police, or of attack by the citizen who is stopped and later complains. The stops and searches described in these cases appeared at first to be inexcusable, but each of them was successfully covered by the UF250 form. I am forced to conclude that "reasonable suspicion" by definition includes many suspicions that are not at all reasonable, and in any case, "suspicion" is such a subjective notion that there is no stop in the street for which the police could not find some explanation that would fit the standards of the statute.

A further difficulty with the administration of the statute is illustrated in the way that the stops and searches were apparently carried out in these cases. Like so much other police work, they were performed in a peremptory and highhanded manner which tended to provoke more or less violent reactions from the citizens involved. Ironically, if the complainants had been guilty of any crime, they might have accepted the search philosophically, but they reacted with fear precisely because they were innocent and were being approached by plainclothesmen.

It will not do to exaggerate the evils of the statute. In the police world, where the most common device to cover a mistake is a criminal charge, it is some comfort to have a procedure which will permit a policeman to account for his search by the less drastic sanction of a stop and frisk. If searches without probable cause cannot be eliminated, there is something to be said for the UF250, which at least reduces the need for false criminal charges.

The stop and frisk law was designed to fill a grey area in the law of arrest and detention. A policeman perhaps has a right, just as anyone else does, to stop a person on the street and ask him a question. The problem arises when the person refuses to answer, and tries to step around him and go on. Does the policeman have a right to detain him? Under the arrest law, it was by no means clear that he had such a right, in the absence of probable cause to believe that a crime had been or was being committed. The stop and frisk law was designed to give him such a right, but as we have seen, the statute was not being widely used during 1966 and 1967. Not only was it under attack in the courts, but the problems it raised for the individual officer were complex. The policy statement for its use was long

—more than a thousand words—and it required a sophisticated policeman to attempt its use. It is perhaps significant that
in the three cases we have discussed, the UF250 forms were
filled out by experienced plainclothesmen from the Narcotics
Bureau. The use of the stop and frisk law was taught at the
Police Academy, in the words of its syllabus, as "a difficult
and unique problem in the law of arrest," which indeed it is.
In the course of Academy lectures I attended, those dealing
with routine problems of patrol, known as Post Conditions,
did not discuss stop and frisk at all. The course did have a
section on "suspicious characters," and the instructors taught,
quite properly, that a patrolman ought to try to find out what
he could about a suspicious person on his beat. One example
of a suspicious character given at the Academy was that of a
man clad in evening dress in a slum neighborhood, and a somewhat less exotic one, given in a study guide for patrolmen, was
"a shabbily dressed youth . . . driving a new Buick." [12] But
neither the instructor nor the book said what a policeman
ought to do if the person under investigation refused to cooperate, and one policeman told me that this hiatus in the law
"leads to some pretty bad arrests." One of them occurred at
a major intersection in Brooklyn during the fall of 1966.

At that time there was a cafeteria located near that corner
which was known as a hangout for narcotics addicts, as well
as for neighborhood people who just wanted a glass of tea. It
faced on a "parkway," so called from the narrow strip of
greenery down its middle which separates the east and west
lanes of traffic and technically is subject to regulations of the
New York City Parks Department.

On October 17, 1966, a college student who lived two
blocks away from the intersection met an old friend in the
cafeteria, and they stayed until it closed. Afterwards, since
the friend lived quite a distance away, they stood outside on
the sidewalk and talked, occasionally pacing up and down a
little. After a half-hour, two policemen stopped them and
asked to see some identification. The two complied. The
police then told them to stand against a wall in a doorway
for a frisk, and the visitor did so, but the college student

refused. They were arrested and taken to the police station, where the student finally submitted to the search, and each of them was issued a summons for annoying people on park property, a violation of park regulations.

The police claimed that the two defendants had been on the grassy strip in the middle of the parkway, and this claim a witness was able to refute; the two had in fact been standing on the sidewalk near the cafeteria. Apparently the summons transported them to the middle of the parkway in order to support the charge of "annoying people." That was a violation of park regulations, but not, at that time, of city or state laws. The arrest, it seemed, had really been made to cover the search, and the police, not having found any contraband and recognizing that they had made a mistake, wanted to impose the least serious charge they could think of to cover the error. At the trial, the patrolman said simply that he had watched the two walking up and down on the grassy plot for half an hour, and that they had got in the way of other pedestrians on four occasions. He did not claim that they had made any noise, or even that they had actively stopped anyone. The testimony was so patently inadequate for a conviction, and it would have been so easy to produce testimony that was adequate, that it seemed likely that the policeman expected and even wanted them to be acquitted. The arrest was sufficient to justify the search; a conviction was unnecessary.

It was just this sort of cover charge that the stop and frisk law was expected to eliminate, and it probably did so successfully in the three cases previously discussed, when the police used the UF250. Before the law was passed, there would have been no way to account for those searches without an arrest upon criminal charges like that on the parkway. This is by no means the same as saying that the stop and frisk law was a desirable piece of legislation. It is true that it removed the need for the police to cover an unlawful search with a criminal charge, but it is doubtful whether it is ever a wise policy to eliminate an abuse by authorizing it.

It is not likely that every stop and frisk in New York results either in arrest or in the filing of a UF250. We received a number of complaints concerning stops on the streets, particularly at the end of 1966 and the beginning of 1967, but in most cases they were impossible to authenticate for lack of witnesses. One complaint of a mass search in Coney Island, for which there were witnesses, illustrates the problems in this sort of case.

We have had occasion before to touch upon the problems of the small Negro ghetto in Coney Island, in connection with the mass police action there in July 1966. By the end of that year, race relations in the community had deteriorated. There was a rise in black nationalist sentiment in the ghetto, especially among teen-age boys, and police detectives, apparently suspecting them of conspiracy, began to question the older people who worked at the Youth Center in Coney Island. On January 9, 1967, I received a call from Rose Winfield, one of the mothers who worked at the Center, complaining that nine boys had been stopped early in the morning, at gunpoint.

That evening my wife Bell and I drove out to the Youth Center. We had seen Mrs. Winfield and many of the same teen-agers as defendants or witnesses in the cases of the previous summer. Some of them had become black ideologues in the intervening five months, and the difference was startling. Most of them had replaced the names by which I knew them with Islamic or African names, and at one point, while I was talking to one of the nine and Bell was talking to another, the young man I was interviewing said, "You're not interested in me, you're interested in that black man talking to your white wife." It was grimly easy to see why the police could have found the young men threatening.

The way one of the older youths told it, they were walking along the street in a group, talking boisterously, when two police cars came cruising by and stopped. One of the policemen said, "Come here," and one of the nine started to run, whereupon an officer jumped out of the car with his pistol drawn and ordered him to stop. All nine were lined up against the wall and frisked. Mrs. Winfield, about a block away, saw the flash of a pistol and the line against the wall. No weapons or contraband were found, and the boys were released two by two, so as to break up the group.

Most of the nine had been arrested before, some of them at the dance in July; if they themselves had not previously been arrested, a cousin or a brother had been. After Mrs. Winfield had made a complaint to the Police Review Board on behalf of the teen-agers, it turned out that their parents did not want to let them testify. They had seen too much trouble to court any more.

It was doubtful whether the case could have been established even if the nine youths had come forward. Naturally enough, no one had thought of recording the numbers on the shields or the squad cars at the time of the stop, and all the policemen in the area, so far from filling out a UF250 form, denied participating in the stop and frisk. It was possible for the Board to have a lineup of all the officers in Coney Island, but even if one of the nine teen-agers had come forward, he might not have been able to identify the officers. This case served only to inspire impotent bitterness in the youths who had been stopped.

I have described here only five instances in which citizens innocent of any crime were searched on the street, but even these few are enough to suggest that the police do not unerringly and by some sixth sense pick wrongdoers for their searches. The grounds of their suspicion do not point with any accuracy toward guilt, and their suspicions are often unfounded, just as are those of the rest of us. The record in other cities tends to confirm this conclusion. One author, very friendly to the use of a program of field interrogations, reports that the Chicago police showed only 3.2 percent of arrests out of a quarter of a million stops, and he himself saw only eleven such arrests in 297 stops.[13] Many authorities on police work will argue that the percentage of arrests is not a reliable index of the value of field interrogation, because it is chiefly intended to act as a deterrent to future crimes. Whether that deterrence is worth the cost in harassment of citizens and its often potentially explosive results is a matter of grave doubt.

The few examples of abusive stops and frisks described here could probably be multiplied in any major city. The practice of field interrogation, with its attendant abuses, is much more intensive in many other cities—Chicago, for one— than it is in New York. The police department in San Diego, California (population about 640,000), has a quota for field interrogations, and in 1965 officers in that city proudly reported 200,000 of them.[14] Professor Herman Schwartz reports that one of his law students who went into a Negro ghetto in Buffalo, New York, in the company of a bearded man, was interrogated eight times in the course of a single evening and was often the target of physical or verbal abuse by police.[15] I cannot report anything as thorough and consistent as that in New York City. On the contrary, all of the cases of street search in New York discussed in this chapter—those in which the complainant was in possession of contraband as well as those in which he was innocent of wrongdoing— show that Department practice on searches during 1966 and 1967 was a patchwork. If evidence of crime was found, the practice was to try to show ordinary probable cause for seizing it. If no evidence was found, many officers followed the old practices of filing a minor criminal charge or denying the entire incident. The small number of stops reported indicates that the stop and frisk law was being used only in a small minority of cases, perhaps for defensive purposes.

SEARCHES OF PRIVATE PREMISES

House searches, as we have seen, present substantially different problems from searches in public places. The stop and frisk law, of course, is not applicable to such searches, and the standards of probable cause are difficult to meet for the search of a house. It is sometimes possible to comply with the requirements through an awkward state of facts, as we saw in the White case of possession of narcotics, but generally, if the police do not witness a crime being committed, they can enter a house only with the use of a warrant, or in the course of making an arrest for a felony. Although the construction of an artificial case for a felony arrest is not unknown, it is unusual. The curious fact is that a great many intrusions on private premises are conducted without any real attempt to establish probable cause. It is a regular practice for detectives to investigate by obtaining access to private places with a bluff, or when the owner is absent, and many citizens regard this invasion of privacy as normal; to this day, no detective story is complete without such an unlawful intrusion. It is in fact one of the standard means of police surveillance, and I myself witnessed a classic example of a search for purposes of surveillance at the beginning of April 1967.

At that time, the Committee to Support the NLF, an extremely militant group opposed to United States policy in Vietnam, occupied a small office a few blocks from mine at the Civil Liberties Union. On the morning of April 5, I found in my mail a letter from Walter Teague III, the chairman of the Committee, which complained that a short plainclothes policeman had shoved his way into the office on March 30 "just to look around." A few days later, two men claiming to be detectives had banged on the door, but it had not been opened. Mr. Teague wanted to know what could be done about the situation. It was a busy day, and by five o'clock that afternoon I had barely begun to think about the problem when the telephone rang. It was Mr. Teague. He said that the police were at the door demanding admittance. He had refused, and he had called us when he heard one of them say, "Get the ax."

I ran around to the Committee's offices and found that Mr. Teague and other members of the group had been unable to resist the gentle blandishments of the officers. The door was open and four or five were inside. As I began to tell them to leave, the tallest man said that Teague had let them in voluntarily. This was patently untrue, since I would not have been there if it were so. Teague pointed out one of the men as the short plainclothesman who had come on March 30, and I demanded to see his identification. He showed it to me and said that he was coming back "every night." The tallest man asked Teague a number of questions. Was this a private club? Did they sell liquor? What was the landlord's name? I di-

rected Mr. Teague not to answer in each case. The man asked
if he could take some of the NLF literature stacked along the
walls, and Teague said that he could not. Then he asked us to
let him into the back room, through a door marked "private,"
and when I said no, he replied, "It would be a shame to kick
it in." I ordered them all to leave again, and they began to
walk about aimlessly, looking at the NLF flags and the posters
and magazines on the walls. I picked up the telephone, called
the Police Department, and asked to talk to the Commissioner.
As I did so, all the officers began to drift out the door. A few
minutes later the Commissioner's investigators arrived to take
statements from me and the members of the Committee.

I later asked Mr. Teague if he knew the reason for the
questions about liquor violations, and he recollected that he
had first seen the short plainclothesman one evening several
months before at a party being given in the office, when the
officer had checked to see if they were selling liquor without
a license. It was easy to picture how the succeeding intrusions
had occurred. The officer, seeing the flags and posters, imagined
that he had stumbled into a revolutionary cell, and he had
come back repeatedly to check on its activities.

I was interested to know what possible excuse could be
given for these intrusions. I was told that the short policeman
claimed that he had seen, presumably during one of his previous unlawful intrusions, a poster in the back room with the
words "Kill the Bastard and all the Birds." He had reported it
to the federal authorities, and *mirabile dictu*, the tallest plainclothesman had been, not a policeman, but a federal agent.
They all suspected that the poster was a violation of a federal
statute penalizing threats upon the life of the President, and
they wanted to get a look at it. It turned out to be beyond the
door marked "private." It was doubtful that such a poster
was a "threat," and quite apart from that, Mr. Teague remembered it as reading "Impeach the Bastard and all the
Birds." The poster was destroyed in a demonstration before I
started looking for it, and I asked the Department what possible difference the wording of the poster could make, since the
men had no right to set foot across the doorstep in the first

place. The Department took the position that this had been too minor an invasion of privacy to support any disciplinary action. The officers did not enter the Committee's offices for personal reasons; they were making a "good faith" investigation of a complaint. They had used no physical force to obtain access, they had taken nothing, and they had made no arrests. This was reminiscent of the hearing officer's reaction to the detention of the two Social Security workers, and I was beginning to see that it was an almost universal attitude within the New York City Police Department. Intrusion simply for "investigation" is such a common practice and so much accepted in all police departments that it is not considered an abuse. In surveying police conduct in 1966 in three other cities, for example, a field survey of the President's Commission found that officers almost never asked for the permission of the occupant before intruding on private premises, and that they had obtained a warrant in only one case.[16]

It was obvious from the officer's remarks that the intrusions upon the Committee's offices were intended to fish for evidence and to harass; the short plainclothesman had practically said as much to my face. This was precisely the practice against which the Fourth Amendment, and the English tradition which preceded it, were directed. As long ago as 1765 a leading English case [17] rejected the use of a vague "general" warrant in a political case very much like this one, where officers of the Crown were looking for evidence of a criminal libel. The fact that in our case the police were intruding on the Committee's offices to investigate a "complaint" made no difference; it is always possible to work up some sort of complaint of a violation of law, particularly one as tenuous as the one used in this case. Tips and other sorts of complaints simply do not constitute probable cause.

Intrusions for political purposes like this one were relatively rare during the period of this study. The search of private premises became almost routine, however, during the intensive 1966–1967 drive against narcotics. On November 5, 1966, the police invaded a fund-raising party given for the much harassed Du Bois Club in Manhattan. The apartment door was apparently unlatched, and several plainclothesmen walked into the party. Witnesses testified that they pushed away at least one boy who asked them for identification, searched a sport jacket hanging on a chair, and cornered the hostess for questioning before the guests, mostly teen-agers, combined to push them out. Uniformed men arrived shortly afterward and arrested the entire party—some eighty-seven persons—for loitering for the purpose of using narcotics, but that story is for the next chapter. This was only the most notorious of many similar raids on parties where the use of narcotics was suspected. In one well-authenticated complaint, the police forced their way into an apartment on the West Side of Manhattan by threatening to get a warrant if they were not admitted. The officers simply walked around the room looking into the ashtrays, and then left. As we saw in the case of the police intrusion into the homosexual party where Gustave Hartman was assaulted, unlawful intrusion and search is one of the forms of harassment employed against outcasts. In the narcotics drive, it was being used as an instrument of harassment in a "cleanup campaign." One officer told me that searches and arrests were being made even when the police knew they could not be supported under the Fourth Amendment; the purpose was for the police to obtain the contraband and get it out of circulation,* while making life difficult for those who possessed it.

Harassment through intrusion on private property perhaps reached its apogee at 622 East Eleventh Street, a hangout for hippies. The most famous of them, for a time, was Ronald Johnson, better known as Galahad, who occupied apartment 11 in the building as a communal pad for anyone who needed it. In the spring of 1967, to be a hippie was a unique losing combination as far as the police were concerned. Hippies were not only outcasts, but outcasts whose life-style was under concerted attack by the Department. Some of them were teen-

* Objects unlawfully seized may be suppressed as evidence, but they will not be returned if they are contraband. The Police Department's Annual Report for 1966 showed over 1,600 pounds of marijuana and 4,337 cigarettes seized.

age runaways, which made them liable to a summary arrest.

Apartment 11, being open to anyone in need, was not quite as private as other private property, and the police took advantage of the fact that the door was always unlocked. The apartment was entered and searched repeatedly until, by the end of April, the occupants were unable to recollect all the intrusions. I was able to authenticate seven in a complaint to the Commissioner on May 9, 1967, but there had apparently been more. It was after one of these, when a flock of young people were arrested, that a policeman at the precinct told the attorney John Mage over the telephone, "These people are bedbugs and should be exterminated." It was easy to see that some policemen simply did not think hippies were entitled, like other citizens, to a warrant.

My complaint to the Commissioner did not appear to make any difference. Officers went right on searching the premises, and on the evening of May 18, 1967, narcotics police staged a massive raid, ransacking the entire apartment. They searched all the people in it and arrested several for loitering.

Shortly afterward we started an action in federal court to enjoin the police from searching persons and apartments and from making arrests in violation of due process of law. It had become obvious that there was a systematic pattern of abuse that would support an injunction on constitutional grounds. The suit was brought under Section 1983 of the Federal Civil Rights Act, which is particularly useful against such massive abuses as our pattern indicated. That injunction was not destined to be granted, but the papers presented in the case were very revealing. An affidavit recounted several intrusions into Galahad's apartment, together with the police raid on the Du Bois Club party in November 1966. The Police Commissioner's sworn reply was most instructive: [18]

(a) There have been a number of entries by police officers into Apartment 11 at 622 East 11th Street in the City and County of New York. These have been occasioned by constant requests received by the police of the 9th Precinct, sometimes from other police departments, but most frequently from parents themselves, to find minors, runaway teen-agers in the "East Village" area of New York City. Usually, the parents themselves have heard that their children are living at Apartment 11 at 622 East 11th Street; they have learned this sometimes through letters written by their children to friends, and sometimes by going through the East Village area themselves, picking up information in coffee-houses and other places frequented by the area's youthful inhabitants. When the 9th Precinct received such a complaint from a parent, a police officer was dispatched, accompanying the parent, to the apartment, named by the parent. The police officer was not there to make arrests or to search the apartment. He was there to preserve the peace, to ensure that no violence occur in the confrontation of an irate parent with any occupants of the apartment. The door to the apartment is open, and displays a "welcome" sign. Anyone knocking at the door is told to "come in". If the minor is there, the minor is simply sent home with his parent. Runaway minors have been found frequently in the apartment.

On May 6, 1967, as a result of this experience with the occupants of Apartment #11 at 622 East 11th Street, police officers requested all of the youths then in the apartment to visit the 9th Precinct Detective Squad offices where a proper check could be made to ascertain if any of the teen-agers or owner of the apartment was the subject of a "missing persons" alarm or a crime. There were then about thirteen teenagers in the company of the owner of the apartment, Ronald Johnson, also known as "Galahad". All of the occupants cooperatively agreed to come to the 9th Squad offices. While they were at the 9th Squad offices, five teen-agers were returned to their parents; the others left. No arrests were made.

The present practice in effect is not to go to the apartment to seek runaway minors, except on a specific complaint of a parent having cause to believe his child is there. Moreover, police officers do not enter the apartment under these circumstances without the occupants' permission.

(b) On May 19, 1967, detectives of the Police Narcotics Squad arrested the persons in Apartment 11 at 622

East 11th Street. The officers had search warrants issued
by a Justice of the Supreme Court, State of New York,
authorizing the search of apartments 12 and 16 of that
building. The warrants were obtained because sales of
illegal drugs to police undercover agents had occurred
in these apartments. In their search of these apartments,
the police found a minor, fourteen year old Rosemary
A——. The girl told them that she had taken drugs both
in apartments 11 and 12 in that building. On the basis of
this admission, the police arrested the persons in apartment 11 as well for congregating together to illegally use
drugs and caused a search to be made of the premises.
The girl, however, refused to identify persons who had
taken drugs with her in the apartment, and the charges
against those persons arrested in apartment 11 were dismissed. . . .

On the night of November 6, 1966, police officers of the
24th Precinct went to an apartment at 251 West 92nd
Street, City and County of New York, after they received
the complaint of a mother of a girl who had attended a
party then in progress at that apartment. The girl returned home apparently under the influence of drugs.
The mother had earlier called the police to say that her
daughter was missing. When her daughter came home,
the mother called the father of the boy who accompanied
her, a doctor, who saw the girl and called the police. Persons at the boisterous party were arrested for disorderly
conduct, as well as the drugs charge.

None of these explanations for the intrusions of the police
constitutes probable cause, and it is apparent that the Commissioner was not really concerned with probable cause.
As in the case of the intrusion upon the Committee to Support the NLF, he inquired only whether his men acted in
"good faith." If they were doing their job by police standards,
that is, if they were really trying to investigate crime, they
would be given the widest latitude. The mere fact that they
violated constitutional rights in the process of enforcing the
laws was not a ground for discipline. A pervasive police attitude about law enforcement, poorly articulated in connection
with other abuses, was being revealed through the problem of
search and seizure.

We had occasion to observe the same attitude at work in connection with police brutality cases in Chapter 3; if the policeman is really doing his job, he is not usually disciplined for an error such as the excessive use of force. However, if the policeman acts out of purely personal motives, the Department feels that his action is not in the line of duty and he may be disciplined. Thus it is that most departmental trials are concerned with matters like the failure of an officer to be at his post. By the same token, when violations of due process are committed for obviously personal reasons, the likelihood of departmental discipline increases. We saw this in the case of police assaults in Chapter 4, and the same rule is applied in the relatively rare case in which an officer intrudes on private premises for personal reasons. In one rather notorious case, an officer was called up on departmental charges for using a search warrant to help an acquaintance, a private detective, obtain evidence for a divorce case against a woman involved in the search.[19] The fact that those charges were made shows how seriously the Department takes abuses committed for personal reasons.

There is a kind of morality in the Department's attitude that a man will be disciplined for abuses committed for personal motives, but not for those performed in the line of duty. This morality, however understandable from a bureaucratic point of view, is dangerous because it means that when there is a conflict between law and organizational goals like "investigation," the organizational goals must come first. Surely this cannot be the proper conclusion for a law enforcement agency.

A further difficulty with the Department's position is that the distinction it draws between duty and personal life is largely artificial. To permit all or most abuses to go unpunished if they are colorably related to a policeman's duties as distinguished from his personal prejudices is to ignore the fact that the two are closely bound up in the policeman's mind. He sees himself as personifying authority, and a threat to him is a threat to that authority. Similarly, when it comes to searches, the policeman thinks his sense of a suspicious situation is superior to the probable-cause requirement of the courts. The Department encourages the policeman to identify himself

with his authority and to make "good faith" judgments which
do not rise to the level of probable cause, either for purposes
of asserting his authority or making an investigation. No doubt
senior officers in the Department believe that these personal
characteristics are useful in detecting and controlling crime.
Beyond that, because the superior officers themselves have
been patrolmen, they are sympathetic to the ideas that an
insult justifies an arrest and that intrusion is a legitimate tool
of investigation.

No doubt the ostensible rationale for the abdication of
police responsibility for the control of intrusions unlawful
under the Fourth Amendment is that such control is the job
of the courts. This attitude is extremely widespread in police
departments throughout the country, and Skolnick has described it as it appears in Oakland, California.[20]

> The worst that can happen to the individual policeman
> for an illegal search is loss of a conviction as a result of
> the exclusionary rule. Superiors within the police organi-
> zation will, however, be in sympathy with an officer, pro-
> vided the search was administratively reasonable, even
> if the officer did not have legal "reasonable" cause to
> make an arrest.

Relinquishing of departmental responsibility to the courts
is acceptable only if the "administratively reasonable" searches
do not lead to intrusions upon innocent people. It is doubtful,
as we have seen, that this is the case.

The Department's permissiveness toward all actions taken
in apparent good faith and in the line of duty is more easily
observed in the case of intrusions on private property than it
is in police abuses on the street. It is possible to keep up a
façade of due process in connection with street abuses, simply
by making them look like legitimate arrests for, say, disorderly
conduct, while the rigorous standards of probable cause make
it nearly impossible to keep up appearances about intrusions
into private premises. The result is that the Department simply
does not try to adhere to standards of due process for such intrusions, while it does attempt to do so in connection with

street arrests. In theory, invasions of private premises ought
to be easier to deal with than other abuses because there is
a clear issue of fact and law; our federal action for an injunction was brought against unlawful searches for just this reason.
The court ruled that there was not enough evidence of a
pattern to justify a preliminary injunction, but the Police
Commissioner did agree to settle the matter by a new order to
his men covering the law of search and seizure. A perhaps
more interesting and valuable consequence was that the
searches at least in Galahad's apartment stopped while the
action was pending.

Up to this point I have not had occasion to say much
about search warrants. Street searches are almost always made
in connection with an arrest, and intrusions into private premises are often conducted without a warrant, purely for investigation, harassment, or the collection of contraband. But if
the police want to enter a house in order to find evidence upon
which to base a prosecution, they will have to have a warrant,
unless they can devise some way to make a lawful arrest in
the house. The process of obtaining the warrant from a judge
is itself open to abuse, in subtle ways that are difficult to
detect.

Consider how probable cause is shown in obtaining a warrant to search for such contraband as, say, policy slips. The
officer usually swears in his affidavit to the court that he has
obtained knowledge of the violation from a reliable informant,
who has perhaps placed a bet. For purposes of probable cause,
the informant need not be named if his reliability can be shown
by some objective means—if, for example, his tips have previously led to convictions. The officer then details his efforts to
corroborate the word of the informant by personal observation.
These two actions, reliable information and corroboration, will
usually support the warrant, and both invite abuses.

The theory behind the privilege to conceal an informant's
name at a hearing on probable cause is that the constant reve-
lation of the identity of informers will destroy their usefulness
and discourage them from giving information.[21] This is per-

haps true, but there can be no doubt that, as Justice Douglas
noted in his dissent in the *McCray* case, "it is not unknown for
the arresting officer to misrepresent his connection with the
informer, his knowledge of the informer's reliability, or the
information allegedly obtained from the informer." Upon this
point, the majority said, "nothing in the Due Process Clause
of the Fourteenth Amendment requires a state court judge in
every such hearing to assume the arresting officers are committing perjury." Nothing in the due process clause, perhaps,
but something, I hope, in these pages indicates that officers
may distort the facts to avoid the exclusion of evidence. The
cloak of anonymity is an invitation to lie even about the existence of an informer, not to speak of his reliability. No one
knows how many "investigative" intrusions by police detectives
have later been passed off as the reported observations of an
informer.

The police have been known to distort the facts about their
personal efforts to corroborate the informer's tip. Surely no
lie is more elusive than this, but on very rare occasions,
through the maneuver of attacking the affidavits which under-
lie the warrant, evidence has been suppressed for this reason.
On January 23, 1967, there appeared in the *New York Law
Journal* the following opinion from Brooklyn Supreme Court:

> *People & C.* v. *John Thomas*—This motion to suppress
> evidence seized in the home of the defendant after a
> search authorized by a warrant is predicated upon
> grounds that . . . the factual matter in the affidavit in
> support of the application for the warrant, but for which
> it would not have been issued, was in fact, false. . . .
>
> The officer's supporting affidavit . . . asserted that on
> May 5 and May 7, 196[6], in the presence and hearing of
> his informant, he made telephone calls by dialing the
> number in the apartment allegedly kept by the defendant
> and in which written records and other paraphernalia
> used in violation of sections 974 and 975, Penal Law, were
> maintained. During the conversations with the defendant
> which thereafter ensued, he asserted in his affidavit, he
> made a number of wagers. The testimony of employees
> of the Telephone Company and documentary evidence
> taken from its files established that the telephone, on the

two days referred to, was disconnected because of the subscriber's failure to pay bills for service and that, accordingly, there was no service into or out of the Apartment. The Appellate Division held in People v. Figueras (NY L.J. February 27, 1964 p. 18/2), that "on the motion to invalidate the warrant and suppress the evidence procured thereunder, defendant was entitled to challenge the truthfulness of the allegations in the affidavit upon which the warrant was issued. False statements of facts in such an affidavit would vitiate the warrant and search" (King v. United States, 282 F. 2d 398).

The bare statement of the officer's informant that there was illegal activity over the telephone referred to and that wagers were being recorded in the apartment in which the telephone was located, does not furnish the required quantum of probable cause upon which to justify the issuance of the warrant (see Court of Appeals decision in People v. Schnitzler, N.Y.L.J. January 16, 1967).

The motion to suppress is therefore granted. Submit order accordingly.

I had a complaint almost identical to this case, another gambling charge in which a motion was made to quash the warrant and suppress the evidence. In that case the defendant proved that he was not at home at the time the officers swore that they had called his number. This complaint was not quite airtight, because someone else could have answered the phone, but it was most unlikely that anyone did—so unlikely, in fact, that the judge granted the motion to suppress.

Many warrants are no doubt issued upon truthful allegations, but they are occasionally executed in a humiliating or destructive way. In one case investigated by Mobilization for Youth on the Lower East Side, the police entered an apartment occupied by a Puerto Rican family under a valid warrant to search for policy slips. The police broke into the apartment by force, either because the defendant refused them entrance or because he asked them to give his wife time to dress. Whatever the reason, when they entered the apartment, the wife was still naked from the waist up and began to scream.

One of the officers had gained access by climbing in a window at the front of the house, and his odd behavior attracted the attention of a young man sitting across the street. He crossed the street and stood on a fence railing to peer in the window. He saw one of the policemen pull the half-naked woman out of bed, slap her, and then sit down with her on his lap and place his hands over her breasts. The second policeman told the first to let the woman alone, and one of her daughters, who had watched the humiliating performance, came and put a sheet around her. Finally, much later, a policewoman arrived, and the woman got dressed and was taken with her husband to the precinct. The saddest part of this tale is that a complaint was made to the Review Board, but it was found unsubstantiated without a hearing.

All the safeguards of due process, all the best intentions of the courts, cannot prevent an act such as this. The courts can do no more than insist that a search be made upon probable cause; only the police can ensure that it is not carried out in a degrading or brutal manner. After the rules are made and the documents are drawn, it is the police who make or break the criminal process. They can destroy due process by distorting the facts, or by simply ignoring its requirements, as they have done in so many house searches. Even if all the other requirements are met and the arrest and search are lawful, such humiliation and brutality as the witness saw from the fence rail are as effective in destroying due process of law as corporal punishment without a trial.

12

SYSTEMATIC
HARASSMENT

IN THE LAST CHAPTER we touched upon police harassment
in connection with the drive against narcotics. Harassment by
searches and other intrusions on privacy is a special case of a
much broader problem in law enforcement; invasion of privacy
is only one of the many weapons used in the campaign against
narcotics and others like it. Let us keep in mind that all the
acts of the police, even when abusive, reflect the prevailing
attitudes in the society, but that this correspondence is particularly close in harassment campaigns. Such a campaign
is not usually undertaken until there is public demand for it.

Unlike most other police abuses, a campaign of harassment
generally has the open approval of the Department, and the
abuses which occur in the course of the drive are actually departmental abuses rather than abuses by the individual policeman. In such a situation the patrolman knows that personal
excesses and errors of judgment committed in the course of the
campaign will be excused by the Department. Participation in
the campaign, so far from raising a doubt about his individual
judgment, is one of his duties. Such a campaign is characteristically directed against an outcast group, whose members are
afraid to protect themselves against the police and who can-

not expect a community outcry in their behalf. The favorite target is a class of petty criminals such as prostitutes or gamblers. Occasionally the police take on a group of noncriminal outcasts such as the hippies, but community feeling about them is ambivalent, and the police may find that the public sympathy is with their target. In the course of the campaign, the customary police efforts to adhere at least to the forms of due process of law are all but dropped, and the individual policeman knows that he is not expected to adhere to them. The Department, or the District Attorney, often makes some effort to restore the appearance of due process by falling back upon the use of vague statutes, which can be applied in a discriminatory manner because their meaning is so flexible. The paradigmatic "harassment statutes" are loitering and vagrancy laws, although the disorderly conduct law, a slightly less vague statute, has been used as well. Systematic harassment, in one or another of its forms, either through vagrancy laws or other means, is a pervasive method of police work in every city in the United States. The leading work on the police use of arrest shows that officers constantly arrest prostitutes, gamblers, and liquor-law violators, and later release them without prosecution.[1] In a city like Detroit, where the Police Department permits arrests on suspicion, the practice is unusually prevalent, but it is not much more difficult to begin it in any jurisdiction which, for example, penalizes loitering or vagrancy.

Because we are accustomed to secrecy in police work, the frankness of the Department in admitting the existence and even the motives for harassment is startling. For example, two devices of very doubtful legality are used in the enforcement of the narcotics and "public morals" laws (gambling, prostitution, and liquor), raiding premises and issuing liability notices, and both are authorized by the written Rules and Procedures of the Police Department.[2] A liability notice may be sent by the Department to the landlord of any place where there has been an arrest for an unlawful business, or where no arrests have been made but "reasonable grounds for suspicion exist." The notice informs the owner that he himself may be liable if the condition is permitted to continue. The procedure frequently results in an eviction, a much more effective tool than arrest for eliminating undesirable tenants in the precinct. A defendant in a prostitution or gambling case is likely to be back on the street after two weeks in jail, but an eviction gets rid of him for good.

While liability notices are commonly sent to the landlords of private apartments, raids are usually made on bars and other public places. The grounds for a raid are the same as for a liability notice: an arrest, or "reasonable grounds for suspicion." After the raid, a "raided premises" sign must be posted, and a patrolman is often stationed inside the premises to prevent "further violation of law." This procedure hurts business drastically at the raided bar, and over the years an enormous amount of litigation has been brought by the owners of such premises. Judges will routinely grant an order, on constitutional or other legal grounds, to remove the sign, but the police go right on raiding premises and putting up more signs. It is plain that the "raided premises" procedure, like the liability notice, is a more powerful tool of harassment than arrest, and the Bar Association of the City of New York has recommended that it be abandoned.

Even more surprising doctrines are taught for the enforcement of the policy and lottery laws. The Department's Rules and Procedures require the maintenance of a file of known gamblers (referred to as KG's). Precinct stations keep a chart, furled like a window shade, which when unrolled reveals the faces of the local KG's. Instructors at the Police Academy lecture on the "blitz" treatment against the KG-of-the-month. He is to be arrested repeatedly, said the instructor in one of the classes we attended. "It's like the bombing we did in World War II. We kept bombing the same city time after time till we reduced it to ashes." It is obvious that the blitz on the KG-of-the-month cannot be conducted within the bounds of due process of law, but the police are open about their treatment of the gambler because they do not expect anyone in the community to spring to his defense. Moreover, it appears that the gamblers themselves are rather chary of opposing the police. Despite the fierce harassment authorized by the Department, I received only a handful of complaints about arrests and searches in gambling cases.

Systematic harassment is primarily reserved for crimes which involve an illegal traffic. These are the "cooperative" or sumptuary crimes, like gambling and prostitution—crimes which have no victims, in the sense that a typical crime of violence has a victim, but on the contrary many willing participants. Although such crimes may involve a widespread and enormously profitable business, the participants who know most about the criminal activity will refuse to testify about it. Under such circumstances, law enforcement officers say, there is no alternative to harassment if the traffic is to be policed at all. Furthermore, the police are often faced by a public demand for immediate action upon a cooperative crime problem like narcotics, and it is then that a cleanup campaign usually begins. In other cases, such as gambling offenses, where there is relatively little public pressure for arrest, harassment is used simply because it is an effective device and the police will not be criticized for using it.

NARCOTICS OFFENSES

We have had occasion to observe how enforcement of the law against possessing narcotics encourages unlawful search, but search alone is not enough to police the narcotics traffic. Officers also make use of dragnet arrests to take people whom they believe to be users of narcotics out of buildings and off the streets. A sympathetic critic of the police who had observed patrols in Harlem told me, "The police have a real problem. They see groups of people standing around on a corner known to be the spot where they make their connection. Some of them may even be nodding. If the police don't pick them up, people in the community complain, 'Why can't these addicts be removed?' So maybe the police pick up the whole bunch and put them in the wagon, just to get them off the street."

Unquestionably the problem which gives rise to the practice is real. Whenever society attempts to deal with any serious social problem like narcotics use through the criminal law, the result is a cooperative crime and a new deviant criminal class. The criminal courts, with their procedural restrictions, cannot cope with the problem, and harassment inevitably begins as a method of control. The neglect of due process, however, invites extraordinary abuses, because a citizen is likely to be arrested any time he is found in circumstances even suggesting a connection with contraband. A principal vehicle for this practice during the period of our project was a statute penalizing any person who "uses, resorts to or loiters about any stairway, staircase, hall, roof, elevator, cellar, court-yard or any passageway of a building for the purpose of unlawfully using or possessing any narcotic drug." [3]

The characteristics of this statute are similar to those of any vague law. It is very difficult to determine what arrests, if any, constitute police abuses under such a statute, because it is difficult to tell what arrests are authorized. What is "loitering," and how is the unlawful "purpose" required by the statute to be proved? The statute is aimed at people against whom there is no definite proof of any connection with narcotics, except possibly previous convictions, or presence in a drug-infested neighborhood. If there is proof of actual possession or sale of drugs, then of course a defendant is not charged with loitering but with the much better defined (and serious) charges of possession or sale. Like most loitering statutes, this one has been used as a means of harassment and control rather than as a true part of the criminal law.

A dragnet arrest under this statute occurred on March 7, 1967, and in a manner characteristic of harassments sanctioned by the Department, the abuse could be authenticated with little effort. It was in fact recorded in a standard form sent by the assistant court clerk to the presiding judge in the Criminal Court (see page 224).

The charges had been dismissed as soon as the fifteen defendants named in this astonishing document were brought before a judge, and a few days later, one of them, Peter Burmeister, found his way to my office. He had been held in the precinct station for five hours after his arrest, locked in a small wire cage in the detectives' room upstairs. The cage gradually filled with the other fourteen men caught during the course

CRIMINAL COURT OF THE CITY OF NEW YORK

Part 1A2, *County of* _____

March 7th, 1967

Charge: Vio. Sect. 1533 Sub. 4 PL

THE PEOPLE OF THE STATE OF NEW YORK
on complaint of

Det. _____

        vs.

Igor Wikul, William Heine, Peter Burmeister, Jose Herrera, Hector Morales, Antonio Bracero, Samuel Torres, Jesus Bracero, Louis Vega, Henry Rodriquez, Rafael Colon, Jose Caban, Pedro Trinidad, Francisco Castro, Michael Arcediano, Jose Rodriquez

TO THE PRESIDING JUDGE

I am in doubt as to whether the facts presented to me in the above case warrant the taking of a complaint on the charge made, as above stated, for the following reasons:

Defendants charged with congregating together (in separate groups) at various locations on Ave. C bet. 6th and 8th Streets at about 2PM, this date, for the purpose of using or buying narcotic drugs.

1–All defendants were gathered together at public thorofares

2–Deponent did not observe defendants commit any overt act

3–None of the defendants made any statement indicating their intent to do so

_____
Assistant Court Clerk

of the day's dragnet, until finally, before they were taken to court, it became impossible to sit down.

Although we wrote to each of the fourteen other defendants, in Spanish and English, we did not receive a single response until Mr. Burmeister himself went out and found one of the men. It was an object lesson in the problem of why it is so difficult even slightly to deter systematic harassment. So long as the police can succeed in directing their actions against petty criminals, there will be no complaints. It is only when the denial of due process of law begins to spill over onto the infuriated middle-class citizen that the abuse becomes notorious.

In Mr. Burmeister, the police had taken on the wrong man. He had once been a technical writer and was then operating a coffeehouse in the neighborhood where he was arrested. After his arrest he tried to go back to technical writing, and the real vice of the statute appeared: he had been arrested on a narcotics charge and that record made it extremely difficult for him to get a job. In the next few months, Mr. Burmeister tried nearly every remedy open to him. In April, he complained to the Police Review Board, and of course, his complaint was found unsubstantiated. It is in the nature of things that no complaint arising out of a campaign of harassment can be found substantiated by the Department. A task force of the President's Commission on Law Enforcement has put its finger on the problem: [4]

> The most complicated situations that arise in current practice are those in which the actions of the officer are clearly illegal or improper but are consistent with prevailing practices of a department. Such practices are commonly found in the police agencies serving large urban areas, where the practices constitute part of the informal response which the police have developed for dealing with problems of a recurring nature. It is, for example, common for police officers to search the interior of a vehicle without legal grounds in high crime rate areas. It is similarly common for police to search gamblers or arrest known prostitutes without adequate

grounds. Since such actions are generally encouraged by superior officers, it is inconceivable that the officer would be administratively criticized or disciplined upon the filing of a complaint. Nevertheless, complaints tend to be processed administratively in the same way as complaints alleging a violation by an officer of administrative policy. As a consequence, the complaint procedure does not serve as a vehicle to challenge and cause a reconsideration of policies which are sanctioned by the department even though not articulated.

In July, Mr. Burmeister went down to the office of the District Attorney to press charges against the arresting officer for abuse of authority. The assistant in charge of complaints refused to prosecute. In fairness to the District Attorney, it must be said that while he might not be willing to prosecute a policeman for making an arrest under the statute, he was equally reluctant to prosecute those who were arrested. He recognized the statute for what it was: a simple excuse to clear the streets. The end result of the combined attitudes of the police and the District Attorney was that the police were making arrests, knowing quite well that no prosecution would ever be brought. I had complaints of more than a hundred arrests under this statute, and in all of them the charges were dismissed upon the motion of the District Attorney. The eighty-seven young people arrested at the fund-raising party for the Du Bois Club in November 1967 were all charged under the loitering statute, and cleared at arraignment after being detained by the police for fifteen hours. Many other youths who had never before been arrested came to us to complain that they had been caught in dragnet arrests at parties when the police, after intruding unlawfully, found one person with marijuana and arrested everyone else for loitering. The charges were always dropped, but the unlawful detention and the unusually damaging arrest record remained.*

The dragnet arrest at a party appears to be an endemic

* Under New York State law the courts do not have the power to expunge arrest records. The Police Commissioner apparently has the power to expunge his own records, and he did so in the case of the 87 persons in this case (*New York Times,* February 27, 1968, p. 45).

abuse in most American cities. Scarcely a week goes by that the headlines do not announce the arrest of several dozen people at a "pot party." If a loitering statute is not available, it is simple enough to charge the whole lot with possessing marijuana. Though the charges are usually dismissed, the dragnet arrest remains of unparalleled value as a tool of harassment. It is the equivalent for private parties of the "raided premises" device used against public places of entertainment.

Dragnet arrests similar to the one involving Mr. Burmeister were part of the Department's campaign of harassment in the East Village, particularly in Galahad's apartment, during the spring of 1967. On May 18, after the complaint about seven previous unlawful intrusions had been made to the Commissioner, the police undertook a thorough search and a mass arrest in the apartment. The search, discussed in Chapter 11, yielded no contraband, but many people in the apartment were arrested anyhow, during a *Walpurgisnacht* of macabre police behavior. There were perhaps fifteen teen-agers sleeping there at the time, and they had all brought a few belongings with them. In the course of the search, policemen emptied their bags, while the young people stood about the room bickering with the officers. After one policeman yanked some beads off the neck of a girl, one of the boys quietly commended him for his courage, and it was then that the officer dared the youth to take a punch at him. When the boy declined, one of the policeman kicked him. One clean-cut visitor from Maine reported that the police took him aside and asked him to take a sock at any hippie in the room. He did not deign to reply. Those arrested that night were arraigned early the next morning on charges of loitering for the purpose of using narcotics, but the cases were dismissed, as usual, on the motion of the District Attorney.

The mass arrest at Galahad's, following so closely upon the case of Mr. Burmeister, at last provoked us to the federal action which was discussed in the preceding chapter. It was to be Mr. Burmeister's final attempt to find redress. The pattern of harassment, using mass arrest and search as a tool, was so widespread that it was obvious the Department accepted it, and no redress could be had from that quarter. The federal action was brought by Mr. Burmeister, Galahad, and others to declare the narcotics loitering statute unconstitutional, and to obtain an injunction against the practice of search and false arrest. The Police Commissioner's affidavit opposing the allegations in the complaint, quoted in the last chapter in connection with the unlawful intrusions into Galahad's apartment, was intended as much as an explanation for the arrests as for the searches. The reason given for the arrest of Mr. Burmeister was as follows: [5]

> On March 7, 1967, Peter Burmeister and fourteen others were arrested in the vicinity of Avenue C and 8th Street, City and County of New York. A detective who saw these persons congregating together around street corners, walking about together, entering hallways knew some of these persons and believed them to be narcotics addicts. He arrested them for congregating together for the purpose of taking narcotics.

On August 30, 1967, the federal court held that the loitering statute was not unconstitutional on its face and that we had not shown enough evidence of its abuse to warrant the issuing of an injunction. Two days afterward (September 1), the entire Penal Law, including the loitering statute, was changed and that made the matter moot. As noted in the preceding chapter, we settled the case for a directive from the Commissioner covering the use of the law of search and seizure.

PROSTITUTION

The public morals laws have always been a difficult and dangerous problem for the police. Prostitution arrests are made by a few hundred plainclothesmen attached to the precincts. For a conviction, the plainclothesman generally has to prove an actual offer by the suspect to perform sexual intercourse. Because it is very rarely that he observes this offer being made to another, most arrests are based on offers made to the policeman himself. Forty years ago, this "vice" work led to some shocking revelations: the police, for example, framed women who would not cooperate with the gangsters who controlled prostitution. Such sensational abuses have apparently been eliminated, but they have left formidable problems of enforcement.

Before the change in the Penal Law of September 1967 and an attendant reorganization of the New York City Criminal Court, prostitution charges were tried in a special part known as Women's Court. In Manhattan, the Police Department itself rather than the District Attorney had acted as prosecutor in Women's Court until May 1967, when the Department suddenly withdrew its lawyers. During the five-month summer hiatus before Women's Court was abolished and prostitution cases were thrown in with other minor violations for trial, there was no prosecutor at all for cases of prostitution.* The judges were faced with the distasteful prospect of themselves cross-examining the defendants, and in a large number of cases they chose to acquit instead. Furthermore, the new Penal Law reduced the severity of the charge; the maximum sentence dropped from six months to fifteen days.

The police received complaints of an increasing number of streetwalkers in the Times Square area. It was rumored that news of the impending reduction in the penalty, together with the lack of a prosecutor in prostitution cases during the spring, encouraged women to come out in the open or even to travel in from other cities. There was a momentary crisis in the enforcement of the public morals laws. The police were faced with a demand from "midtown businessmen and . . . City Hall" [6] for increased enforcement of the prostitution laws, at a time when the tools for their enforcement were particularly inadequate. Thus began a drive against prostitutes that proved to be the classic among cleanup campaigns.

The results were strange. While the plainclothesmen who enforced the prostitution laws continued and perhaps intensified their work, an enormous number of girls during the summer were charged by uniformed patrolmen with disorderly conduct. Part of the reason, of course, was that a prosecutor

* This is not so odd as it sounds. Many other minor charges, such as traffic infractions, are tried summarily without a prosecutor.

was available for disorderly conduct cases. It seems, however, that the prostitution laws would not have been suitable for a cleanup campaign even if there had been a prosecutor in Women's Court. Each prostitution case required a solicitation, and while the plainclothesmen could and did stretch the facts of solicitation to include girls who were merely loitering, they could not pick up very many at a time without damaging their own credibility. More important, the number of plainclothesmen was limited, and it was absurd for a uniformed officer to pretend that a girl had solicited him. It was impossible to have a massive "drive" against the women without using uniformed men and dragnet arrests. The vehicle for the drive had to be the third paragraph of the old disorderly conduct statute, penalizing the act of congregating with others and refusing to obey a police order to move on, whenever a breach of the peace might be occasioned. Prior to the campaign, women had rarely been arrested for failing to move on, but arrests under that section rose from about five a week during the month of May to over three hundred in the last week of August.

It was a well-conceived system. Patrolmen simply ordered women standing around Times Square to move on, and if they failed to do so, they were arrested. Jacques Nevard, then press spokesman for the Department, said: [7]

> It's unprofitable and uneconomic to make solicitation arrests required to substantiate a prostitution charge.
>
> We're trying to sweep the streets so that people can walk without being assaulted by these brazen women, and it's more effective to arrest them for disorderly conduct or loitering.
>
> And, of course, we believe the arrests are perfectly legal.

The problem with the scheme was that no one but the police thought that the arrests were legal. A simple refusal to move on was not enough to make out a case of disorderly conduct. Congregating with at least two others and some act tending to a breach of the peace were also elements of the offense, which was obviously directed against unruly crowds rather than lone women. The police made no attempt to supply these requirements, and the District Attorney's office dismissed the cases without trial literally by the hundreds. By September 22, 1,231 of the 1,316 cases had been dismissed,[8] and the assistants privately expressed their embarrassment about them. Like the loitering statute in narcotics cases, the disorderly conduct statute was being used for harassment arrests without any intention of prosecution.

Some of the judges of the Criminal Court were even more exercised than the District Attorney. Judge Amos Basel said:

> I don't doubt that most of them are prostitutes, but it is a violation of the civil liberties of these girls. Even streetwalkers are entitled to their constitutional rights. The DA moved in all these cases to have the charges thrown out, but in every case the girls were arrested after it was too late for night court so they were kept over night with no substantial charges pending against them.

Some girls resisted the arrests, assuming that they could not be arrested if they did not solicit anyone. In an extraordinary attack upon cover charges, another judge commented from the bench upon one woman's complaint that she had been kicked by a policeman as a result of her refusal to be taken: [9]

> I just want it understood for the record that as long as I sit here, and I am sitting here for the rest of the week, all these cases that are being brought in by the Police Department with respect to girls walking in Times Square neighborhood or anywhere else unless they commit any crime they are going right out the window and everyone that is going to be brought in is going to be paroled.
>
> I don't care if they had a hundred arrests for prostitution, unless they are brought in properly and you have evidence against them, they are going right out of the door.
>
> I don't want any defendants manhandled by anybody in the station house or out on the street.
>
> Officers don't have to protect themselves by adding the additional count of resisting a police officer when they are being illegally arrested.

At first the change in the Penal Law on September 1 brought some slight comfort to the District Attorney, but none to the judges. The revised code contained an expanded and still more impenetrably vague provision against loitering "under circumstances which justify suspicion that [the defendant] may be engaged or about to engage in crime." The District Attorney agreed to begin to prosecute for the arrests if they were made for loitering instead of disorderly conduct. Exactly the same kind of dragnet arrests were made; only the charges were changed. It was a classic example of the way vague legislation lends itself to systematic harassment. When the police are urged to arrest citizens because they belong to an outcast group, there is no way to do it effectively without a law that penalizes "loitering" or "vagrancy."

After October, it appeared that the harassment and the cold weather had driven the women off the streets; the arrests dropped off to almost nothing. Judge Basel delivered the *coup de grâce* to the cleanup campaign on November 9, 1967, when he ruled that the loitering statute was inapplicable to prostitution; the press reported the District Attorney's concession that he was correct.*

The best remedy for an abuse like the cleanup campaign in Times Square, as for any systematic harassment, is an injunction. Those very characteristics which make it impossible to obtain redress from the Police Department tend to supply the basis for judicial action. A pattern of repeated false arrests, when officials admit both the facts of the practice and their motives in pursuing it, creates the framework for a civil rights action. We were ready to attempt the remedy in this case, as we had done in the case of the searches and arrests of the Lower East Side, but we found that the Police Department had been wise in selecting the target for harassment. None of the girls who came to my office was willing to take the offensive against the police. Two girls who had been repeatedly picked

---

* The reasoning is rather technical. The statute penalized loitering under circumstances which justified suspicion of a "crime." Only felonies and misdemeanors are crimes; prostitution is a "violation" and suspicion of a violation is not enough for arrest.

up for disorderly conduct and loitering did come in to complain, but they later jumped bail on those charges and were never seen again. There simply were no plaintiffs for an injunction action. A systematic "blitz" is one of the abuses against which there really are effective judicial remedies, and yet those remedies can be used relatively infrequently because the typical victims of such treatment are unwilling to take any action. It is only when the victims are recent fugitives from middle-class respectability, as occasionally happens in the enforcement of the narcotics laws, that an effective action against the harassment can be mounted.

The complicity of the public in police abuses is most clearly revealed by the continuation of this kind of systematic harassment. In this chapter we saw roundups of suspected narcotics addicts urged by the neighbors and mass arrests in Times Square encouraged by the city and local businessmen. The police engage in the wholesale arrest of pariahs because the public urges them to do so, and because the public will obviously not object to the unconstitutional treatment this inflicts upon the victims of the roundups. And so the public participates in what we have called the police ethic—if a man is "dangerous," that is, if he has a criminal background or is a potential criminal, then he ought to be arrested.

The connection between public morality and the police ethic is less obvious in the harassment of known gamblers, which continues even though the public cares very little about strict enforcement of the gambling laws. In a broader sense, however, public morality is still at work here through the impulse to control social conduct by criminal penalties. Whenever the legislature decides to penalize conduct which has no victim—running a gambling establishment, for example— law enforcement begins to change from traditional patrol and detective work. Undercover participation in the illegal business is the first and most obvious step, but it is too slow, uncertain, and expensive to control conduct as widespread as gambling or traffic in contraband. Unconstitutional harassment of a class of people more or less closely connected with the business becomes an accepted part of police work, either because of direct public demand or as the indirect result of legislation.

Subtle effects upon the personality of the policeman himself have been observed in Oakland, California, by Jerome Skolnick.[10] As the legislature tries increasingly to dictate social conduct through criminal law, the officer tends to define his problems in terms of a criminal class and to find more and more people with whom he comes in contact to be suspicious. "If the policeman's job is to observe deviations from 'normality,' a more rigid definition of normality will make him more watchful and suspicious." Morals legislation enhances the tendency of the policeman to regard members of any outcast group as potential and perhaps actual criminals. Furthermore, the simple increase in the number of crimes and the problems of controlling them strengthens the temptation to look for such shortcuts in enforcement as systematic arrest and search. Finally, the policeman is convinced by the public outcry for such legislation that the press and the citizens care less for the lawful conduct of law enforcement than for the control of antisocial behavior. Policemen are clever enough to know that the impulse to control morality through punishment runs directly against the increasingly rigid protection of due process of law by the courts, and they recognize that any lingering public demand for due process, as compared with the demand for a crime cleanup, must be largely hypocritical. Every new sumptuary crime creates a new class of criminals, and the public as well as the police believe that they must be controlled by harassment.

It is no accident that statutes penalizing ill-defined conduct like loitering are used as tools of systematic harassment. Such laws embody the police ethic that potentially dangerous persons ought to be arrested and that a guilty intention is the equivalent of a crime. They do not require any criminal act for an arrest, but only *presence* in a place where an antisocial act has occurred or might occur. It is this presence against which we have repeatedly seen the police take action. The New York statute which penalizes loitering for the purpose of using narcotics implies that the impulse of the police to penalize mere presence is ethical. By using the statute, the police channel their activities in a direction which is familiar to us: not toward the enforcement of law, but toward the control of a potentially criminal group. Systematic harassment has the same purpose; it sanctions arrest as a weapon against a group associated with antisocial behavior, regardless of whether the members of the group are engaged in that behavior at the time of their arrest. The loitering statute provides a natural vehicle for systematic harassment, because the statute and the harassment alike are directed against the individual and his group rather than his actions. In passing the statute, the legislature makes clear that it approves the police ethic— arresting the "potentially dangerous" man—and the dragnet arrests which result.

13

FIREARMS

ON MAY 11, 1966, a police officer on his beat in Brooklyn stopped a twenty-two-year-old man driving an automobile with Vermont license plates. While the officer was trying to check whether the car had been stolen, the young man suddenly started up and drove off. The officer commandeered a car driven by another citizen and gave chase. The fugitive was apparently a skillful driver and evaded his pursuers for blocks while the officer shouted at him to stop. But as he made a sharp left into another street, the commandeered car cut diagonally across the intersection and pulled up even with the Vermont car. The officer extended his revolver out of the window and shot the driver, who died in the hospital a few hours later.

It appeared that the car really had been stolen; car theft is in most cases a grand larceny, and thus the officer had killed a fleeing felon. The young man's parents were grief-stricken, and the driver whose car had been commandeered, after telling the facts, expressed the opinion that the Vermont car could have been stopped without killing the driver. Yet the facts as he told them did not justify even bringing, not to speak of winning, a civil action under the law as it existed on May 11, 1966. Shooting the driver was not a police abuse at that time because it was authorized both by the criminal law and by the Police Department regulations.

Criminal law and police regulations in this country have traditionally permitted an officer to shoot at a fleeing felon whether he is physically dangerous or not. During the period when this study was conducted, that law was at last changed in New York. The revised Penal Law of New York State, effective on September 1, 1967, provided that an officer could not justifiably use deadly force except to defend his own life or the life of another person against deadly force, or to apprehend a felon who had used or threatened to use deadly force. As a practical matter, this probably meant that an officer might not shoot unless the felon had a weapon and had made some attempt to use it. It was no longer justifiable to kill the driver of a stolen car.

Reformers had long urged a change in the traditional rule, and a task force report of the President's Commission on Law Enforcement recommended precisely the law that the revised Penal Law embodied.[1] The traditional rule was at best grotesquely illogical. Capital punishment was not authorized for all felonies, and most particularly, it was not authorized for the crime of escaping from custody. It is impossible to see why it should be permissible to execute without trial a man who could not have been executed after trial. Of late years, the traditional rule has become even more absurd because capital punishment has been abolished in New York except for the extraordinary cases of murder of a police officer, or murder by a prisoner serving a life sentence. Even before capital punishment was abolished, in 1965, public agitation had made it increasingly difficult to execute a man under due process of law. Only one execution pursuant to a death sentence took place in New York in 1964, and yet in the year after July 1, 1964, twenty-seven people were killed in justifiable homicides by New York City policemen (in the same period, three police officers were killed by citizens).[2] The law cannot authorize such a large number of summary executions while permitting virtually none by due process of law.

Quite apart from these considerations, some curb on the use of firearms was obviously necessary in New York and elsewhere. Police killings, whether justifiable or not, have been one of the most important sources of ghetto animosity toward the police; in 1964 the shooting of a suspect touched off an enormous outburst of anger in Harlem. Failure to institute a reform, long overdue, which might help to prevent even one of these uprisings would be the worst sort of legislative irresponsibility. As Police Commissioner Howard R. Leary remarked: [3]

> . . . permitting the police to shoot suspected criminals, who are not a danger to life and limb, would, I believe, not only increase the risk of riots in sensitive communities, but also subtly increase the tolerance of—indeed glorification of—violence which is a significant problem in our society. (Similarly, one must consider the effect of killing someone upon the police officer involved. Our department has had to retire men or reassign them to non-patrol functions because of emotional problems caused by having been the killer in a situation that was technically a justifiable homicide under the traditional rule.)

Despite the logic and the necessity for this elementary reform, opposition to any restriction on the police use of firearms has been growing. As this is written, a bill to again expand the right to shoot has passed in the state legislature. Throughout the country, in the wake of three years of violent ghetto uprisings, a repressive wave is growing out of the impulse to put down unarmed looters by shooting to kill. Restrictions on the use of firearms are being rejected and, in New York, even repealed. This legislative wave tells us again, if we need to be reminded, that it is hardly reasonable to ask the police to change when society is demanding that they remain the same.

Strictly speaking, the last few pages of the present chapter have been out of the mainstream of this study. It has never been my purpose to quarrel with the laws so much as to get at the abuses in the way they are administered. The law governing the use of deadly force has been discussed here at some length, however, both because it is an important, changing issue in police work and because a grasp of the law as it was during 1966 and 1967 is essential to understanding its aberrations.

It is impossible to do more than sketch the nature of the problem here, because the use of firearms is one of the most difficult police actions to investigate. It is hard enough to document cases where officers have drawn their pistols without authorization, let alone those where they have fired them. Every effort is made, not only by the officers but by the city itself, to explain away any use of firearms, because the consequences—personal, political, and financial—can be extremely serious. Even if a policeman's use of firearms is not followed by a major civil disturbance, there may still be a civil damage suit or a grand jury investigation. The complaints that I have received are difficult to authenticate, but they suggest that whenever a citizen is killed by an officer, there is a tendency to supply the elements that will justify the policeman in shooting at him.

One evening in the summer of 1966 (when it was still justifiable to shoot any fleeing felon), police attempted to stop three teen-agers in a car after they had run through a stop sign. The driver instead stepped on the gas, and the officers, supposing the car to be stolen, gave chase. The car finally crashed into the center rail of an elevated highway, and the boys fled, jumping over the edge of the road onto a ramp. A patrolman shot down the ramp and killed one of them, claiming that the boy had cut him with a knife in the effort to escape. The car, as it turned out, had not been stolen, but lent by an uncle of one of the boys.

The curious twist to this case was a telephone call to our office from two witnesses. They had watched the crash from an apartment overlooking the highway, and listening to a radio broadcast afterward, they realized that it did not describe the facts as they had seen them. The witnesses had watched the boys jump out of the car and run across the road, and had seen a patrolman shoot at them as they ran down the ramp. They did not see any physical struggle between any of the boys and a policeman, and they did not think the gap between the boys and their pursuers was ever smaller than ten feet. These two were the most disinterested of witnesses, because they knew nothing about the teen-agers at all. They called the Civil Liberties Union simply because they could not decide where they ought to report their observations.

Any conclusions about this case must be tentative, because a civil suit brought by the dead boy's parents through a private attorney is still pending and will probably remain unresolved for several years more. It is characteristic of cases where there has been a killing, not only that it is difficult to determine the facts, but that the investigation and subsequent lawsuit are extremely protracted. It is not really possible to complete such a case in two years, the period allocated for this study, but even from the fragmentary evidence that we have, it appears that the police may have distorted the facts in this case to justify the shooting. The likelihood of such distortion implies that reforms in the law governing the use of deadly force will some-times be evaded, even when the legislature can be induced to accept them. Such reforms are still useful, however, because, as we saw in the case of the exclusionary rule (Chapter 12), many officers will comply with the rules in a straightforward manner.

Such reforms would be more effective if they restricted the occasions upon which officers were authorized to draw their weapons without firing them or even intending to fire them. Somewhat surprisingly, there is no such restriction. There is nothing in the law or in police regulations, either in New York or anywhere else so far as I can discover, which prevents an officer from drawing his pistol when he would not be au-thorized to shoot it. The most widespread if not the most serious abuse of firearms is in drawing the weapon unnecessarily; for every time it is fired, the gun is probably drawn many times. In previous chapters we have considered a number of cases where the gun was used as an instrument of arrest, or worse yet, of mere detention. In the case of the Social Security em-ployees stopped while driving through Harlem, for example (Chapter 11), one of the officers admitted that he had drawn his pistol, and no one in the Department seemed to find this

in the least surprising. It is obvious that the purpose of drawing the weapon in such cases is to "get the drop" on the suspect,
to prevent him from running away or assaulting the officer. In
short, the gun keeps the suspect quiet, and from the policeman's point of view it probably appears to make his job easier.
From the citizen's point of view, of course, such indiscriminate
use of guns is terrifying. It is a serious defect in police practices, and as long as there is anything like a stop and frisk law,
there certainly should not be a privilege to conduct the stop
at gunpoint. Mere suspicion cannot justify such a serious, ag-
gressive action against a citizen. Moreover, officers occasionally
show poor judgment in drawing their revolvers, just as they
do in stopping and frisking people. Sometimes, as we have
observed in previous chapters, policemen point a gun at a
crowd simply in the hope that it will not become unruly, and
sometimes—though relatively rarely—the gun goes off.

One reason that the use of the pistol as a tool of arrest is
broader than its use as a weapon is that law enforcement authorities feel an officer ought to have considerable discretion
for an arrest in a "tight spot." When a policeman is arresting
an unwilling prisoner or trying to extricate him from a hostile
crowd, he should not have to wait for an assault that is serious
enough to warrant his shooting someone before he draws his
pistol.[4] As a practical matter, this problem is usually not so
difficult as it seems at first, because it is easy to summon assistance, and in fact my experience in this study indicates that
officers arrest recalcitrant and disorderly prisoners every day
by calling for assistance and without drawing their revolvers.

There is perhaps a second reason, in the minds of law enforcement officials, why the right to draw and the right to fire
a pistol are not commensurate. Policemen envision situations
where they face unknown dangers; for example, officers may be
ambushed as they break into a house to execute a warrant or
to make an arrest. This is a real problem, but it is far away
from the point. There can be few objections to police going
into a blind situation with guns drawn; the abuse has to do
with drawing the weapon on an obviously unarmed man simply
for purposes of detention. Neither of these reasons, in fact,

appears sufficient to justify such an action, and it would be a small but valuable reform to restrict the use of firearms by policemen to situations either where the men would be clearly justified in using them, or where the circumstances are undeterminable (entering a darkened house, for example). In other situations, the balance ought to fall on the side of the citizen's freedom from intimidation by weapons.

OFF-DUTY USE OF GUNS

One of the most controversial of the rules of the New York City Police Department provides that: [5]

> Members of the force shall carry their regulation service revolvers at all times, except that any Colt or Smith and Wesson revolver designed to shoot the .38 special cartridge may be carried:
> a. When assigned to detective or plainclothes duty.
> b. When assigned to desk duty.
> c. When off-duty and not in uniform.

The use of firearms by off-duty policemen presents all the dangers discussed earlier in this chapter, including the tendency to stop suspects at gunpoint and to tailor the story of any shooting to fit the legal requirements, together with the additional danger that the pistol may be drawn in some purely personal, off-duty dispute. This is probably rare, but it unquestionably does occur.

Such encounters occasionally lead to a complete misunderstanding; when the officer is unidentified, the citizen may imagine that he is faced with a murderer or a thief. In one case, two hospital attendants were driving across a bridge from Manhattan to the Bronx on an evening in October 1966, when another driver cut recklessly in front of them. At the next red light, both drivers began to argue, and got out of their cars. The second driver was seen to open his jacket and put his hand on a gun, whereupon the first jumped back into his car and started down the boulevard, blowing his horn in the hope of attracting the attention of the authorities to the presence of a madman. When a police car finally did stop the other driver, the hospital orderly was amazed to see him show police identification. He was still more astonished to receive a summons for, among other things, blowing his horn without cause. The charges were dismissed at a five-minute trial in traffic court, when the officer admitted, in response to a question from the bench, that it was the defendant who had stopped the police car.

At times, the appearance of the off-duty revolver in personal arguments conjures up one's worst fears about the possible abuse of weapons. On April 27, 1966, three men in their twenties who had been to school together—one of them was then a graduate student working as a welfare investigator—went out to a party. Late in the evening, they stopped at a bar on West Nineteenth Street. It was in a drab industrial neighborhood only two blocks from my office. All three drank several beers and fell into conversation with the regulars of the place. One of them identified himself by name as a police detective. He questioned them about their political views, and finding them to be generally liberal, he asked if they had ever had any trouble with the FBI. He was particularly interested in the most noticeable of the three, who was six and a half feet tall, with bright red hair. He kept trying to find out whether the young man, whom he called "Red," had ever been in trouble. The policeman began to mutter about "taking care of Red," and the bartender finally asked the three young men, in a low voice, to leave, but it was too late. The detective followed "Red" onto the street, staggering slightly, and the other two came anxiously after. They looked on, frozen, as the detective drew a gun and said, "I'm going to take care of you, Red." The young man went gingerly back to the bar, but when he tried the door, he found that the bartender had prudently locked it and turned out the lights. The detective finally put the gun in his pocket, then took "Red's" arm and marched him to the avenue where, to their immense relief, the young men were able to stop a passing squad car. Red was taken in the car to the precinct, while the other two walked. In the detective's room upstairs, the detective began to question them, but other officers intervened and finally permitted all three to leave.

Admirable officers that they were, they made no attempt to "cover" the acts of the detective by an arrest.

"Red" and his two companions came to my office two days later, and a complaint was filed with the Department. It was followed by a number of interesting developments. First, the detective was demoted to patrolman by the simple fiat of the Commissioner and without a hearing. The status of detective is granted solely at the pleasure of the Commissioner, and it is not subject to the state civil service law. Thus a detective can be demoted without a hearing, while a sergeant, lieutenant, or captain cannot. Reduction to patrolman status, resulting as it does in a substantial cut in pay, is a very severe penalty in itself. Furthermore, no other punishment could be imposed against the officer as a patrolman without the hearing required by the civil service law. The case was sent to the Deputy Commissioner for a trial without any preliminary proceedings at the Review Board, a sure sign that the case against the officer was strong.

The departmental trial was unusually simple, yet effective. The tall redhead who was the chief complaining witness was not there to testify; he was not even in New York City. Under direct questioning by the police prosecutor, the two other witnesses, young, respectable, and credible, briefly recounted the events which took place inside the bar and afterward. The policeman did not take the stand to deny the allegations, and in fact there were some aspects, even of the cross-examination of the two young men, that the defense lawyer seemed to neglect. For example, he made no attempt to determine whether the boys had egged the officer on to perform some violent act and in effect had thus entrapped him. I do not maintain that such evidence would have excused the act of drawing the pistol, but only that it was worth exploring by the defense to mitigate the penalty. In the end, the charges of pointing the gun and taking the chief witness to the station house without just cause were sustained, and the officer was suspended for ten days in addition to the original penalty of reduction in rank.

This case provides a lot of food for thought when it is compared with other departmental trials. It resulted in swift and

yet comparatively severe discipline, although the chief prosecution witness did not appear and only a token defense was
entered. Many other cases, apparently as strong, did not even
get to trial, and if they did, yielded little result. Although the
respectability of the victims undoubtedly had some bearing
on the outcome, it could not have been determinative, because
other cases with middle-class witnesses and victims have been
dismissed. The determining factors in this case seem to be
three. In the first place, the dispute was purely personal. It was
not the typical street situation, where the officer is trying to
put a stop to a disturbance or at least responding to defiance.
Those are situations where, as we have repeatedly observed,
the Department tends to be lenient because the officer is at
least asserting his authority in a threatening situation. Second,
the officer did not attempt to transform the situation into a
disturbance by making a cover arrest for disorderly conduct
or for anything else. Once again, unhappily, the moral from
the policeman's point of view is that he should have made
that arrest. Finally, in this case a pistol rather than a fist or
club was misused, and that is a serious complaint indeed.

At last we are left with the conundrum which so often faces
us in police abuses: Why did the officer do it? Here, we have
a little more information than usual. It seems that he had been
to a rally that night to support United States policy in Vietnam.
He was so exasperated to see young men out of uniform, and
probably opposed to the war, that he became argumentative.
Belligerence is not enough, however, to explain his suspicions
about the young men, his apparent belief that they were connected with some criminal activity. To understand those
suspicions, we perhaps need to know something about the ingrained habits of a lifetime of investigative work, combined
with the insularity of the policeman's existence. Arthur Niederhoffer, now a sociologist but formerly a policeman, has suggested the results: [6]

> A good detective must be suspicious; he needs the
> intuitive ability to sense plots and conspiracies on the
> basis of embryonic evidence. Specially trained experts in
> the Los Angeles and New York City Police Departments

use computers to perform factor analysis on data obtained
from seemingly unrelated crimes, attempting to detect a
pattern indicative of some vast conspiracy. The existence
of syndicates like the Mafia and Cosa Nostra does much
to convince the police that their vigilance alone prevents
such organizations from destroying the United States.
Suspicion becomes second nature to many policemen.
Cynical as they are, they can at the same time be very
moralistic about others' behavior. Their common complaint is that "nowadays there is no respect for law and
order." Projectivity makes them enemies of Communists
and unspecified "do-gooders." At the same time it
strengthens their attraction to reactionary political groups.

Though the genesis of the abuse in this case may be extraordinary, what is utterly unique in my experience is the
fact that the off-duty officer identified himself, so that disciplinary action could be taken. In another, almost identical
case, I was told that there had been an argument in a bar, one
of the parties had pulled a revolver, and both had backed off
hastily. After they left, the bartender had said that the armed
man was a policeman, but the bartender could not be induced
to remember anything about the incident afterwards.

It is difficult to draw any final conclusions about the use
of firearms from the evidence presented in this chapter, because the law has been in a state of flux during the entire
period of this study. It may change yet again before these
words are published. It is not clear how successfully reforms
in the law regarding the use of deadly force by the police can
reduce the number of people killed by policemen. Even before
revision of the law was attempted, most police shootings were
justified upon the ground that the action was taken in response
to an immediate threat of deadly force from the citizen.
Twenty-five of the twenty-seven justifiable homicides by policemen recorded in the year after July 1, 1964, were explained by
the Department in this way; they would have been justified
under any conceivable revision of the law. It is equally clear
that no revision has had the effect of limiting the indiscriminate
use of weapons for stops and arrests. This is not so much the

fault of the legislature as of the Department, which could and should issue regulations forbidding the use of weapons for arrest or detention except under circumstances when they might lawfully be fired. Finally, if we wish to effectively reduce the chances of abuse either in drawing or firing weapons, we are going to have to recognize that the situations in which guns are carried, especially off duty, must be limited.

14

REMEDIES
AND FAILURES

ALL THE AGENCIES which affect redress for police abuses—
the man on the beat himself, the District Attorney, the courts,
and the Police Department—have been considered in the past
chapters. For the most part, I have emphasized the nature of
the abuses, and the remedy, or lack of it, has been included as
part of that story. The most basic point in this book is that
the pattern of police abuses continues because, for a number
of reasons which will be more fully explored in the last chapter,
most people in our society do not wish to change the pattern.
If they really wanted change, they could exert enough pressure
on the agencies of the legal process to bring it about. Before
we go on to that more general point, however, we must survey
more carefully how those agencies work, and how they might
work better to give redress to the citizen.

THE MAN ON THE BEAT

The police themselves are the most formidable obstacle to
redress for police abuses. An arrest, together with the necessary
testimony, is used to cover almost all street-corner abuses. The
testimony is usually effective in covering the abuse for perfectly
natural reasons—for example, because there is no one in

court to contradict it except another policeman, and he will not do so. The graded structure for advancement in the Police Department, together with its tradition of hostility to outsiders, tends to create almost complete solidarity up the police chain of command. This protects any individual officer from criticism, even by people higher up in the chain, and it reinforces the effectiveness of cover charges and other obstacles to redress, simply because substantially all policemen share similar values and because they are forbidden by their code to betray one another's mistakes.

These are characteristics which the New York City Police Department shares with every other urban police department in the country. The habit of covering an error by an arrest and the obligation always to back up another officer are familiar traits of all policemen, and have been as long as anyone can remember. To a startling degree, the obligation at least to back up a fellow employee is also common to other bureaucracies with a vertical system of advancement. I saw this obligation broken once, for example, in the Transit Authority, when a Negro subway conductor protested the way in which a white transit policeman was treating some Negroes on a subway platform. The conductor was fired by the Transit Authority, and tried and convicted on a criminal charge of obstructing an officer. At that price, only the most heroic will break the code.

The police themselves, then, block the road to most other remedies, even before other institutions intrude. The resourcefulness and solidarity of the police in covering an abuse is always the most startling and disappointing aspect of police misconduct for the uninitiated citizen who is arrested. It often destroys any lingering faith in the process of justice as a whole, as well as in the police.

THE DISTRICT ATTORNEY

The next hurdle along the road to redress is the office of the District Attorney. It is the DA who has the greatest power, outside the Department, to curb police distortions of fact, as well as to scotch at least the cover charges in police abuses.

The prosecutor has the power to decide whether the testimony of the police is so inherently fantastic as to preclude a good-faith prosecution; he has the even greater power to decide whether the defense is so strong as to preclude the likelihood that the police story is true. By refusing a prosecution, the District Attorney brings the most effective of sanctions against the police. Such a refusal is likely to bring reform in police practices more quickly than any other device.

During the two years of this study, the office of Frank Hogan, the Manhattan District Attorney, was moving in the direction of reform, as we observed in connection with the cases of criticism of policemen (Chapter 6). At the close of 1967, some of his assistants were willing to go much further than they had been in 1965 in trying to find out whether a prosecution was being brought in good faith. Mr. Hogan's office, however, is the only one which has made any use of its potential for reform. The District Attorneys and their assistants in Queens, the Bronx, and Brooklyn are notably less sensitive to the issues. Their style continues to be one of cynical scoffing at allegations of police abuse. This is a shocking attitude for the public prosecutor to take; his job is to find out the truth, not to put defendants in jail indiscriminately.

The power of any district attorney to protect the police and perpetuate abuses is nearly as great as his power to eliminate them, and unfortunately most prosecutors in the United States have chosen to side uncritically with the police. They use an arsenal of weapons against civilian complaints, extending from the extraction of releases in return for dismissing cases up to the prosecution of citizens for making "false" complaints against policemen. All in all, with the exception of the Manhattan office, few prosecutors have shown any inclination to use their public powers to control police abuses.

THE COURTS
CRIMINAL TRIALS

The role of the courts in blocking redress for police abuses has not been much emphasized in past chapters. In general, I have tried to use as examples those cases which were successfully defended in Criminal Court, treating the courts as a sort of neutral medium, a window into the workings of the police. Nevertheless, the courts do play an important role in protecting the police from criticism. It is the job of the trial courts to find the facts upon the cover charges brought by the police. They have the power to shield police officers from effective complaints by citizens, and they use it all too often. In the ordinary assault case, where a police officer is not a complainant, a judge is perfectly willing to listen to the defense that in fact it was the complainant and not the defendant who committed the assault. Such cross-complaints are entertained all the time. But when a police officer is the complainant, a defense based on police abuse is not so hospitably received, because the defense is an attack upon the authorities. The judge sees in it an effort to impeach a witness, the policeman, upon whose credibility he is compelled to rely in thousands of cases. Beyond that, to grant credence to a defense based upon such abuse is to open the door to a civilian complaint and perhaps to a suit for damages. If the judges seem doubtful about defenses based upon police abuses, the reader can imagine their reaction to an attempt to prosecute a police officer. Police officers prosecute citizens for assault as a matter of course, but I have yet to see a citizen take out a summons against a police officer for assault and get his case to trial.

The situation should not be exaggerated; there is no doubt that many courageous judges can transcend any "official bias," as the cases in this book have demonstrated. It is equally clear, however, that it is unduly hard to win a criminal case when the defense involves criticism of a police officer. The fact that I have found the office of the prosecutor a more hopeful center of reform than the judiciary in New York City is perhaps a measure of how difficult the situation can be.

Outside of New York City, the situation in the urban trial courts is undoubtedly worse. The quality of the judiciary in the lower courts is poorer, and the official bias is even more ironclad. One of the few benefits accorded by the sheer volume of criminal cases in New York City is that there are a large number of judges. The defense lawyer does not face the prob-

lem he does in a small town, where there are but few magis-
trates and he is at the mercy of their prejudices.

An important difference between the procedure for misdemeanor cases in New York and that in many other cities is
that the quality of defense for the indigent in New York is
better, if only by default. In New York City, a poor defendant
facing a trial for any offense that might result in a jail sentence
always has either a lawyer from the Legal Aid Society or one
appointed by the court. Incredible as it may seem, some of the
largest cities in the country—Baltimore, Detroit, and Chicago,
for example—conduct the greater part of their misdemeanor
trials without defense counsel, and for that matter, frequently
without a prosecutor. This means that many of the criminal
cases recounted in this book, if they had occurred in other
cities, would have been tried without defense counsel. The
trials which result from such practices are a travesty of
justice.[1]

Defendants in most jurisdictions outside New York City
have one potential advantage in avoiding the consequences of
official bias: they are entitled to a jury trial in misdemeanor
cases. In police brutality cases, this right can be extremely
important, when the defendant is charged with assaulting a
policeman and the judge has a bias in favor of the police. The
jury cares something, but less than the judge on the whole,
for protecting public officials in cases where an obvious error
has been made. The right to a jury trial, however, is utterly
worthless if the defendant does not have a lawyer, and in fact
this right is usually waived in misdemeanor trials outside New
York City simply because the quality of defense is often so
poor.

APPELLATE REVIEW

The right of appeal is relatively ineffective in reviewing decisions of the lower courts in cases where police abuses are alleged. In most such cases, there is a sharp conflict of fact
between the defendant and the police officer, and when that
conflict has been resolved against the defendant by a trial
judge, it is very rare that his judgment will be reversed by

a higher court. Out of five cases appealed in connection with this study, only one was reversed, and that was done with the consent of the District Attorney. The situation is much the same in all jurisdictions. Federal Judge J. Skelly Wright, formerly of the Fifth and now of the District of Columbia Circuit, has emphasized the role of the appellate courts in controlling police misconduct by rejecting incredible testimony,[2] but he is the exception. Most appeals courts are reluctant to become involved in disputes with the trial courts over questions of fact.

Because of their limited powers to review the facts, appellate courts, especially the United States Supreme Court, have established rules of law intended to limit the discretion of the police and reduce the incidence of police abuses. The *Mapp* rule excluding unlawfully seized evidence was one of the first and most effective of these. The rules requiring the police to warn defendants of their rights before interrogating them or subjecting them to an identification lineup are partly intended to bring an outside observer, in the form of a lawyer, onto the scene as quickly as possible.

With the exception of the exclusionary rule, most of these rules have little effect on the street-corner abuses we have considered in this study. If the police have roughed up a "wise guy" and charged him with disorderly conduct and assault, rules governing confessions and identifications make very little difference. There is, however, one judge-made rule in some states which is of some importance for street-corner cases: the rule that reasonable resistance to an unlawful arrest is not a crime. I emphasize it here because it is the least known of all protections for the defendant. Very often there are witnesses to the incident in the street which is the basis of the arrest, and they are in a position to testify to the defendant's conduct as well as to that of the police. The prevailing rule (formerly in effect in New York) makes it possible for the accused to defend himself against cover charges of disorderly conduct and assault, for example, by showing through witnesses that there has been no disorderly conduct. Without this rule, the idea of an unlawful arrest becomes meaningless, because the police can sooner or later find a way to arrest anyone they like. The more outrageous or abusive they are in originally stopping a citizen, the more likely they are to provoke resistance, and any such resistance, even pulling one's wrist away from the handcuffs, becomes a misdemeanor.

Apart from these purely practical considerations about the value of witnesses and the likelihood of abusive arrests, the common-law rule seems in principle to embody a wise policy. It would be shocking to permit a citizen to be convicted of a crime just because he had refused to submit to a highhanded arrest. Even under the present rule, the police system of cover arrests produces a catastrophic contempt for the legal process. If the courts could convict a man even on those rare occasions when he might have proved through witnesses that he was unlawfully arrested, the situation would deteriorate still further. There is no more certain way to encourage hatred of the judicial process than by making it unlawful to resist official abuse, and it seems most unwise for a democratic society to kill by law the impulse in its citizens to resist such abuse. While it is true that resistance often leads to grief for the resister, to make that resistance criminal will only cause people to fear the courts as they now fear the police.

Fantastic as it may seem, the common-law rule has been abolished in many states, and on March 6, 1968, it was abolished by the New York State legislature. We are at present faced with a wave of repressive "anticrime" legislation throughout the country, and it seems likely, given the general public ignorance about the importance of the right to resist reasonably, that the right may be abolished everywhere. It is at present not clear whether the right is a constitutional right, but unless the courts decide that it is, the right may disappear forever.

CIVIL DAMAGE ACTIONS

Because of the length of time it takes to complete civil actions, I have not made an exhaustive attempt in this study to test their effectiveness as remedies. Any opinions I give here must be sketchy at best.

Success in the criminal action against the complainant generally governs the effectiveness of the civil claims. In every jurisdiction, the criminal charges customarily brought to cover any police abuse act as an effective bar to a civil action, if a conviction is obtained. The civil case is usually based on claims of false arrest, malicious prosecution, and assault. The first two are barred as a matter of law by a conviction, and the suit for assault can be covered by a criminal charge of assault from the policeman. The civil action, then, is an effective remedy only when the criminal charges are dismissed or are never brought.

The civil action may be brought in either state or federal court, and each alternative presents its own special difficulties. In New York the state court action can be filed against both the city and the officer as an individual. The claim against the city must be filed within ninety days after the claim arises,[3] however, and in some cases this requirement interferes with the effectiveness of the civil remedy. More important, such actions ordinarily consume six years from the time of the incident until the time of judgment, because the city does not often settle them and the court calendars are extremely congested. Since the present study covered only two years, we could not have completed even one such case.

It requires a plaintiff with a nearly perfect case and a great deal of patience and staying power to complete such a case, let alone win it. Most victims of police abuse, particularly poor people, cannot undertake protracted litigation except when they have been subjected to some disabling injury, and many lawyers do not consider the suit worthwhile without a serious injury. Astonishingly enough, despite all these obstacles the city pays out substantial damages for the peccadillos of its officers. Professor Walter Gellhorn of Columbia reports that in 1965 a total of $169,482 was recovered on thirty-five claims.[4] This is not an enormous amount of money, but it is enough to indicate that some very serious cases were settled in 1965.

Nevertheless, it is doubtful that damage claims are an effective deterrent to police abuses. To some extent, the use of the civil courts may even exacerbate abuses by encouraging the police to bring criminal cover charges. If the civil damages paid by the city were large enough, the financial pressure might be enough to bring about a greater push from the top for change, but the damages are in fact infinitesimal compared to the Department's budget. In short, a state damage action is valuable for the individual client in serious cases, but it is hardly an instrument of reform.

Section 1983 of the Federal Civil Rights Act, the chief vehicle for federal actions against the police, has been on the books since Reconstruction, but it has been applied to police abuses only in the past few years. The statute provides:

> Every person who, under color of any statute, ordinance, regulation, custom or usage, of any State or Territory, subjects, or causes to be subjected, any citizen of the United States or other person within the jurisdiction thereof to the deprivation of any rights, privileges, or immunities secured by the Constitution and laws, shall be liable to the party injured in an action at law, suit in equity, or other proper proceeding for redress.

It was widely held for many years that this statute did not cover summary punishments by the police because it was thought that no federal law or constitutional right was violated. As recently as 1961, the Civil Rights Commission concluded that Section 1983 was ineffective.[5] In the same year, however, the Supreme Court broadened its interpretation of the scope of the statute, and it came to be widely used during the Southern civil rights struggle, when there was small hope of redress from the state courts. As a vehicle for obtaining damages, the statute after ninety years is still in the experimental stage.

The greatest value of Section 1983 as an instrument of reform lies in the use of the injunctive power. The statute provides for an injunction as well as damages for a deprivation of federal rights, and when a pattern of unconstitutional acts by the police can be shown, the federal suit is the logical remedy. There is still a problem created by the fact that federal courts do not like to interfere with the enforcement of state laws. When an attack is made upon a state statute—such as the loitering law in the case of the searches in the East Village (Chapter 11)—the federal court will generally abstain from striking down the law (except where freedom of speech is involved), holding that it ought first to be interpreted by the state courts. This results in a somewhat anomalous situation, where the federal courts will enjoin unconstitutional actions which are not authorized under state law (such as unlawful searches) but will not enjoin unconstitutional actions (such as vagrancy arrests) which are authorized by state law.

The federal injunction is the appropriate action against any practice authorized by the Police Department that is not at the same time authorized by state law. A good case, to my way of thinking, would be an action under Section 1983 against the police regulations authorizing the posting of "raided premises" signs and the issuing of liability notices to landlords (see Chapter 12). These are authorized by the Department upon mere suspicion, and there is not the slightest authority for them under state law; they are purely local regulations. This particular litigation was never attempted in my office because no plaintiff ever came in seeking such assistance, but I think the regulations could be eliminated or much improved through the federal courts. Section 1983 is an extremely powerful tool of litigation; the mere pendency of such a case attracts so much public notice in a city like New York that it frequently suffices to put a stop to the practice complained of, at least for a short time.

Apart from situations where systematic harassment can be shown, a federal action does not seem more useful in New York City than a state court action. By the terms of Section 1983, the action must be brought against an individual rather than a municipality. This reduces its relative value in New York City, where an action can be brought in state court against the city—which is usually better able to afford damages than the officer—and where a jury or a judge may actually award some damages.

The situation is otherwise in many states. The doctrine of sovereign immunity, protecting the municipality from damage actions, and abolished by statute in New York, survives in many states. Since the plaintiff must sue the individual officer in either state or federal court, he may as well go to federal court in those jurisdictions. Moreover many local judges, particularly in smaller communities, are extremely hostile to claims against the police. Outside New York City, then, a federal action will frequently be the best vehicle for any damage action based upon the abuse of power by a police officer.

REVIEW OF CIVILIAN COMPLAINTS

Review of complaints is a subject difficult to summarize for New York City alone, and much more so for other cities. Methods of review are under constant study and attack, and they are changing. Review of complaints in New York City will be considered in detail here, and then more generally as it illuminates the problem of review throughout the country.

My tendency has been to discuss departmental review as a step following the dismissal of criminal charges, although from a theoretical point of view the two are not necessarily connected. The Department has the power to prefer charges against an officer regardless of the disposition of the criminal charges he has brought against the citizen. For example, it is possible for the Department to discipline a policeman for using excessive force even though the citizen has been convicted of resisting arrest, if superior officers believe that more force was used than the resistance warranted. As a practical matter, however, review of civilian complaints is intimately bound up with the disposition of the criminal cover charges. If the criminal charges explain or justify the acts of the officer at all, then a conviction will serve to protect him from departmental charges, unless his actions have been so disproportionate to the offense as to result in death or maiming. The Review Board will not generally hold a hearing until after the criminal charges are disposed of, and the Department will not prefer charges which encroach upon any criminal charges brought by the policeman. When we discuss review of civilian complaints, then, we are talking about a remedy which is available after the criminal charges are cleared away, or in the infrequent case when no such charges are brought. It is the third hurdle to redress for police abuses, and by far the most complex and controversial of all.

At the time of this writing there are two steps in the usual departmental review of civilian complaints, neither of which involves review by civilians outside the Department. A complaint of abuse of authority is first brought to the Review Board. It is investigated by one of the high-ranking officers on the Board's staff, and unless the facts are obviously for or against the officer, it is referred to a hearing examiner (a Department employee, but not a policeman) for a formal hearing upon sworn testimony. The transcript of the hearing is considered by the Board, made up chiefly of long-time employees of the Department. If the complaint is found substantiated, the officer has a right under the state civil service law to a trial before the Commissioner or his deputy, to determine whether he should be punished. In this two-tiered review, the Police Commissioner has almost complete control. For example, if he chooses to bypass the Review Board to send a complaint directly to departmental trial, or if he chooses to have it investigated by some officer outside the Review Board, he is free to do so, and he occasionally does. This was done in several cases discussed in past chapters, including the Du Bois Club riot (Chapter 10) and the intrusion into the offices of the Committee to Support the NLF (Chapter 11).

The two years of our project afforded an unusual opportunity to observe changes in the workings of the Review Board. The civilian board, dominated by appointees from outside the Department, was in operation for such a short time—four months in 1966—that it is impossible to say whether it did a better job than the present board composed of employees of the Department. Nevertheless, as I have had occasion to observe before, the period of civilian review did bring to the Board methods of investigating and hearing more rational and open than those which existed before the institution of the Civilian Review Board. The change brought in hearing examiners from outside the Department and centralized the investigative staff at the offices of the Board.

Under the old system (pre-Civilian Review Board), the investigation was assigned to the command where the officer worked, and a ranking officer in that command held the hearing. Grotesque abuses occurred in that system, including:

a. Efforts to discourage the complainant or his witnesses. Officers were known to tell the complainant that he could be sued for libel if he lost out in his complaint. In one case, the investigator went to the high school attended by one of the witnesses, a sixteen-year-old girl, and asked the school authorities to show him her record. Sometimes complaints were simply buried and ignored, as we saw in the case of Steven Sellers (Chapter 7).

b. Efforts on the part of the hearing officer to conciliate by explaining the actions of the policeman instead of undertaking an objective evaluation of the facts. The experience of all administrative agencies has shown that it is poor policy for the one who investigates to sit in judgment also; it results in prejudice for or against the complainant. The present Board has a conciliation procedure in which the staff will try to settle a complaint if the citizen is willing, but conciliation is, as it should be, separate from the hearing procedure.

These are rather typical abuses for any administrative agency when it does not have a centralized staff beholden to no one but the agency for preferment, and when it does not have rational and neutral hearing procedures. Conversely, the bench marks of any rationally organized administrative agency must be a staff responsible only to that agency, and hearing examiners who are divorced from other functions of the agency. The brief period of civilian review brought these reforms, if it did not permanently bring about civilian review.

There are still some defects in the current Board's procedures. One is that its hearing process is too closely linked to the criminal case against the complainant. Ordinarily, a hearing is not held until after the criminal case is over, and this leads sometimes to an inordinate delay. In the Coney Island riot case, it took a year and a half to dispose of the criminal charges and, consequently, to get to a hearing (Chapter 10). Both complainants and policemen (or district attorneys) have contributed to this situation. The attorney for the complainant sometimes delays the Review Board hearing until after the criminal trial because he suspects that the hearing will be used as a fishing expedition for the criminal case—to determine, for example, the names of his witnesses. Policemen may believe the same with respect to the prosecution's witnesses. Even in cases where the names of witnesses are already public knowledge, the Board still often delays the hearing until after the criminal case is over. This is often unnecessary and prejudicial; the decisions of the Board should not be made dependent upon those of the criminal courts.

Furthermore, the Board is much too secretive about the basis for its findings. It simply reports to the complainant whether his case was found substantiated or not, without elaborating further. The report which is sent to the complainant should instead evaluate the evidence and show how the Board's conclusion was reached.

Everything I have said so far concerns the internal procedures of the Board's staff, rather than the men at the top who constitute the Board itself and decide its cases. All the procedural niceties will not make the Board a viable avenue of redress if these men are not determined to give that redress when it is warranted. One of the central purposes of this book has been to learn how fair the decisions of the Review Board are, and it is time now to come to grips with that elusive question.

I am bound to say, at the outset, that my conclusions must be largely subjective, for in the nature of things the evaluation of evidence is a matter of opinion. From the manner in which the Board has decided many of the cases described in past chapters, I feel it is clear that its members tend to participate too much in the police ethic. If the policeman is on the job and attempting to do what is at least arguably his duty, he will be given the widest latitude for errors in judgment. If he is in good faith searching for contraband, the fact that the search is totally unconstitutional will not result in the preferring of charges; if he is making an arrest for a disturbance of the peace, the fact that he loses his temper and clubs the culprit will not result in the preferring of charges. On the other hand,

if the officer is on a "frolic of his own," as the old legal phrase
has it, the likelihood that charges will be preferred is higher.
Obviously, there is some legitimate distinction to be made between overzealousness in the line of duty and sheer personal
assertiveness. But the difference, it seems, is not so great that
the first should simply be ignored. Perhaps it should receive
a lesser penalty, but it should not be entirely excused, particularly when policemen are encouraged as much as they are
to identify themselves with the authority vested in the job.

We had an opportunity to make a concrete contrast between
the attitudes of long-time employees of the Department and
those of newcomers, during the period when the hearing examiners from outside the Department were waiting for their
statutory year to pass so that they could begin to sit as they
had done before the referendum. The members of the Board
acted at this time as hearing examiners, and in some cases they
showed a tendency to try to explain and justify to the complainant the actions of the officer, instead of sitting in objective
judgment. Hearing examiners originally from outside the Department, both before and after the hiatus, appeared to be
much more objective.

In New York, public debate about police abuses tends to
revolve around the Review Board, but in fact, of course, the
Board's effectiveness is always limited by the effectiveness of
the Police Commissioner's trial proceedings. An officer cannot
be disciplined except by the Commissioner, and no city ordinance creating or abolishing a board of review can change that
situation.

Departmental trials are conducted at a very high level of
procedural sophistication. Both the Department and the officer
are represented by counsel, and the cases are tried, with the
strictest adherence to rules of evidence, before a Deputy
Commissioner who essentially sits as a judge. The Deputy
Commissioner is severely fair. The decisions may in fact be
better considered than those emanating from the City Criminal
Court upon charges against citizens. The Department has
worked very hard at its discipline, disposing of 982 cases in
1966 alone.

Nevertheless, the quality of the trials has varied—chiefly, I think, because of the varying attitudes of the prosecuting officers toward their cases. The same could be said of assistant district attorneys in criminal cases, but there is a structural defect in the Department's procedures, inherent in the fact that the prosecution is in the hands of the Department. If it chooses to play down some aspect of the case, as I believe was done in the Nichols frame (Chapter 9), that aspect becomes invisible.

The choice of charges which reach the Deputy Commissioner is heavily influenced by internal organizational goals, as distinguished from the effort to improve police work in the community. In 1966, for example, 42 percent of the charges presented to the Deputy Commissioner involved being AWOL or lax in patrol, while all the complaints of the sort discussed in this book (assault, misuse of revolver, and false statements) constituted only 8.9 percent of the charges.[6] The emphasis on organizational goals to the exclusion of almost everything else was dramatically highlighted on July 19, 1968, when the Commissioner dismissed a patrolman for bringing discredit on the Department by living with a woman. (Both parties were unmarried.)

Like the cases before the Review Board, departmental charges tend to be tailored so as not to encroach on criminal charges, pending or decided, against the complaining witness. In the Kaplan case (Chapter 7), where three people were arrested because of their complaint about a political sticker on a police car, the charges touched only upon the fact that the sticker had been on the car and not on the abuse of power in making the arrest. Similarly, in the case where a gun was fired in a bar on Christmas Eve (Chapter 3), the charges concerned only false statements and other failures to cooperate with the investigation, but not the assault on the complainants or any other major abuse of power against them, which might have cast doubt on the validity of the criminal charges. This is not a very straightforward approach to discipline. If the Department's investigators think the complainant is innocent of the criminal charges, they ought to say so and make sure that the charges are dropped, instead of avoiding all issues pending in the criminal courts. To fail to recommend that criminal charges be dropped under such circumstances defeats the ends of justice and implies that officers will be permitted to protect themselves if they can just make the criminal case stick.

Let us now take a broad look at the entire departmental procedure, Review Board and trial together, with a view to its overall effectiveness. The first thing that must strike a neutral observer is the ponderousness of the proceedings. A full investigation by a high-ranking officer is followed by a formal hearing and a lengthy process of decision upon the transcript. This in turn is but the threshold to another, still more formal hearing, this time with a prosecutor. Some of this procedural nicety is unavoidable, indeed valuable. The police are civil servants, and they are properly entitled to a full hearing before being dismissed or disciplined on account of charges of misconduct. We have only to remember the loyalty-security problems of government employees in the fifties to realize that the alternatives to a fair hearing open the door to a host of abuses more serious than delay. But there is a real question whether the procedure could not be shortened, and the Review Board is the obvious place to look for an abbreviation of the proceedings. It often appears that the elaborate Review Board hearing is only a façade for rejecting cases, because the strongest cases are frequently sent to trial without a hearing—and sometimes by the Commissioner's own investigators, without even reaching the Review Board. This impression is considerably strengthened when all the members of the Board hold other jobs in the Department as well as their Review Board jobs.

The variety of reviewing procedures in American police departments is bewildering. The two-tier system, or some variation of it, is the one characteristic of review that seems prevalent everywhere. Even in those cities which have civilian review boards, the decision about discipline is in the hands of the police commissioner. Apart from that, review of civilian complaints throughout the country is a crazy quilt.

If we take independence from influences adverse to neutrality in the individual case as the touchstone of proper administrative procedures, we may get some grasp of the situation. Independence may exist at three levels, the investigation, the hearing, and the decision, and it may take the relatively unusual form of independence *from* the department (civilian review) or independence *within* the department (working solely for the reviewing agency and not for anyone else). Considering these standards, a survey of methods of review shows that most departments in the country fail even to afford independence within the department to the review proceedings. As we saw in Chapter 3, very few departments rely exclusively on a special unit to investigate complaints, and many have no formal hearing procedures.[7]

On the other hand, some cities, notably Philadelphia and Rochester, have civilian review boards. Philadelphia has an odd combination—a civilian review board, but no centralized investigative staff. I suspect that this must limit the effectiveness of the board; [8] even though it is independent of the police department, it must still receive rather slanted investigative reports, because it has no assistance from investigators who are responsible solely to the board. An investigative staff at least independent within the department seems to be the basic ingredient of orderly procedure, because such a staff supplies the basis for any decision made at the top. On this score, most American police departments have failed to offer even the elements of adequate review.

This survey of the avenues of redress for police abuses has been a tale offering but faint hopes. All the devices—negotiation with the office of the District Attorney, defense of the criminal charges, departmental review, and civil actions— are sometimes effective, but in only a small percentage of cases. Furthermore, they tend to cancel one another out. We have noted that if the District Attorney dismisses a case, he frequently insists upon a waiver of claims. The pendency of a civil or a criminal action connected with a police abuse brings the process of departmental review to a halt. All the institutions, considered together, tend to protect the police, even when they do not go so far as to punish the citizen.

None of these institutions is immune to reform; each of

them has been reformed substantially in the past, and many
of them now function more effectively in some cities than in
others. Our discussion of their failings may help somewhat to
indicate the direction that change might take.

THE DISTRICT ATTORNEY

At the simplest level, district attorneys in New York and elsewhere should abolish their most obvious practice in support
of police abuses: the extraction of releases in return for
the dismissal of cases. This measure has apparently been
taken in the District of Columbia. Further development of the
prosecutor's role in limiting police abuses, particularly the
use of his discretion in dismissing cover charges, which has
been started in Manhattan, presents more subtle problems. Apparently the Manhattan District Attorney's office is able to be
more sensitive than others to the problem of police abuses because the assistants there are chosen by merit, not by politics.
They are not permitted to practice privately while they are
prosecutors, and because of the low salaries for assistant district attorneys, older lawyers are constantly leaving while new
ones come in. As a result, the office is not much subject to
political pressure and it is somewhat responsive to social
change. As a task force of the President's Commission on Law
Enforcement has said, freedom from politics and the awarding
of jobs on merit are basic reforms for any prosecutorial function,[9] but they seem especially important for the control of
police abuses.

THE COURTS

In New York City, the most elementary reform needed to improve the trial of cases in which police abuse is raised as a
defense is the institution of a jury trial for misdemeanor cases.*
A jury chosen from a cross section of the city should alleviate
the problem of occasional judicial bias in favor of the testimony
of police officers.

---

* Since this was written, the United States Supreme Court decided
Duncan v. Louisiana May 20, 1968. It appears to provide for a constitutional right to a jury trial in serious misdemeanor cases such as those
described in this study.

A general improvement in the quality of defense counsel for indigents is needed everywhere in the country. Perhaps I should say "quantity" rather than "quality," because in many cities no counsel at all is given, and in New York the Legal Aid lawyers are able enough, though their case load is so enormous as to preclude their adequately considering each case.

For a long time to come, the most important place to fight police abuses is still going to be the criminal courts. No system of review can change the situation unless persons abused can be acquitted in criminal court, and those acquittals will require a lot of hard work and organization. Until society becomes enlightened enough to demand better police practices, the injured are going to have to fight the abuses themselves. This means that the most important element in any "review" of police action is solid community organization and adequate legal defense. In cases from poor neighborhoods, I have invariably observed that the abused defendant accused of disorderly conduct and resisting arrest or assault has a better chance of acquittal if he is connected with a community organization. Witnesses are often members of the organization, and they can come forward without feeling that they are alone. When the witnesses are not members of the organization, the members can nevertheless seek them out and expect to be greeted with trust rather than suspicion. Similarly, a lawyer who is willing to take the time to work with the neighborhood groups and go to see the witnesses is essential. The neighborhood law offices sponsored by the federal Office of Economic Opportunity would be ideal vehicles for this purpose, if the poverty laws did not forbid them to take criminal cases. As a first tiny step in reform, that law should be changed.

Appellate courts should take a somewhat more expansive role in overseeing the fact-determinations of the lower courts than they have traditionally done. The United States Supreme Court has limited the discretion of the police, but in so doing it has perhaps increased the tendency of the police to present a version of the facts that will avoid its rulings. Closer appellate scrutiny is needed to make sure that the rules are not being evaded.

I will say little here about the substantive rules made by the courts. It has not generally been the purpose of this study to discuss the laws so much as their administration, although one judge-made rule—the right to reasonably resist an unlawful arrest—has been explored in these pages. Appellate courts and state legislatures should recognize that to destroy that right is to invite unlawful and discriminatory arrests.

REVIEW OF CIVILIAN COMPLAINTS

The possibilities for reform of departmental review in New York City are severely limited by the terms of the local law abolishing civilian review, which forbids anyone to review a complaint who has not been a departmental employee for at least a year. Nevertheless, greater independence *within* the Department is still possible, and the members of the Review Board, who at present divide their duties between its cases and other jobs in the Department, should be appointed to work solely for the Board.

Some action should be taken to streamline the cumbersome two-tier system of review. I myself was once of the opinion that since the current Review Board is composed of police employees anyhow, it would not make much difference if it were abolished. Most of the cases which are now sent to the Commissioner for trial would still be tried, and one step would be eliminated. While there is some virtue in this view, I now think that it ignores the positive effects of the Review Board hearing on police-community relations. That hearing airs the facts in all major cases—those that are found unsubstantiated as well as those sent to the Commissioner for departmental trial; when departmental charges are not preferred, it helps to show why by revealing weaknesses in the complainant's case. For example, in one case a police officer was charged with kicking a citizen. I thought the case against the policeman extremely strong until the officer's lawyer brought out on cross-examination at the hearing that the complainant had been involved in an almost identical incident in London many years before and had subsequently been convicted of assaulting the officer. Suddenly, the complainant's veracity was in doubt.

If the only instruments of discipline were the Commissioner's investigators and the departmental trial, cases like this would be dropped (just as they are now), but no one outside the Department would know why.

From this point of view, the Review Board's function is chiefly to expose the facts, and the present procedures of the Board do not seem best suited for it. After a laborious formal hearing, no findings of fact are issued to the complainant or the public. It would be less cumbersome and more to the point to have one neutral person interview the witness (with counsel present) and then make detailed findings of fact. The Board should then issue its decision, giving a reasoned analysis of the facts. One step in the process of review would be enormously expedited, and the complainant and the public would better understand the results.

In addition, in New York City and elsewhere, when demonstrations, civil disturbances, and other situations threaten to bring on the abuses of mass police action, the abuses can be forestalled by sending civilian observers and film teams to expected trouble areas. This is analogous to civilian review, but for mass action it is more effective.

Outside New York City, the possibilities of review are much broader. It is theoretically possible to have a review procedure independent from the police at all levels. As the police do not fail to point out, there is no reason why such an agency should oversee only police abuses, and when metamorphosed into a general independent review board for all official abuses, the agency is better known by its Scandinavian name of "Ombudsman." In most jurisdictions, an Ombudsman for all officials is more feasible politically than a civilian review board solely for the police. The public seems to be able to unite on the proposition that "bureaucrats" make mistakes, but not that "the police" make mistakes. It is true that the investigative techniques of the Ombudsman have traditionally been more restricted than those of a trial board; he has not usually gathered facts or held hearings himself, but has relied instead upon the records of other agencies. For American purposes, however, there is no real reason why he should not have a full investigative staff. Civilian review should take the path of the Ombudsman with expanded powers, and a field survey of the President's Commission has made that recommendation.[10]

In the confusion of debate over effective investigation of police complaints, we tend to assume that some sort of review on a case-by-case basis is the most effective tool of reform. The truth is that any method of sifting the facts after an event is over, particularly when it is directed to identifying and punishing a particular person, is of very limited value. The problem of proof is always difficult. Inevitably, any person who makes a serious accusation against a public servant has the burden of proving it to a reviewing body, and he can carry that burden only in a small minority of cases; usually, there will be no witnesses to corroborate his allegations. Worse, he himself will often be charged with a crime, and his credibility will be in serious doubt. On those occasions when the defendant is not arrested, he will frequently be unable to identify the officer who is supposed to have abused him. The problem of identification becomes still more difficult when the complainant is injured in a civil disturbance, where there are dozens of officers, and yet such injuries are among the chief sources of complaints against the police. In general, then, under any system of review, relatively few abuses are going to be punished.

It is doubtful, in any case, that the threat of punishment is a very effective deterrent to police abuses. Few of us now believe that the threat of punishment much deters crimes by private citizens, and it is hard to understand why the belief still persists that stringent discipline will deter abuses by the police. It is a tired old truism that crime by private citizens is a social problem, and that it can be reduced by changing the social conditions. A man commits a crime for a reason, and it is important to give him a reason for doing something different, as well as to try to discipline him for what he has done. Police abuses of the sort we have discussed here are crimes, and they are fully as much the result of social conditions as other crimes, if not more so. The policeman's ethic—to eliminate those who threaten authority and convict the guilty any way he can— seems to him a logical compromise between due process and law enforcement because citizens and his superiors tell him it is.

At least in some cases, the limitations of review can be alleviated by changing the emphasis of review from punishment of a particular officer to recommendations for changes in procedure and regulations. This has been a traditional function of the Scandinavian Ombudsman, and American review boards can (and sometimes do) undertake such a rule-making function. Insofar as abuses are systematic, or are really based on a failure to grasp an element of law or proper police work, new rules can be effective. For example, the rule restricting harassment of people handing out political leaflets (Chapter 7) seems to have been generally followed by policemen. The rules will not be effective, however, if they conflict with customs endorsed at the precinct level. No review can bring about much change as long as policemen are unwilling to testify, and their immediate superiors are unwilling to criticize them, concerning abuses that are sanctioned by the police ethic.

The inherent limitations of a case-by-case approach to review raises the problem of reform within the Police Department. I have no doubt that considerable improvement is possible, if only because of the history of abuses in New York and other cities. The situation is better in New York than it is in many other communities, and it is a great deal better here now than it was a generation ago.

The police problems of forty years ago are sadly memorialized in the reports of the first presidential Commission on Law Enforcement, published in 1931 and collectively called the Wickersham Report. In those days officers were mortally stupid —the *Report on the Police* found that 75 percent of the policemen in the country were mentally unfit, by Army intelligence test standards, to perform their duties.[11] It was the age of the "dumb cop," but if the present study has proved nothing else, I hope it has shown that the dumb cop is practically extinct. The abuses described here have mostly been the work of experienced, intelligent men. Sometimes they were misusing their intelligence, but of the fact that they had it there can be no doubt.

Since the days of the Wickersham Commission, police de-

partments in all major cities have improved the quality of
their men, and the incidence of most abuses has certainly declined. The one abuse that has perhaps increased is lying. The
new protections for the accused and the public sensitivity
to police brutality have caused the police abuses of those days
in part to disappear and in part simply to go underground.
Insofar as they have disappeared, there has been a clear gain,
but insofar as they have gone underground, we are faced with
a new problem.

The problem is to find what departmental reforms can reduce the prevalence of the existing police abuses, whether
new or time-honored. It does not appear that the fault
is with the quality of the recruits. In New York, as in most
cities, they are much like other young men of the same age and
background. Nor is the fault in their training. Most of the work
in the Police Academy seems to be adequate as technical
education, although some areas of systematic abuse, like arrests for loitering or gambling, do seem to indicate a failure
to teach the requirements of due process. These practices,
chiefly centering around minor harassment arrests—such as
those for gambling—can be improved if the Department will
attempt to define more clearly when such arrests may lawfully
be made. However, these improvements cannot bring about
basic change, because police recruits in New York City and
elsewhere alter their standards after they enter the Department
and come in contact with older officers at the precinct level.[12]
These factors are much the same for every major urban department, and proposals for reform at the precinct level should be
as applicable to other cities as they are to New York.

There has been much discussion in the last few years about
higher standards of academic education, including possibly
a college degree, for the men who are offered jobs in the Department. This is a superficially attractive idea, but it is a shot-
gun approach that fails to deal with the basic problem. The
simple fact is that police work in our society tends to create an
authoritarian outlook, and this tendency is reinforced by practices in the precinct. As we saw in the case of the police ser-
geant-lawyer who arrested two schoolteachers for handing out

leaflets, education is no guarantee against abuse of power. Of course, the sergeant did not and probably would not abuse the defendants physically, but it may well be that education would only transmute summary punishment by violence into simple false arrest. That would certainly be a clear gain, but it would hardly be worth the cost of higher education.

A more complex situation is presented by the fact that, for a great many police jobs, a college degree does not seem necessary or appropriate. Patrol is one of the most essential and arduous jobs in the administration of a city, but a college degree scarcely seems to prepare for it. A noted student of the police has remarked that a college degree would be unnecessary for a recruit but insufficient training in itself for an administrator in a large department.[13] The implication is that higher education should be required to rise into the higher ranks but should not be required for a recruit. At the present time this is not the case; civil service procedures for promotion to lieutenant and captain are based on only two factors: seniority and the results of a competitive examination. Education is not considered.

The impulse to require more academic training for policemen is rooted in the hope of getting men with a new orientation who cannot be so easily molded to the police ethic. While I sympathize with this endeavor, I think, for the reasons I have just given, that it is a little beside the point. A direct attack should be made upon the monolithic adherence to the police ethic and the unofficial code of secrecy. One way this can be done is by selecting officers for command positions or specialized jobs by different standards than those by which patrolmen are selected. The innovation would not prevent qualified patrolmen from rising in the ranks, but it would require them to obtain proper specialized training in order to do so. Such a reform has been suggested by Professor Richard Blum and enthusiastically expounded by the President's Commission on Law Enforcement.[14] The change would serve a twofold purpose: it would encourage educated men to enter positions where academic training might be useful, and it would tend to reduce the monolithic secrecy of the police. It was earlier suggested that "the system" in police departments by which abuses are covered is sanctioned by officers in command positions, and the ethical judgments which tend to lead to police abuses are encouraged throughout the department. This situation continues partly because there is almost total solidarity in the department; virtually every man in a command position has at one time been a patrolman and has had to accept all the precinct mores. This manner of appointment and promotion must be broken open somewhere to let people who are not thoroughly assimilated filter in.

Just where this break should be made in the ranks is an open question. The President's Commission has recommended an excellent plan for a three-part police department, including a Community Service Officer, an unarmed young apprentice policeman working in neighborhoods; a police officer, doing routine patrol work; and a police agent, a specialized officer similar to a detective.[15] I think this is a useful concept, and it may be an excellent way to bring more Puerto Ricans and Negroes into the department (initially as Community Service Officers). I would add that officers above the rank of sergeant should also be recruited from outside as well as from within the ranks of patrolmen, and receive special training for their job. This would check the abuses which so often result from police solidarity and obtain specially trained men for the police. It will, of course, require changes in the civil service laws, but I can see no alternative if there is to be reform.

Apart from these proposals for new methods of recruitment, there are other, less sweeping changes which can help to alter the character of the police department. I think that police attitudes will be subtly affected for the better by a change in the "emergency" or "military preparedness" aspect of police work. At the present time, policemen are required to carry guns while they are off duty, in order to be ready to rush into action if a crime should be committed. This reinforces the solidarity of policemen and the suspicion of and social separation from outsiders. I think that the rule exists partly for this very reason, and it ought to be changed for the same reason. When a man is off duty, he ought to be a citizen, not a threatening instrument of force.

Minor changes should also be made in the manner of appointing detectives. Technically, in New York and elsewhere, the appointment is usually made by the Police Commissioner, and it is by custom based upon some particularly good piece of police work. There is nothing basically wrong with this system, but too many policemen believe that an enormous number of arrests, or a few violent arrests, will lead to advancement. Recommendations to the Police Commissioner for promotion are made by local commanders, and inevitably ambitious patrolmen must assimilate the opinions of their superiors. It seems that the commissioner ought to take more direct control of the appointment process, to ensure that patrolmen do not believe that practices which create poor community relations —such as an accumulation of false arrests—will contribute to promotion.

It will not surprise me if these proposals encounter the most severe opposition from law enforcement officials; it is easy to imagine their reaction to a proposal to introduce outsiders into the police ranks. Limitations on the use of deadly force have already been reversed by the New York legislature, and it is apparent that we are not faced with a public mood that is hospitable to any limitation on police powers. This is a time that dramatizes the thesis that the police really do approximately what society wants them to do, and society has naturally rejected efforts to change the policeman's methods. The Patrolmen's Benevolent Association spelled it out in the simplest terms by the success of its referendum rejecting civilian review of police complaints in New York City. The referendum told us that if we wanted to reform the police, we would have to reform the electorate.

15

THE POLICE
AND SOCIETY

PREVIOUS CHAPTERS HAVE SHOWN that the anatomy of street-corner abuses is unchanging. The policeman on the beat sees his job to be one of maintaining tranquillity and perpetuating the established routine. Any person out of the ordinary is suspicious; if he is recognizably deviant, then he is potentially criminal. Potentially criminal also, and a severe threat to good order, is any challenge to the policeman's authority. A challenge may come either from the deviant, simply by his failure to respond to an officer's order, or from the ordinary citizen who is openly defiant. In either case, the challenge will be met by anger and one or more weapons out of the arsenal of legal sanctions, from a summons up through summary corporal punishment. Criminal charges, beginning with disorderly conduct and ranging up to felonious assault, are commonly laid to cover the actions of the policeman and to punish the offender. In the eyes of the police, arrest is practically tantamount to guilt, and the police will supply the allegations necessary for conviction; the courts are treated as a mere adjunct to their purpose. Distortion of the facts becomes the most pervasive and the most significant of abuses. The police ethic justifies any action which is intended to maintain order or to convict any wrongdoer/(i.e., anyone actually or potentially guilty of crime). In studying search and seizure, for example, we found that the police tend to justify a search made "in good faith"—really looking for a crime—regardless of whether it is a lawful search or not. Once again, the facts are distorted so as to justify the search in the eyes of the courts, although there is less distortion in connection with house searches than with searches of persons on the street.

We have seen that some abuses do not precisely fit our conception of the tendencies in police behavior that give rise to abuses—those, for example, which are committed for personal reasons like family revenge or professional advancement. Although it is significant that these are the abuses which are generally condemned by policemen themselves, it is important to observe that such actions shade off subtly into duty-oriented abuses, because the Department encourages the man to identify himself with his authority. Other abuses, such as those that occur during mass police action, seem to be similar in origin to ordinary street abuses, but are distorted out of all recognition by mass frenzy. Finally, a few abuses are chronic because they are systematically encouraged by the Department. In condoning systematic abuses, the Department itself acts upon much the same rationale that the individual policeman uses to justify isolated street abuses. When the Department authorizes an action in violation of due process, such as a roundup of prostitutes, it does so to preserve order ("a clean city") and to harass a group of people who are considered undesirable. The chief difference between isolated and systematic abuses is that there is less distortion of the facts about the latter, because the individual officers find it unnecessary and thus make no attempt to cover their own actions. Except in the case of systematic harassment, then, distortion of fact is the thread than runs through all abuses, however different they may seem. The distortion of fact, and indeed every abuse, is rationalized by the need to maintain authority and catch wrongdoers.

The tendencies in police behavior which give rise to abuses do form a sort of "police character": a man, suspicious of out-

siders, who is concerned with order, reacts aggressively to
threats to his authority, and regards every attempt to control
that authority with cynicism. Other authors have attempted to
mold this character, or a similar one, into a sociological or
psychological framework. Neiderhoffer, for example, has ana-
lyzed the policeman according to the characteristics of an
"authoritarian personality." [1] For our purposes, terms like this
are tautological; the word "authoritarian" either reiterates what
we know already about policemen, or else it is irrelevant. To
get at the roots of police behavior, I should have to go to a
deeper psychological level, and the fragmentary nature of the
evidence collected here, together with the fragmentary nature
of the available psychological studies, prevents me from performing the task adequately. It is enough here for us to know
that the characteristic police reactions are a logical product
of the police role (e.g. maintaining order) and the traditions of
the Department (e.g. secrecy).

The important point for us here is that police abuses *do* form
a pattern, and that they reveal one aspect of police character.
Police abuses are a set of consistent responses in similar situations, and not very surprising responses at that. The policeman
identifies with the office with which he is vested, and con-
siders a threat to that office the most serious of threats to good
order. It is misleading to say that his views are unlawful or
unethical. They may participate in a different ethic, and perhaps even in a somewhat different law from the criminal law
of the modern, liberal state, but unquestionably there are ethics
and law at work here. It is a "good guys versus bad guys"
ethic, free of the strictures of procedure: the person who is
"wise to a cop" has no respect for authority and deserves to be
punished. Deviants are undesirable, and the police should ride
herd on them to keep them from intruding on the rest of
society. A criminal ought to be caught and put in jail the
quickest way that one can get him there.

Is this really such an unfamiliar canon of ethics? Doesn't it
rather ring of the opinion reflected in most of our newspaper
editorials and shared by thousands of citizens? We should
realize that the appeals courts ask an extraordinary act of will

from the policeman. They ask him to be concerned solely with "enforcing law," not with simply catching wrongdoers. It is an abstract distinction that most of us treat with the same suspicion as does the policeman, and the policeman continues to ignore it partly because we encourage him to do so.

Max Weber distinguished between the substantive rationality and the formal rationality of legal systems.[2] A substantively rational system obeys generally consistent, if poorly articulated, norms of ethics and law. The formally rational legal system is more coherent and logically consistent. It is the typical system of a society governed by an impersonal bureaucracy dealing at arm's length with citizens. Our criminal law is becoming increasingly rational in the formal sense, as economic and political relations become more abstract, while the police continue to adhere to a kind of substantive rationality. Formal rationality is increasing partly because the rough rules of the police are simply inadequate to the social changes taking place in our society, and to the ideal of equal justice. The conflict in which the police are placed—between their own code and the formal code—is the conflict of modern city administration, and indeed, of the people who live in the cities. The question which the citizens of New York, and of every city which pretends to a liberal administration, must ask themselves is whether they would rather have the police follow their old-fashioned rules, or whether they really want the police to adhere to the formally rational (and substantively different) rules of due process of law. It is clear that there is something in most of us that does not want the police to change; the landslide vote against a civilian review board demonstrated that, if nothing else. We want efficiency, quick work, order above all, though we claim to want due process and equal justice as well. Without basic changes to eliminate the obvious injustices in our society, we cannot expect to have all these, but if all else fails, we think we would like to preserve at least the appearance of order ("peace and quiet"). It is for the police to play the tough, no-nonsense half of this conflict. The enlightened feel a little guilty about their own impulse to coerce respect by force, and it is easier for them to turn the police into a whipping boy than to admit to such instincts themselves. The police do all the "wrong" things—club people who are outcasts or defiant of authority—but the unfortunate truth is that much public disapproval of their actions is sheer hypocrisy. Many, perhaps most, citizens feel that it is desirable for a policeman to coerce adherence to his code by punching a "wise kid" or ransacking an apartment without a warrant. They hide from themselves the fact that every act which coerces obedience from a man by unlawful means is by definition an act of oppression. For people who accept such practices, much as they may recoil from the consistency with which they are applied by the police, virtually no abuses are recorded in this book.

For legislators and judges the police are a godsend, because all the acts of oppression that must be performed in this society to keep it running smoothly are pushed upon the police. The police get the blame, and the officials stay free of the stigma of approving their highhanded acts. The police have become the repository of all the illiberal impulses in this liberal society; they are under heavy fire because most of us no longer admit so readily to our illiberal impulses as we once did.

The welter of statutes intended to control morality by penalizing the possession of some contraband, or the act of vagrancy or loitering, pointedly reveals the hypocrisy in the administration of our laws. The legislature passes such statutes, knowing quite well that their enforcement encourages a host of police abuses, including unlawful searches, dragnet arrests, and systematic harassment. The links between these abuses and morals legislation is no accident; the impulse in each is the same. It is the drive to legislate the lives of others and to force them to adhere to an accepted mode of life; that impulse cannot be enforced without abusing the rights of citizens.

Viewed in this light, the distortions of fact by policemen, which we have pronounced at once the most dangerous and the most pervasive of abuses, do not seem quite so shocking or unnatural. Lying is a bridge between the substantively rational rules of the police and the formally rational ones of the criminal law, by which the first are made to appear to conform to the second.

The actions of the police probably embody a natural tendency of any group of bureaucrats, working out in the field where their decisions have low visibility, to avoid the effect of restrictive regulations that conflict with existing practices. A book similar to this could perhaps be written about welfare workers or even public school administrators. The effects of the conflict between rule and practice are more dramatic in the case of the police than of other bureaucrats because the victims of their practices wind up in jail, and more prolonged and exaggerated because of the traditional solidarity and secrecy of the police. Like many other minor bureaucrats before them, however, the police continue to adhere to their old customs because they know that their superiors and much of the rest of society approves. They have no motive to change.

Up to this point, I have made little effort to choose between the substantively rational rules of the police and the formally rational rules of the courts. Even without a choice between the two, the distortion of facts by the police is an inherently dangerous practice. In our society, law enforcement officers are expected to respond to civilian legal directives, and if they fail to do so, then the power of society to change its laws is significantly decreased, and the police in effect control the criminal law. But the covert adherence to another set of laws is not nearly so serious if in fact those laws are superior to, or just as good as, the stated laws. If the formally rational rules are unworkable or unnecessary, to avoid them is a relatively minor failing, because in the long run the laws themselves will probably change. It is not the function of this book to make value judgments about the effectiveness of the formal rules, but the problem cannot be ignored entirely if we are to understand the effect of police abuses. We must at least look a little more deeply into the formal rules.

Let us consider, as an example, the requirements of "probable cause" for an arrest and search. The limitations of probable cause are established to make sure that the police arrest only people whom a neutral and rational observer would suppose to be guilty. A system of dragnet arrest and search would probably catch more persons carrying contraband than the application of probable cause, but the courts attempt to make a prior judgment so that those who are obviously or probably innocent will not be harassed. Any rule that relaxes the requirements of probable cause necessarily lowers the standards of suspicion and tends to include more innocent persons. As we have seen, police methods, when they depart from probable cause, do tend to punish innocent people together with the guilty. The point for use here is that the courts have made a policy judgment to exclude as many arrests of the innocent as possible, consistent with catching the obvious criminal. The rule of the courts, apart from being formally rational, also embodies a substantively rational rule *different* from that of the police, and the formal nature of the rule is intended to control police action and enforce the underlying substantive principle. The substantively rational police rule favors investigation so long as it is done in good faith, a policy judgment which is properly for the courts rather than the police to make because the courts are better equipped to strike the balance between investigation and freedom. The police rule inevitably favors investigation—favors the authorities, in short. It is apparent, then, that the rule of the courts is not dryly logical or lacking in practical effectiveness, but is simply based on a judgment different from that of the police about the needs of society.

There are two principles underlying such procedural rules: first, that the elaboration of legal rules is properly a matter for the courts, and second, that the balance is properly struck on the side of personal liberty. Our society is suspicious of both these principles; it finds the police rules easier to grasp than the court rules. Though the incidence of police abuses may be reduced by institutional reforms, the police rules cannot change finally until society decides to disapprove of them. More citizens must come to accept the principle that the term "law enforcement" refers to enforcement of the laws and not to the arrest or harassment of defiant or deviant citizens. More citizens must come to accept the principle that all police abuses constitute the enforcement of a private code by unlawful means and that, as such, they are inherently oppressive. Too many people, in fact, understand this already and yet secretly (or openly) approve the acts of the police because they fear the defiance of others as much as do the police. They recognize that nearly every form of defiance of an authority, whether it be from a "wise" teen-ager, from the hippie way of life, or finally, from an open revolt by students or black people, is a demand for a new way of life both social and economic. They fear that demand for change enough to use force to oppose it, and unless that fear disappears, they will continue to condone police acts of oppression, and police rules will not change.

The saddest aspect of police abuses is that they defeat their avowed purposes. The rationalization for street abuses is that they create or at least maintain respect for authority. Punishment for the wise guy is supposed to "teach him a lesson," but the system of police abuses creates only contempt for authority. A man, and especially the already defiant black man in this country, does not feel respect when he is clubbed, when he is charged with a crime, and when he loses his only job because he has been convicted. Words cannot convey the despair, the hatred, induced by a system which injures a man and then brands him as a criminal. It is not enough to say that the behavior of all the administrators involved—the officer, his superiors, the prosecutor, the judge—is understandable. The system within which the police work is evil, for the simplest of reasons: because it injures people and destroys their respect for the legal process. It is not for nothing that ghetto people have chosen police abuses as the symbol of oppression; it is because they actually *are* acts of oppression.

This brings us back to the importance of police abuses and the urgency of the problem they present. They are hardly the only acts of oppression in our cities, but they are the easiest to recognize. The anger they instill is part of the fuel for the violent uprisings in our cities during the past five years. As an indispensable condition for ending those uprisings, the police must change their allegiance from a private code to a publicly recognized rule of law, and it is only when society itself demands this change that it will take place.

ANALYTICAL APPENDIX

THE FIGURES that follow summarize the work and the findings of the Police Practices Project of the Defense and Education Fund of the New York Civil Liberties Union. They are to be viewed with some caution because the cases, after all, were not chosen at random. The complainants are people who chose to contact our office rather than another, and the authentication of the complaints, as we have seen, is at the mercy of the institutions of justice. This analysis is at best suggestive of the nature and sources of civilian complaints.

From March 1, 1966, to July 31, 1967, the project received a total of 441 complaints. Of these, 123 were accepted by the project for further investigation and litigation, usually because corroborating evidence was available. Seventy-one complaints were finally authenticated—that is, corroborating evidence was found and no conviction was obtained to cover the abuse. These 71 complaints constitute 57 percent of the complaints accepted and 16 percent of all those received. Seven police departmental trials resulted, and eight officers were disciplined (some accepted a reprimand without trial). The complaints can be broken down into categories as follows (the totals are not cumulative because some complaints involved a number of abuses):

	Total complaints	Authenticated
Assault by officer	87	10
Assault with false arrest	77	18
False arrest	69	17
Search—house	25	11
Search—outdoors	27	7
Entrapment	6	—
Frame	34	3

	Total complaints (cont.)	*Authenticated (cont.)*
Unlawful confession	9	—
Misuse of firearm	14	7
Improper identification	4	—
Wire tap	2	—
Not permitted to talk to attorney	8	1
Racial slur	8	1
Detention w/o charge	5	3
Discrimination	3	3

The ethnic background of the complainants is interesting. Of 441 complainants, 178, or 40 percent, are Puerto Rican or Negro. Of the 71 complainants in the authenticated cases, 29 (again 40 percent) are Puerto Rican or Negro. Looking only at the complaints involving allegations of police assault, however (assault or assault/false arrest), we find the following:

	Complaints (assault or assault/false arrest)	*Authenticated*
Total	164	28
Negro or Puerto Rican	106	16
% Negro and Puerto Rican	65%	57%

This result suggests that though any citizen may be abused by a policeman, summary corporal punishment, rather than some milder sanction such as simple arrest or a summons, is more likely to be used against a Negro or Puerto Rican.

In the effort to learn some basic facts about the genesis of the use and abuse of force by police officers, I have attempted to extract all complaints involving assault which arose out of defiance of the policeman (e.g., failure to move on), and verbal defiance in particular. The results are extremely rough because the definition of defiance is rather subjective. In many of the 318 complaints not accepted by the office, furthermore, the origins of the citizen's problem are unknown. The figures are:

	Total complaints (cont.)	*Authenticated (cont.)*
Assault & assault/false arrest	164	28
Defiance present	91	20
% defiant	55%	71%
Verbal defiance as a % of total defiance	56%	60%

Arrest on criminal charges, of course, proved to be the endemic problem. In all the 164 complaints about assault, 80 percent of the complainants had been arrested, either upon a related or an unrelated charge. Out of the 71 authenticated complaints of all types, the complainants in 59 (or 76 percent) of the cases were arrested.

NOTES

Introduction

1. U.S. National Commission on Law Observance and Enforcement (Wickersham Commission), *Report on the Police* (Washington, Government Printing Office, 1931), p. 130.

2. U.S. National Commission on Law Observance and Enforcement, *Report on Lawlessness in Law Enforcement* (Washington, Government Printing Office, 1931), p. 88.

Chapter 1. A Puerto Rican in Seward Park

1. People v. Jose Rivera, Dkt. No. 6794/66, Criminal Court of the City of New York, Pt. 2B3, Manhattan, minutes of trial, June 30, 1966.

Chapter 2. Bitterness on Sugar Hill

1. People v. Samuel Johnson and Harold Bell, Dkt. Nos. B5616–17/66, C9145–46/66, Criminal Court of the City of New York, Pt. 2B3, Manhattan, minutes of trial, July 28, 1966.

2. Patricia Wald and Joel Hoffman, "Report and Recommendations on the disorderly Conduct Statute of the District of Columbia," mimeographed staff document, President's Commission on Crime in the District of Columbia (July 15, 1966), p. 25.

3. Quoted in President's Commission on Law Enforcement and the Administration of Justice, *The Task Force Report on the Police* (Washington, Government Printing Office, 1967), p. 181. (This report is hereafter referred to as TFRP.)

4. Nathan Goldman, *The Differential Selection of Juvenile Offenders for Court Appearances* (Washington, National Council on Crime and Delinquency, 1963), p. 106.

5. Kenneth B. Clark, *Dark Ghetto: Dilemmas of Social Power* (New York, Harper & Row, Publishers, 1965), pp. 4–5.

6. Jerome H. Skolnick, *Justice Without Trial: Law Enforcement in Democratic Society* (New York, John Wiley & Sons, Inc., 1966), p. 45.

7. *Ibid.*, p. 48.
8. TFRP, p. 195.
9. "New Police Board Finds Complaints Are Off Sharply," *New York Times,* January 9, 1967, p. 1.
10. Irving M. Piliavin and Scott Briar, "Police Encounters with Juveniles," *American Journal of Sociology,* LXX (September 1964), 206.
11. John H. McNamara, "Uncertainties in Police Work: The Relevance of Police Recruits' Background and Training," in David Joseph Bordua, ed., *The Police: Six Sociological Essays* (New York, John Wiley & Sons, Inc., 1967), p. 176.

Chapter 3.   Defiance and Force

1. William A. Westley, "Violence and the Police," *American Journal of Sociology,* LIX (August 1953), p. 38.
2. TFRP, p. 182. Albert J. Reiss, Jr., "Police Brutality—Answers to Key Questions," *Trans-Action,* July–August 1968, p. 16, reports 37 instances of excessive force in 3,826 encounters with citizens, in a three-city survey.
3. McNamara, "Uncertainties in Police Work," pp. 213–14.
4. Westley, "Violence and the Police," p. 38.
5. People v. Lingo and Hernandez, Dkt. Nos. B2660/66, Y1255/66, Criminal Court of the City of New York, Pt. 2B3, Manhattan, minutes of trial, September 13–14, 1966.
6. Dkt. No. 162697, Criminal Court of the City of New York, Bronx, minutes of trial, June 28, 1966.
7. TFRP, p. 182, mentions a similar case.
8. Cases collected by William Liebovitz.
9. Westley, "Violence and the Police," p. 38.
10. *New York Times,* June 3, 1966, p. 41; December 15, 1966, p. 1.
11. Philip Zimbardo, "Psychology of Police Confessions," paper presented at the American Psychological Association Symposium on Confessions, September 3, 1966.
12. Dkt. No. YO 297/67, Criminal Court of the City of New York, Pt. 3, Queens, minutes of trial, July 6, 1967.
13. Harold Beral and Marcus Sick, Note, "Administration of Complaints by Civilians Against the Police," *Harvard Law Review,* LXXVII (January 1964), 499, 504, 506.
14. President's Commission on Law Enforcement and the Administration of Justice, *Field Survey V: A National Survey of Police and Community Relations* (Washington, Government Printing Office, 1967), p. 217.

Chapter 4.   Force and Revenge

1. People v. Joseph Mimmo, Dkt. No. B4824/66, Criminal Court of the City of New York, Pt. 2B3, Queens, minutes of trial, February 2, 1967.
2. "Car Grazed, Teens Assail Grazer and Collide with Law," *New York Daily News,* July 8, 1966, p. 41.

Chapter 5.   Defiance and Arrest

1. People v. Gerald Zuckerman, Dkt. No. B6838/66, Criminal Court

of the City of New York, Pt. 2B3, Bronx, minutes of trial, January 18, 1967.

2. People v. Gerald Zuckerman, Dkt. No. 6838/66, Criminal Court of the City of New York, Pt. 1B, Bronx, minutes of preliminary hearing, November 14, 1966.

3. McNamara, "Uncertainties in Police Work," p. 222.

4. Dkt. No. C16167/66, Criminal Court of the City of New York, Pt. 1C, Manhattan, minutes of trial, December 20, 1966.

Chapter 6.   Criticism of the Police

1. People v. Weissman, 138 Misc. 542, 247 N.Y. Supp. 372 (Sp. Sess., App. Pt., 1, Dept. 1930).

2. People v. George and Elinor Fischer, Dkt. No. 6629–31/67, Criminal Court of the City of New York, Pt. 1C, Manhattan, minutes of conditional examination, June 1, 1967.

3. People v. Gilda Kaplan, Marshall Kaplan, Harriet Weingarten, Dkt. No. C15664–66/66, Criminal Court of the City of New York, Pt. 1C, Manhattan, minutes of trial, November 29, 1966.

4. Murray Kempton's column in the *New York Post,* October 27, 1966, contains an elegant account of the case.

Chapter 7.   Outcasts

1. James Mills, "The Detective," *Life,* December 3, 1965, pp. 90–123.

2. Dkt. Nos. C13930/67, C13934/67, A11630–32/67, Criminal Court of the City of New York, Pt. 2A2, Manhattan, minutes of trial, August 31, 1967.

3. New York City Administrative Code, §755(2)-7.5.

4. Press et al. v. Leary, Civil Action No. 2402/67, U.S. Dist. Ct., S.D.N.Y.

5. Skolnick, *Justice Without Trial,* p. 49.

6. Oscar Lewis, "The Culture of Poverty," *Scientific American,* CCXV (October 1966), 19.

7. Quoted in TFRP, p. 180.

8. Westley, "Violence and the Police," p. 39.

9. Robert Paul Wolff, "Beyond Tolerance," in Robert Paul Wolff, Barrington Moore, and Herbert Marcuse, *A Critique of Pure Tolerance* (Boston, Beacon Press, 1965), pp. 37–38.

Chapter 8.   Force, Arrest, and Cover Charges

1. McNamara, "Uncertainties in Police Work," p. 168.

2. *Ibid.,* pp. 226, 228.

3. *Ibid.,* p. 194; Arthur Niederhoffer, *Behind the Shield: The Police in Urban Society* (New York, Doubleday & Company, Inc., 1967), Ch. 5.

4. Westley, "Violence and the Police," p. 39.

5. Carl Werthman and Irving M. Piliavin, "Gang Members and the Police," in David Joseph Bordua, ed., *The Police: Six Sociological Essays* (New York, John Wiley & Sons, Inc., 1966), p. 93.

6. Richard H. Blum, "The Problems of Being a Police Officer," *Police,* January 1961, p. 12.

7. William A. Westley, "Secrecy and the Police," *Social Forces,*

XXXIV (March 1956), 254.

8. Blum, "Problems of Being a Police Officer," p. 10.

9. TFRP, p. 195.

10. President's Commission on Law Enforcement and the Administration of Justice, *Field Survey V*, pp. 189 ff.

11. TFRP, p. 186.

12. *Ibid.*, p. 195.

13. Miller Dixon v. District of Columbia, D.C. Cir. Dkt. No. 21084/67.

Chapter 9. Frames

1. Dkt. No. B5860/66, Criminal Court of the City of New York, Pt. 2B, Manhattan, calendar minutes, July 26, 1966.

2. See Selwyn Rabb, *Justice in the Back Room* (Cleveland, The World Publishing Company, 1967).

3. For promotion to sergeant, for example, in 1966 the City Department of Personnel weighed "Seniority and Performance" as 40% of the score. (The competitive examination counted 60%.) The highest departmental recognition, the Medal of Honor, counted for only 3 points of seniority and performance, or 1.2 points in the overall score. *City of New York, Department of Personnel, Notice of Examination No. 1453* (1966).

4. Bruce Smith, *Police Systems in the United States*, 2nd rev. ed. (New York, Harper & Row, Publishers, 1960), p. 241.

5. McNamara, "Uncertainties in Police Work," p. 189.

6. Aspects of the following case are described in *New York Times*, June 23, 1966, p. 1; June 24, 1966, p. 25; August 2, 1966, p. 22.

7. *New York Post*, February 16, 1968, p. 1.

Chapter 10. Mass Police Action

1. See, e.g., "Revolt in the Newark Ghetto," *Life*, July 28, 1967, pp. 16–28; Thomas Hayden, "The Occupation of Newark," *New York Review of Books*, August 24, 1967, p. 14; cf. "Day of Protest, Night of Violence," photographic report by ACLU of Southern California on police misconduct of June 24, 1967, in Los Angeles.

2. "Coney Island's Slums and Tidy Houses Reflect Big City Problems," *New York Times*, July 24, 1967, p. 29.

3. Hayden, "Occupation of Newark."

4. People v. Cherry, 307 N.Y. 308, 311 (1954).

5. "New Police Plan Used on Crowds," *New York Times*, July 25, 1966, p. 16.

Chapter 11. Search and Seizure

1. 367 U.S. 643 (1961).

2. Sarah Barlow, "Patterns of Arrests for Misdemeanor Narcotics Possession: Manhattan Police Practices 1960–1962," mimeographed report of Mobilization for Youth (New York, 1967). The figures I use are drawn from Mrs. Barlow's Appendix J, which is not included in the mimeographed version because of its size.

3. Suspicious readers may suggest that this second set of figures accounts for the first, but it is not so. In absolute numbers, the total of

allegations of abandonment went from 308 to 483 for all policemen, and from 205 to 311 for narcotics officers. The decline in arrests, however, emphasized the existence of the "dropsy" arrests and gave rise to the impression that the *number* of such arrests had increased astronomically. The *percentage* of such arrests did increase astronomically (more than three times, from 14% to 47%).

4. "Narcotics Arrests Up 37.3% in City," *New York Times,* December 15, 1966, p. 42.

5. Brinegar v. United States, 338 U.S. 160, 181 (1948).

6. Skolnick, *Justice Without Trial,* p. 215.

7. New York Code of Criminal Procedure §180-a.

§180-a. Temporary questioning of persons in public places; search for weapons.

1. A police officer may stop any person abroad in a public place whom he reasonably suspects is committing, has committed or is about to commit a felony or any of the offenses specified in section five hundred fifty-two of this chapter, and may demand of him his name, address and an explanation of his actions.

2. When a police officer has stopped a person for questioning pursuant to this section and reasonably suspects that he is in danger of life or limb, he may search such person for a dangerous weapon. If the police officer finds such a weapon or any other thing the possession of which may constitute a crime, he may take and keep it until the completion of the questioning, at which time he shall either return it, if lawfully possessed, or arrest such person.

8. People v. Peters, 18 N.Y.2d 238, 245 (1966), *aff'd* — U.S. — (1968); People v. Sibron, 18 N.Y.2d 603 (1966), *rev'd,* — U.S. — (1968).

9. President's Commission on Law Enforcement and the Administration of Justice, *Field Survey V,* p. 330.

10. Herman Schwartz, "Stop and Frisk," *Journal of Criminal Law, Criminology, and Police Science,* LVIII (December 1967), 433, 444 n. 63.

11. TFRP, p. 39.

12. Joseph A. Murray, *Study Guide for Patrolman* (New York, Arco Publishing Company, 1966), p. 23.

13. Wayland D. Pilcher, "The Law and Practice of Field Interrogation," *Journal of Criminal Law, Criminology, and Police Science,* LVIII (December 1967), 487–89.

14. TFRP, p. 184.

15. Schwartz, "Stop and Frisk," p. 453, n. 146.

16. President's Commission on Law Enforcement and the Administration of Justice, *Field Survey III: Studies in Crime and Law Enforcement in Major Metropolitan Areas* (Washington, Government Printing Office, 1967), Vol. II, § 1, p. 92.

17. Entick v. Carrington, 19 *Howell's State Trials,* col. 1029.

18. Burmeister et al. v. Leary, Civil Action No. 2149/67, U.S. Dist. Ct., S.D.N.Y.

19. *New York Times,* December 6, 1966, p. 52.

20. Skolnick, *Justice Without Trial,* p. 223; to the same effect, see TFRP, p. 29.

21. McCray v. Illinois, 386 U.S. 300 (1967).

Chapter 12.   Systematic Harassment

1. Wayne R. LaFave, *Arrest: The Decision to Take a Suspect into Custody* (Boston, Little, Brown and Company, 1965), Chs. 22–24. See also TFRP, pp. 187–88.

2. For liability notices see New York City Police Department Rules and Procedures, Ch. 8, §31, and for raided premises, Ch. 8, §27.

3. P.L. §1533(5). This section was replaced on September 1, 1967, by one substantially more vague: §240.35(9).

4. TFRP, pp. 28–29.

5. Burmeister et al. v. Leary, Civil Action No. 2149/67, U.S. Dist. Ct., S.D.N.Y.

6. Sidney Zion, "Prostitution: The Midtown Roundup," *New York Times,* October 1, 1967, § 4, p. 1. This is one of a series by Mr. Zion in *The New York Times* dealing with the Times Square cleanup: September 26, 1967, p. 62; September 27, 1967, p. 48; September 29, 1967, p. 63; October 1, 1967, § 4, p. 1; November 10, 1967, p. 41.

7. *Ibid.,* September 26, 1967, p. 62.

8. I am indebted to Robert Croog of Columbia Law School for culling these figures from the records of the Manhattan Criminal Court.

9. Dkt. No. C14481–2/67, New York City Criminal Court, Pt. 1A2, Manhattan, calendar minutes, August 23, 1967.

10. Skolnick, *Justice Without Trial,* p. 206.

Chapter 13.   Firearms

1. TFRP, p. 189.

2. New York City Police Department statistics.

3. Howard R. Leary, "Law, Social Order and the Use of Deadly Force," speech given at the Georgetown University Law Center, Washington, D.C., March 21, 1967.

4. See George Mullins, "Justified Use of Force Under the Revised Penal Law," *New York Law Journal,* June 15, 1967, p. 14.

5. NYCPD Rules and Procedures, Ch. 25, §23-0.

6. Niederhoffer, *Behind the Shield,* pp. 109–10.

Chapter 14.   Remedies and Failures

1. The sad story is briefly recounted in President's Commission on Law Enforcement and the Administration of Justice, *The Task Force Report on the Courts* (Washington, Government Printing Office, 1967), pp. 30 ff., appendices B and C. The issue whether the U.S. Constitution requires appointment of counsel for a crime less than a felony is unsettled as of this writing.

2. Jackson v. United States, 353 F.2d 862 (5th Cir. 1965).

3. This statement covers a number of unsettled issues. In suits for false arrest and malicious prosecution, the phrase may mean 90 days after the criminal charges are dismissed. For an assault claim, the law clearly means 90 days after the assault. N.Y.S. Gen. Mun. Law §50(e).

4. Walter Gellhorn, *When Americans Complain* (Cambridge, Mass., Harvard University Press, 1966), p. 184.

5. U.S. Civil Rights Commission, *The Fifty States Report* (Washington, Government Printing Office, 1961), p. 69.

6. Figures kindly supplied by the New York City Police Department to Robert Croog, Columbia Law School.

7. Beral and Sick, Note, "Administration of Complaints by Civilians," *Harvard Law Review*, LXXVII, 499, 504, 506. The situation may have improved since 1963.

8. President's Commission on Law Enforcement and the Administration of Justice, *Field Survey IV: Police and the Community* (Washington, Government Printing Office, 1967), II, 239.

9. President's Commission on Law Enforcement, *Task Force Report on the Courts*, p. 73.

10. President's Commission on Law Enforcement, *Field Survey V*, pp. 246 ff.

11. U.S. National Commission on Law Observance and Enforcement, *Report on the Police*, p. 61.

12. McNamara, "Uncertainties in Police Work," p. 194; Niederhoffer, *Behind the Shield*, Ch. 5.

13. Richard H. Blum, *Police Selection* (Springfield, Ill., Charles C. Thomas, Publisher, 1964), pp. 58–59.

14. *Ibid.*, p. 59. TFRP, p. 108.

15. *Ibid.*

Chapter 15. The Police and Society

1. Niederhoffer, *Behind the Shield*, p. 107.

2. Max Rheinstein, ed., *Max Weber on Law and Economy in Society*, trans. Edward Shils (Cambridge, Mass., Harvard University Press, 1954), Chs. 7 and 8.

BIBLIOGRAPHY

This short list does not purport to be a complete bibliography of leading works about the police, though of course many of the most important writings on the subject are included here. For a more compendious bibliography, the reader is referred to the one in David Joseph Bordua, *The Police: Six Sociological Essays* (New York, John Wiley & Sons, Inc., 1967). The works cited in the foregoing chapters are as follows:

BOOKS

Blum, Richard H., *Police Selection*. Springfield, Ill., Charles C. Thomas, Publisher, 1964.

Bordua, David Joseph, ed., *The Police: Six Sociological Essays*. New York, John Wiley & Sons, Inc., 1967.

Clark, Kenneth B., *Dark Ghetto: Dilemmas of Social Power*. New York, Harper & Row, Publishers, 1965.

Gellhorn, Walter, *When Americans Complain*. Cambridge, Mass., Harvard University Press, 1966.

Goldman, Nathan, *The Differential Selection of Juvenile Offenders for Court Appearances*. Washington, National Council on Crime and Delinquency, 1963.

LaFave, Wayne R., *Arrest: The Decision to Take a Suspect into Custody*. Boston, Little, Brown and Company, 1965.

McNamara, John H. See Bordua, David Joseph.

Murray, Joseph A., *Study Guide for Patrolman*. New York, Arco Publishing Company, 1966.

Niederhoffer, Arthur, *Behind the Shield: The Police in Urban Society*. New York, Doubleday & Company, Inc., 1967.

President's Commission on Law Enforcement and the Administration of Justice, *The Challenge of Crime in a Free Society.* Washington, Government Printing Office, 1967.

_____, *Field Survey III: Studies in Crime and Law Enforcement in Major Metropolitan Areas.* Washington, Government Printing Office, 1967, 2 vols.

_____, *Field Survey IV: Police and the Community.* Washington, Government Printing Office, 1967, 2 vols.

_____, *Field Survey V: A National Survey of Police and Community Relations.* Washington, Government Printing Office, 1967.

_____, *The Task Force Report on the Courts.* Washington, Government Printing Office, 1967.

_____, *The Task Force Report on the Police.* Washington, Government Printing Office, 1967.

Raab, Selwyn, *Justice in the Back Room.* Cleveland, The World Publishing Company, 1967.

Rheinstein, Max, ed., *Max Weber on Law and Economy in Society,* trans. Edward Shils. Cambridge, Mass., Harvard University Press, 1954.

Skolnick, Jerome H., *Justice Without Trial: Law Enforcement in Democratic Society.* New York, John Wiley & Sons, Inc., 1966.

Smith, Bruce, *Police Systems in the United States,* 2nd rev. ed. New York, Harper & Row, Publishers, 1960.

U.S. Civil Rights Commission, *The Fifty States Report.* Washington, Government Printing Office, 1961.

U.S. National Commission on Law Observance and Enforcement (Wickersham Commission), *Report on Lawlessness in Law Enforcement.* Washington, Government Printing Office, 1931.

_____, *Report on the Police.* Washington, Government Printing Office, 1931.

Werthman, Carl, and Irving M. Piliavin. See Bordua, David Joseph.

Wolff, Robert Paul, Barrington Moore, and Herbert Marcuse, *A Critique of Pure Tolerance.* Boston, Beacon Press, 1965.

PERIODICALS

Beral, Harold, and Marcus Sick, Note, "Administration of Complaints by Civilians Against the Police." *Harvard Law Review,* LXXVII (January 1964), 499, 504, 506.

Blum, Richard H., "The Problems of Being a Police Officer." *Police,* January 1961.

Hayden, Thomas, "The Occupation of Newark." *New York Review of Books,* August 24, 1967.

Lewis, Oscar, "The Culture of Poverty." *Scientific American,* Vol. CCXIV (October 1966).

Life, July 28, 1967.

Mills, James, "The Detective." *Life,* December 3, 1965, pp. 90–123.

Mullins, George, "Justified Use of Force Under the Revised Penal Law." *New York Law Journal,* June 15, 1967.

New York *Daily News,* July 8, 1966.

New York Post, October 27, 1966; February 16, 1968.

New York Times, June 3, 23, and 24, July 25, August 2, December 6 and
    15, 1966; January 9, July 24, 1967; February 27, 1968.
Pilcher, Wayland D., "The Law and Practice of Field Interrogation."
    Journal of Criminal Law, Criminology and Police Science, LVIII
    (December 1967), 487–89.
Piliavin, Irving M., and Scott Briar, "Police Encounters with Juveniles."
    American Journal of Sociology, Vol. LXX (September 1964).
Reiss, Albert J., Jr., "Police Brutality—Answers to Key Questions." *Trans-
    Action,* July–August 1968.
Schwartz, Herman, "Stop and Frisk." *Journal of Criminal Law, Crimi-
    nology and Police Science,* Vol. LVIII (December 1967).
Westley, William A., "Secrecy and the Police." *Social Forces,* Vol. XXXIV
    (March 1956).
————, "Violence and the Police." *American Journal of Sociology,*
    Vol. LIX (August 1953).
Zion, Sidney, articles concerning prostitution, *New York Times,* Septem-
    ber 26, 27, and 29, October 1, November 10, 1967.

UNPUBLISHED SPEECHES AND PAPERS

American Civil Liberties Union of Southern California, "Day of Protest,
    Night of Violence." Photographic report on incidents of June 24,
    1967, in Los Angeles.
Barlow, Sarah, "Patterns of Arrest for Misdemeanor Narcotics Possession:
    Manhattan Police Practices 1960–62." Mimeographed report by
    Mobilization for Youth, New York, 1967.
Leary, Howard R., "Law, Social Order and the Use of Deadly Force."
    Speech given at the Georgetown University Law Center, Washing-
    ton, D.C., March 21, 1967.
New York City Police Department, *Rules and Procedures.*
Wald, Patricia, and Joel Hoffman, "Report and Recommendations on the
    Disorderly Conduct Statute of the District of Columbia." Mimeo-
    graphed staff document, President's Commission on Crime in the
    District of Columbia, July 15, 1966.
Zimbardo, Philip, "Psychology of Police Confessions." Paper presented at
    the American Psychological Association Symposium on Confessions,
    September 3, 1966.